EDEN ON THE MARSH
An Illustrated History of
SAVANNAH

Pictorial Research
by Mary Elizabeth Holland

"Partners in Progress"
by Francis Hullar

Introduction by Eugenia Price

Produced in Cooperation with the
Coastal Heritage Society

Windsor Publications, Inc.
Northridge, California

EDEN ON THE MARSH

An Illustrated History of

SAVANNAH

—Edward Chan Sieg—

Windsor Publications, Inc., — History Book Division

Publisher: John M. Phillips
Editorial Director: Teri Davis Greenberg
Design Director: Alexander D'Anca

Staff for *Eden on the Marsh*
Senior Editor: Nancy Evans
Production Editor: Karl Stull
Assistant Editors: Gail Koffman, Lane Powell
Director, Corporate Biographies: Karen Story
Assistant Director, Corporate Biographies: Phyllis
    Gray
Editor, Corporate Biographies: Judith Hunter
Editorial Assistants: Kathy M. Brown, Patricia
    Cobb, Lonnie Pham, Pat Pittman, Deena Tucker,
    Sharon L. Volz

Designer: J. R. Vasquez

Honorary Advisors:

Windsor Publications and the Coastal Heritage Society wish to acknowledge the following individuals,
who lent valuable assistance in the preparation of
this volume:

Carson Branan
Robert A. Burnett
Robert E. James
James R. Lientz, Jr.
John Rousakis

Library of Congress Cataloging in Publication Data:

Sieg, Edward Chan, 1928-
    Eden on the marsh.

    "Produced in cooperation with the Coastal Heri-
tage Society."
    Bibliography: p. 206
    Includes index.
    1. Savannah (Ga.)—History. 2. Savannah (Ga.)—
Description. 3. Savannah (Ga.)—Industries.
I. Coastal Heritage Society (Ga.) II. Title.
F294.S2S49   1985   975.8'724   85-20250
ISBN 0-89781-115-1

*Endsheets: Louis Wagner
streaks down Waters Ave-
nue in the 1911 Gran
Prix as spectators line the
southside racecourse to
view the world's greatest
cars and drivers. Wagner's
Fiat won first place in
1908, but wrecked in
1910, and withdrew due
to mechanical problems
in 1911. Courtesy, Dr.
Julian Killen Quattle-
baum, Sr.*

*Title page: Pulaski Mon-
ument commands the
foreground in this litho-
graph, circa 1855, after a
painting by J.W. Hill.
From the I.N. Phelps
Stokes Collection. Cour-
tesy, The New York Pub-
lic Library and the Astor,
Lenox and Tilden Foun-
dations*

CONTENTS

INTRODUCTION

Fulfilling a request to write an introduction for a book is not a new experience for me, but it has been a long time since I've introduced a work for which I feel such unbridled enthusiasm. I am, at the moment, in the difficult midst of my own research for the third in a quartet of novels laid in old Savannah and taking time out to read *Eden on the Marsh* has not only been enlightening, but a surprisingly stimulating interlude. I am grateful to my friend, Scott Smith, director of the highly creative Coastal Heritage Society at Savannah's Old Fort Jackson, for giving me the privilege of this introduction.

There are other books about *portions* of Savannah's complex and fascinating history—books on its wonderfully restored old houses, its founder, General James Edward Oglethorpe, its historic river, its forts—but talented, perceptive Edward Chan Sieg has here filled Savannah's biggest book need in *Eden on the Marsh*. I thank him from my heart for having given the time, and brain-bending concentration required to set down this sweeping, highly readable overview of Savannah's history from that first climb up the steep riverfront bluff by Oglethorpe and his settlers in 1733 to today. The author has not neglected the muscle and heart of the old city by writing only about its wealthy merchant and planter class. They are here, of course, but he has also included other immigrants—the Scottish, Jewish, Irish, and German people, who came willingly to find a better life—and the blacks, who came unwillingly on slave ships and who not only helped build Savannah's commerce and architecture, but who now as productive citizens still give the city much of its vigor, expertise, and cosmopolitan ambiance.

Savannah has been called by many names other than Eden on the Marsh. Travel writers call it the South's Beautiful Lady. A disillusioned newsman in the 1800s wrote an embittered poem about Savannah in which he described the city as "a hotbed of rogues . . . where Satan has fixed his headquarters on earth and outlawed integrity, wisdom and worth." Perhaps Savannah is both of these things, but it is far, far more. People from all walks of life and of all ages are strangely drawn to the very name—Savannah. I have learned this firsthand from readers of my novels laid here.

I promise that you will find the "more" of Savannah in these pages of rare photographs and lucid writing. Edward Chan Sieg has, in my opinion, superbly captured the important points in its history *and* its singular mystique.

Eugenia Price
St. Simons Island, Georgia

Left: *Blossoms lend grace to Johnson Square. Photo by Chan Sieg*

Page 9: *In the 1840s, railroad construction across the marsh transformed the small town of Savannah into the cotton capital of the South. Courtesy, Chatham-Effingham-Liberty Regional Library, Thomas Gamble Picture Collection (hereafter, CEL Regional Library, Gamble Collection)*

Pages 10-11: *National Maritime Day celebrates the voyage, in May 1819, of the S.S. Savannah—the first steamship to cross the Atlantic. Painting by John Stobart; photo by Beth Holland*

PREFACE

Tradition has it that the first game of golf played in the New World was essayed on a field near Savannah in 1796. Nearly two centuries later a Savannahian, Hollis Stacy, reached the pinnacle of the golf world by becoming the U.S. Women's Open champion. That a woman in her early twenties would bridge the gap between the origin and fruition is a testament to the traditional, conservative, laid-back history of Savannah during its first two hundred or more years and a shining example of just how far the old town has come. It was just one generation ago that Savannah women who took sports seriously were considered odd; two-piece bathing suits were frowned upon.

This is not to imply that Savannah's past is without innovation. Savannah's history is filled with dashing men and strong-willed women, as fiercely individualistic as any in American history. They rebelled against Oglethorpe's rules, against the royal Governor Reynolds, against Great Britain, against the Union, and finally, against the Supreme Court. But when William Scarbrough sent the first steamship across the Atlantic and back, Savannah's investment brokers could see no future in a venture which lost money on its first trip. Devastated by fire in 1820, Savannah refused to buy the idea of fireproof buildings put forth in newspaper ads by its own favorite architect, William Jay, and famed Hermitage plantation owner, Henry McAlpin. Instead, the first fireproof building was built in Charleston two years later. Jay had left for good, leaving a legacy of four buildings which are now the elite of Savannah's architectural treasures. McAlpin began an even more farsighted enterprise when he laid a set of railroad tracks for his brick factory. With horse-drawn cars, it was the first such construction in America. But other interests in Charleston got the railroad started in the United States, and only when the new transportation threatened Savannah's economic life did the city change its policies and proceed to outdo the nation in the rapid development of rail transportation.

Technical advances have not often stirred Savannah's imagination to the point of developing them. The automobile focused world attention on Savannah as early as 1908 when the Vanderbilt Cup Races were held on a track just outside the city. The *Savannah Morning News* reported excitement so high that spectators outnumbered the population four-to-one. The races were held again in 1910 and 1911, but the scheduled 1913 contest was postponed—reportedly because many citizens found the engines noisy and the crowds troublesome. Savannah had retreated again into its unpaved pose, trying to halt the inevitable. But after World War I, the future of the automobile was obvious. Two decades after that first race, the state of Georgia finally had a paved road connecting with Florida.

To understand the paradoxical nature of the little city on the marsh—which has received so much national acclaim for its excellent design of squares and streets, which has been touted as an "All-American City," and is considered so historically significant that not only the Historic District but the Victorian District, the Isle of Hope, and the residential suburbs of Ardsley Park and Chatham Crescent (developed between 1910 and 1930) have been placed on the National Register of Historic Places—one has only to look into the peculiar circumstances of its birth.

Savannah was born from the mating of humanitarian idealism and imperial necessity. Conceived by Oglethorpe as a haven for unfortunates, the colony was also designed to protect the important trade center of Charleston from Spanish threats in Florida. The first colonists were lured with lavish promises of a "land of milk and honey." The oppressed of Europe came to Georgia in droves. Few of the early settlers had any experience in agriculture, house-building, or military matters, but they were expected to perform all these tasks, make silk, and stay sober. (Oglethorpe allowed daily portions of beer, ale, and wine—but not rum.) After ten years of struggling, Oglethorpe left Savannah safe from the Spaniards, but still threatened by the French, Indians, and even the Charlestonians who had already become jealous of Savannah's intrepid businessmen. With Oglethorpe gone, the town was left to make its own way, find its own security, and establish its own identity. For 2-1/2 centuries, Savannah has sought the fulfillment of a promised Eden.

ACKNOWLEDGMENTS

It is no easy task to condense the accumulated lives and actions of many people over 2-1/2 centuries into a slim, illustrated volume. The author wishes to express his indebtedness to the hundreds of sincere and ardent writers whose work constitutes the bulk of the information in this volume. If by omitting or choosing some traditional material over some other the contents of this brief work smack of flippancy or less than serious intent, the author adds his apology to his gratitude. This is not a history book in the formal sense; it is rather a book about historical events and persons.

Thanks are also due to many institutions and individuals whose shared materials lend authenticity to this manuscript: the Office of the Mayor of Savannah; the Georgia Historical Society; the Ships of the Sea Museum, David Guernsey, director; the Tybee Museum; and especially the National Park Service personnel at the Fort Pulaski National Monument, Dan Brown, director, and John Beck. Individuals of particular importance include: Mrs. Lilla Hawes, Savannah's most eminent living source of local history; Mrs. Judy Nichols of the Chatham-Effingham-Liberty Regional Library; Mr. Scott Smith, director of Old Fort Jackson; and Dr. John D. Duncan, who first introduced me to the little secrets of Savannah's past.

As for the tedious task of correcting the manuscript, I am indebted to Nancy Evans, a rare editor who makes criticism with gentleness and makes punctuation palatable. Finally, to Beth Holland—researcher, editor, typist, and constant friend—without whom this work might never have been completed, all praise must be given.

CHAPTER I

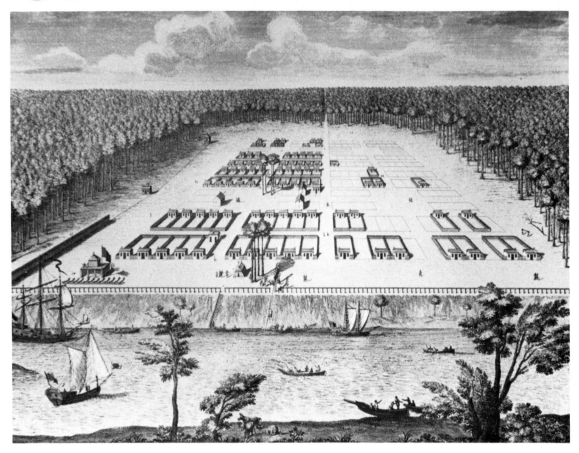

Peter Gordon, one of the first settlers, published this view of Savannah in 1734 at the request of the Trustees. Gordon did not find his Eden in Savannah. Instead he became associated with the Malcontents and left the city. Engraving by Fourdrinier. Courtesy, Old Fort Jackson

IN SEARCH OF SOLVENCY

The thirty-second degree of north latitude passes through the Holy Land near Jerusalem. It slices through Africa, transverses the Atlantic, and pierces the coast of the New World near Savannah. In the second decade of the eighteenth century Sir Robert Mountgomery concluded that since the Garden of

Eden was known to have been near Jerusalem, then the same idyllic conditions must be found a few miles upstream on the Savannah River. Armed with a land deal from the Carolina Proprietors and letters of introduction and endorsement, he set forth in England in 1717. There Mountgomery made an elaborate presentation promising massive profits for all who would invest in his "New Eden." Sir Robert was certain that in one year after investment, he would virtually be able to corner the market in potash. Unfortunately, he failed to raise the money.

In 1562 a pair of events shaped the history of North America and were particularly influential in the founding of the Georgia colony 170 years later.

A French colony was established at Port Royal, South Carolina, by Jean Ribaut. Though unsuccessful, it alerted the Spanish who protested in vain. Two years later, under Laudonniere, the French settled in North Florida. Spain retaliated by sending Menendez de Aviles to establish a permanent settlement at St. Augustine. Spain underscored its claim when De Aviles massacred the French. Thus, St. Augustine is indeed the "oldest *permanent* settlement" in the United States. After this effort, the French concentrated on territory explored by Cartier much farther north.

The second event of 1562 was more far-reaching in its effect on the founding of Georgia. John Hawkins, the first of the

great English seadogs, carried a cargo of 300 human beings from Guinea on the coast of Africa to Haiti. There he traded them for "ginger, sugar and pearls at large profit" and returned to England. With Queen Elizabeth's tacit approval, English seadogs then began a systematic pillaging of Spain's wealth. In the inevitable war that followed, piracy was given official approval and the names of Hawkins, Sir Francis Drake, Oxenham, and Cavendish were etched in English naval history. Spanish cities of trade—Valparaiso, Cartagena, Santo Domingo, Nombre de Dios—were attacked, held for ransom, or sacked entirely. Successes of the privateers encouraged Queen Elizabeth to bolder actions. In 1578, while Drake was sailing the *Golden Hind* around the globe, the Queen gave Sir Humphrey Gilbert a patent granting him the right "to inhabit and possess at his choice all remote and heathen lands not in the actual possession of any Christian prince." This was a clear challenge to Spain that it must be able to "inhabit and possess" its territories in order to hold them.

What had begun with Hawkins in 1562 became officially licensed in the same year the great armada was defeated. In 1588 the Guinea Company was organized in London with an official permit to "carry on traffic" in human cargo from Africa's west coast.

When Oglethorpe established the Towne of Savannah in 1733, it was, to a

Right: *James Edward Oglethorpe, an idealist and a man of action, founded and preserved the colony of Georgia through its first decade. Courtesy, CEL Regional Library, Gamble Collection*

Below, left: *An almost life-sized Indian by local artist Liz Toschach is one of several early-Savannah paintings and murals in the Tybee Museum.*

great extent, the inevitable outcome of the two events of 1562. James Edward Oglethorpe, born in 1696, was the son of a knight whose family traced its lineage back to Edward the Confessor, the last of the Saxon kings. Young James attended Eton and Oxford, leaving the latter to enter service under Prince Eugene of Savoy. At age twenty, Oglethorpe already had a reputation for his military prowess. Elected to the House of Commons in his mid-twenties, he was soon known for his espousal of humanitarian causes. He published pamphlets and made speeches against the impressment of British seamen, against the conditions in English prisons, in favor of the oppressed Protestants of Salzburg, and pleading for equality of treatment in trade matters with the West Indies and American colonies. Sympathetic to the plight of the growing numbers of debtors in England, Oglethorpe and his friend, Lord Percival, conceived a plan for a new colony based on idealistic and humanitarian principles.

This plan departed from the usual colonial schemes in that it was not organized along strictly business lines. Neither a proprietorship nor a stock company, Georgia was to be a trusteeship with twenty-one men, headed by John Percival (later the Earl of Egmont), administering the colony. These Trustees would receive no salary, own no land in the colony, hold no office there, and receive no income from the productivity of the colonists. It was, in effect, the first large-scale, non-profit enterprise in the Ameri-

Facing page, bottom right: *"Tybee Light," famous in poem and song as the easternmost landmark of Georgia, is from a 1764 engraving. Courtesy, CEL Regional Library, Gamble Collection*

Left: *In the fall of 1979, hurricane David swept across the marshes around Savannah. Two and a half centuries earlier, outbreaks of harsh weather numbered among the many problems facing the settlers who pursued the dream of a new Eden. Photo by Beth Holland*

Below: *In calmer weather, the prospect of paradise may have been renewed.* © Grant Compton, 1985

The Georgia colony was named for George II, from the German House of Hanover, who ruled England from 1727 to 1760. Courtesy, V. & J. Duncan Antique Maps & Prints

cas. Funding would come strictly from donations. The Trustees would carefully select the colonists according to their qualifications and character, preference given to worthy persons on a basis of real need. By eliminating self-interest, Oglethorpe and Percival laid the foundation for a uniquely humanitarian and idealistic enterprise.

They were realistic men, however, understanding the low probability of success that depended entirely on idealism and charity, so they introduced a profit motive. Under mercantilist principles, the colony would not be allowed to establish manufacturing and at the end of a year—New Eden being so fertile—the colonists would be independent of charity and producing more than they needed for sustenance. This surplus would flow back to England—at England's prices—and be

traded for English products. The colonies would be a market for English goods. The promise of a constant market would please everyone and assure the contributors that their money was indeed going to a worthy cause. But the two designers had an even better selling point. They produced pamphlets and reprints describing in glowing terms the Georgia climate and fertility as exactly coincident with those Near and Far Eastern climes which produced so many exotic products desired in England—particularly silk. England's textile industry was growing by leaps and bounds but the cost of raw materials was a major retardant of profits, so the very mention of a cheap source of silk, which had to be entirely imported at prices set by other nations, was much like mentioning oil in Texas.

Finally, there was the matter of Charlestown (which became Charleston after the Revolution), a rich city threatened by the Spaniards and Indians. The Trustees took great pains to assure the use of the new colony as a buffer against further intrusion on England's interests.

With tidy answers to all the anticipated negatives, they capped their proposal by naming the colony after King George II. As expressed in the charter:

His Majesty having taken into his Consideration the miserable Circumstances of many of his own poor Subjects, ready to perish for Want; as likewise the Distresses of many Foreigners, who would take Refuge here from Persecution; and having a princely Regard to the great Danger the Southern Frontiers of South-Carolina *are exposed to, by Reason of the small Number of white Inhabitants there, hath out of his fatherly Compassion towards his Subjects been graciously pleased to grant a Charter for incorporating a Number of Gentlemen by the Name of THE TRUSTEES FOR ESTABLISHING THE COLONY OF GEORGIA IN AMERICA.*

Of all the English colonies, Georgia probably was the most publicized with speeches in Parliament, sermons from pulpits, ads in the papers, pamphlets, and announcements. Soon after the charter was granted, the application list had far more people than could be handled by the donations then in hand. The first colonists were carefully screened, and Oglethorpe agreed to accompany them at his own expense as a representative of the Trustees. In November 1732 the *Anne* sailed for the New World with James Oglethorpe, some 114 colonists, and as the press reported, "on Board 10 Ton of Alderman Parsons' best Beer. ..." On February 12, 1733, after transferring to small boats at Port Royal, they anchored at the chosen site of Savannah, clambered up the steep forty-foot bluff fronting the river, and for the first time, dusted their feet in the sand of the New Eden.

Oglethorpe served the colony in multiple roles: as the leader, he was arbiter and judge of all disputes; as engineer and architect, he designed, laid out, and named the town's streets; as commander, he organized the militia and guard system, built forts along the coast, and led expeditions against the Spaniards; as supreme authority, he did whatever he thought was needed regardless of English regulations (particularly when it came to money); as diplomat, he gained the alliance of Georgia's Indian nations and made treaties which greatly expanded the colony's land holdings (Oglethorpe took a group of Indians back to England and presented them to London society which helped continue the donations needed by the Trustees); he settled problems with South Carolina's Indian traders by forbidding them to trade in Georgia; against the inclinations of the Trustees, he permitted Jews to settle in Savannah; he established a number of other towns (running up bills that were the constant concern of the Trustees, but at the same time spending huge sums of his own); and finally, having defeated the Spaniards at Bloody Marsh, Oglethorpe returned to England, successfully faced a court-martial hearing on his activities in

the New World, and then retired from colonial involvement.

February in Savannah is even crueler than T.S. Eliot's April. It is a month when one may safely predict heavy thundershowers, freezing rains, hail and sleet, gale-force winds from several directions, sunny days with spring breezes, azaleas opening, birdsong, and—ever so often—snow. It was one of these Februarys which greeted the first settlers in 1733.

Whatever the weather, the settlers were obviously pleased to be "home" after the long crossing. Joseph Fitzwalter, a gardener, wrote: "I take it to be the promised land." Even Oglethorpe, who had come a few days before the main body to select the site and make friends with the local Indians, was moved to write the Trustees: "... I went myself to view the Savannah River. I fixed upon a healthy situation about ten miles from the sea. The river here forms a half moon, along the South side of which the banks are about 40 foot high. ... Upon the riverside in the center of this plain, I have laid out the town. ... The landskip is very agreeable, the stream being wide and bordered with high woods on both sides."

Oglethorpe wrote this on the tenth day after the settlers disembarked. For an entire week they had labored to unload their supplies and provisions, trying but failing to erect a crane to lift cargoes up the forty-foot bluff. Oglethorpe had already laid out the town and the common ground (property of the Trustees), had begun fortifications and land-clearing, and the first house was already under construction. He had won the loyalty of nearby Indians who expressed a desire to learn about Christianity and to send their children to English schools.

In this first letter from his tent overlooking the river, Oglethorpe seemed optimistic, but within it were augurs of the troubles ahead. "Our people are all alive," he wrote, "but ten are ill with the bloody flux, which I take to proceed from the cold and their not being accustomed to lie in tents." Having failed to complete the crane, he saw the need for skilled labor and wrote a single sentence characteristic of his take-charge attitude: "Not being able to get Negroes, I have taken ten of the Independent Company to work for us, for which I make them an allowance." With this single action, Oglethorpe established two principles he would follow throughout his tenure in the colony: his adamant opposition to the permanent use of slaves—though he was perfectly willing to "rent" black carpenters and masons from Charlestown who were instrumental in building Savannah—and his willingness to spend the Trustees' funds whenever and in whatever amounts he deemed necessary. Oglethorpe merely had to sign a chit which would be redeemed in England.

The communication gap between the Trustees in London and the colonists in Georgia made accurate bookkeeping virtually impossible. Demands of any kind from either side required nearly four months reaction time. Problems were usually solved locally before instructions could be received. The Trustees, wishing all possible success for their venture, made express prohibitions against the worst of what they took to be immoralizing influences. The proscribed list included "papists, Negroes, and rum." Lawyers were not encouraged to settle in the new colony for fear they might stir up trouble over property rights; neither were Jews invited, although the Trustees commissioned Jews to solicit funds for the colony. Before the first year was celebrated, every one of these prohibitions was a source of trouble.

The demands placed on the charity colonists were heavy. Each agreed to remain in Georgia for three years during which time he would serve in a kind of communal capacity in clearing land, building houses, and learning the basic skills of military training. He would receive a town lot for his house, a five-acre gardening plot in the Trustees' common ground, and—to make a total of fifty acres—a farm lot farther from town "in the woods." During the first year he was expected to aid in clearing the town site, help build housing and common buildings, labor as a soldier and pull a shift at guard duty, erect fortifications, unload ships, learn to be Christian to Indians with "rude dress, painted faces, and sliced ears," become skilled at agriculture, plant 100 mulberry trees for each of his ten acres to feed the silkworms, go to church regularly, behave decently, stay sober, attend meetings, and never gripe.

It never occurred to the Trustees that their process of selection resulted in a body of colonists totally unqualified for the hardships and vicissitudes of life in New Eden. In designing the colony Oglethorpe and Percival had envisioned a land of small farmers, each his own proprietor, defending his land, and cultivating mulberry trees for the profits expected by the royal government in England. Such agrarian equality, they believed, would prevent bickering and jealousy. Grants of 500 acres of land *were* available to prospective colonists who wished to come at their own expense and who could afford the appropriate servants to attend the land.

The colonist did not own his fifty acres, so he could neither sell nor mortgage it. He could occupy the acreage only as long as he cultivated it properly. Women could not inherit rights to land. The restrictions of the Trustees did not stimulate a high level of motivation, particularly when the closest neighbors in South Carolina had no such restrictions.

The Trustees' seemingly heavy-handed position was not indefensible, however. They reasoned that men who had already proven themselves failures—for whatever the causes—might well fail again if not removed from those temptations which lead to failure. Slaves, for example, were all very well under certain conditions, but for a lazy man to have a slave. ... The problems of rum were self-evident. Percival's own misgivings about certain of the "chosen" were noted in his journal. After selecting the men who were to hold the highest positions in the colony—magistrates and bailiffs—he noted: "All of

them not worth 20L." Before a later shipload was to embark, he had interviewed eight carpenters, of whom he remarked: "One had . . . been obliged to Sell his bed, and another was to Sell his tools to pay his Creditors. . . . Miserable objects most of them."

To their credit, the Trustees warned the colonists that life in Savannah would be hard, but nothing could deter the men and women seeking a better life. Sir William Wise, an old nobleman come upon hard times, summed it up succinctly: "It's better to be on Charity than to starve to death!" He was to become the victim in one of the first great crimes in the colony. Richard White and Alice Riley were Sir William's assigned Irish servants. White tied Sir William's hair around the old man's neck, while Alice shoved his head in a bucket of water. They were both executed, Alice after a suitable delay for the birth of her child.

Oglethorpe believed rules were not made to apply to him. Whenever he saw fit, he acted in accordance with the dictates of his own conscience. He did not hesitate to rent slaves from Charlestown to help build Savannah, he bought a

boatload of Irish indentured servants for resale to the more affluent colonists (despite the ban on papists), and he petitioned the Trustees for exceptions to the inheritance rules for certain widows. But on the matter of rum, Oglethorpe was constant. As long as he remained on the premises, the colony functioned reasonably well; but the moment he left, chaos moved in.

After Oglethorpe's first trip to Charlestown, he returned to find work not progressing, bickering and jealousies, and much absenteeism for drunkenness. Rum, believed Oglethorpe, was the root of all evil. He wrote repeatedly to Percival that were it not for rum, all would be well. During the first terrible summer when fevers and fluxes raged through the colony and so many died, Oglethorpe blamed it on the indulgence in liquid spirits that attended his absence. Despite Oglethorpe's rantings about the evils of drinking, people were dying and the colony was in real trouble. Without notice, a shipload of refugee Jews arrived in the colony. Oglethorpe accepted the offer of assistance from Dr. Nunis, a physician on board, whose ministrations soon restored confi-

The Jerusalem Lutheran Church at Ebenezer, a few miles north of Savannah on the Savannah River, recalls the earliest days of the colony when persecuted German and Austrian Protestants, many from Salzburg, found refuge in Georgia. The Reverend John Martin Bolzius was the religious teacher and leader of the Salzburgers. In 1736, after two years of considerable hardship and illness in their first settlement, Bolzius petitioned Oglethorpe for a better location. Within the year the Salzburgers settled in New Ebenezer where Oglethorpe laid out a town of four squares on a plan similar to Savannah's. From Historical Collections of Georgia, *by George White, 1855*

dence of recovery to the colony. As a result, Oglethorpe allowed them to remain.

Meanwhile, in London, applications for passage to Georgia were pouring in from all over Europe. Many of these requests were from religious sects suffering persecution. Salzburgers, Moravians, Huguenots—all became part of Savannah history. They were hard-working, humble, and religious people who for the most part were of a higher character than the native English selected by the Trustees. Probably the most influential were the Scot Highlanders, proud and aggressive military men, from whose ranks would come a never-ending list of heroes in all the wars to come. Oglethorpe settled them at Darien near the southern border, close to the Spanish threat. They thrived there.

In the ten years that Oglethorpe remained involved with Georgia, the Trustees sent over approximately 2,000 settlers. This early mix produced a truly American microcosm with influences from many nations, pockets of varied cultures, and a level of religious tolerance as high as any colony could boast.

Oglethorpe had intended to return to England after laying out the town and assigning lots to the settlers, but the heavy toll of fevers that first summer convinced him that he was needed. Problems mounted and he was delayed until the following year. When he left, the colony was reported to be in good shape. Thomas Christie, Recorder, wrote that where once had been trees that hid the houses, now he could "... scarce see any Trees for Houses." Samuel Eveleigh, a Charlestown businessman, wrote to Oglethorpe in October of 1734: "I found a great alteration every way for the better from what it was when I was last there.... There are about four score houses built and forty more going forward, besides several additions making to their former ones. Muir is building a two-story house joining to his former one. ..."

Construction was of the most readily available material—wood. The average house was twenty-four by sixteen feet,

raised off the ground, with a sleeping loft under the roof. A fire during the first winter underscored the need for brick, at least in the fireplaces.

Colonist Elisha Dobree wrote numerous pleading letters to the Trustees. In January 1735 he wrote: "As we have no fresh beef nor pork out of the Store, eating so much salt meat heats the blood and causes the scurvy ... I am sorry that I have reason to inform Your Honourable Board that the workmen at Tybee are almost continually drunk and that the lighthouse is not like to be quickly built. ..."

The ideal of agrarian equality was all very well on paper, but it did not translate to the soil and climate of Savannah. The flat, sandy bluff of the townsite provided equality in the parceling of house-lots, but the farmlands farther inland were by no means equal. Although some settlers actually had rich, easily cultivated land, some found themselves practically under water while others wrestled with useless topsoil. In addition, other inhabitants made life miserable—cockroaches, sandflies, ants, and dragon-like alligators. Early on, Oglethorpe handled the alligator fear in revealing fashion. Soon after the colonists landed, a twelve-foot gator was hauled up the bluff—causing a panic. Oglethorpe called some of the young boys over, gave them sticks, and had them beat the poor gator to death, proving to all onlookers that the Georgia gator was no match for stout English youths.

Reports of chamber pots freezing in the night, of icy winds and rains that made work impossible, and of heat and drought that parched the summer crops went back to the Trustees. To top it off deer, opossums, and raccoons ate the gardens and "other vermin" attacked all that was growing. The Trustees were besieged with conflicting reports about the colony's progress. Letters confirming their hopes for success were intermixed with ones predicting the certain doom of the experiment. Sir Robert Walpole, Chancellor of the Exchequer, held power over the budget of the government and

John Wesley found his ministry in the Georgia colony beset with frustrations. The discipline Wesley attempted to impose did not sit well with the struggling colonists who sought merely to survive in the alien land. Embroiled in scandal and fearful of arrest, Wesley left Savannah to follow a course which ultimately brought him world prominence as a great Protestant leader. Courtesy, V. & J. Duncan Antique Maps & Prints

kept the Trustees in line by forcing them to appeal for funds annually rather than including the colony in the regular budget. There was never enough money from donations. The anticipated money crops were not forthcoming and the very real threat of the Spaniards was ever present.

From the colonists' first landing at Savannah, the Spaniards had lodged protests. Diplomatic solution became less likely as Oglethrope pushed farther south into Spanish territory, building forts to protect the main colony at Savannah. In 1736 Oglethorpe began constructing a fort at Frederica on St. Simons Island. Guarding the Inland Passage, Fort Frederica was to balance the Spanish stronghold nearby at St. Augustine.

Oglethorpe invaded Florida after an incident in Spanish territory (Amelia Island) where two Englishmen were killed. He ravaged the countryside all the way to St. Augustine, where he burned the town. Lacking mortars and heavy artillery, Oglethorpe was unable to take the fort. When expected reinforcements from Carolina failed to arrive, he gave up the campaign and returned to Frederica.

In retaliation for Oglethorpe's invasion, Spain landed a large force close to Frederica. At the battle of Bloody Marsh, Oglethorpe's forces surprised the Spanish advance troops and sent them retreating. Believing the English force to be larger

The Reverend George Whitefield, co-founder of Methodism and successor to John Wesley as minister to Georgia, blazed a fiery path of piety through the colonies as one of the nation's first great traveling evangelists. From Historical Collections of Georgia, *by George White, 1855*

than it was, the Spaniards took to their ships and left Georgia. It was the last invasion of English territory in America by Spanish armies. Actually, Oglethorpe had tricked them with false intelligence reports. The Spanish force vastly outnumbered Oglethorpe's which consisted of a single regiment, some irregulars, and friendly Indians.

Georgia's population in 1737 was about 5,000; after the failure at St. Augustine no more than a few hundred remained. Most fled to Charlestown where land and slaves were available. A group of 121 dissenters who called themselves the Malcontents had petitioned the Trustees for a change of status concerning land ownership, slave labor, and trade restrictions, but their petitions were turned down. They removed to Charlestown en masse in 1741.

John Wesley had found the place intolerable. In 1736 he accepted the call to the colony, fully prepared to impose the

spirit of God on settler and Indian alike. Wesley's ardor and strict discipline did not sit well with the realities of life in Georgia, however, so he quickly encountered resistance and finally, failure. Accused of improper conduct by a jealous husband, John Wesley was scheduled for trial and punishment when he "shook off the dust of . . . [his] feet, and left Georgia" one evening after vespers and walked to Carolina. He wrote that Georgia was ". . . a Settlement of Opposums, Raccoons and the like Inhabitants." Being run out of the colony was preceded by a number of accomplishments—he established the first Sunday school in America, fostered the growth of education among the settlers and the Indians, and published his first book of hymns.

John Wesley was succeeded by George Whitefield, who many called the greatest orator of his time. Before departing England, Whitefield learned from John's brother, Charles Wesley, that many children were wandering the colony parentless and homeless. Within a month after arriving, Whitefield knew his task—to save the children. He returned to England to raise money for his project. Undaunted by the negative reaction that attended any mention of the Georgia colony, he managed to obtain a grant of 500 acres, funds for building an elaborate orphanage, and a staff of thirteen.

Returning to Savannah early in 1740, Whitefield rented the largest house in town from David Douglass as a temporary headquarters and within a week was taking in children—by the ear! With unbounded energy he rushed through the streets of decaying Savannah collaring children for his orphanage. By March he had laid out the site and begun construction on the elaborate Bethesda complex which is still in operation.

Whitefield, like Wesley before him, made his own rules. He feared no man, confronted anyone, and defied whom he chose—including Oglethorpe.

Whitefield had summarily plucked the two young Milledge children from the home of their brother, John, who had in-

After a stormy history as an orphanage, a school, and a college, Bethesda was a well-established institution of national reputation by the 1890s. Founded by the Reverend George Whitefield in 1736, the orphanage was co-educational until 1801 when it became the Bethesda Home for Boys. From Art Work of Savannah, *by Charles H. Olmstead, 1893*

herited the family responsibility from his father. Young John was industrious, ingratiating himself with Oglethorpe who requested the return of the children to their proper home. Whitefield replied that John's "Brother and Sister were at their proper Home already ... [Furthermore,] you can tell General Oglethorpe I said so." A few days later, Whitefield and his assistant, James Habersham, left for a trip to Pennsylvania. John Milledge took the children back home where, despite the hardship, they eventually prevailed and became one of Georgia's most influential families.

In Philadelphia, Whitefield confronted Ben Franklin who did not fully approve of placing the orphanage in Savannah. Whitefield preached such a sermon that even the thrifty Mr. Franklin emptied his purse afterward.

Savannah did not provide the proper environment for Whitefield's ambition, however. After establishing the orphanage he moved north where his contributions to the new denomination of Methodism were, like Wesley's, monumental.

Within a decade of its founding, the colony was inextricably in debt. Rumors of mismanagement of the Trustees' funds, of graft and corruption and favoritism by appointed officials kept the colony in turmoil. With so many duties and tasks, even the industrious colonists were in danger of going under. Oglethorpe's military forays took them away from their essential labors. As a result, much land went uncleared, gardens went to seed, and houses crumbled from lack of repair.

The dream was ending.

Before Oglethorpe's victory at Bloody Marsh in 1742, Parliament was debating the wisdom of continuing the colony. It was suggested that the borders be drawn

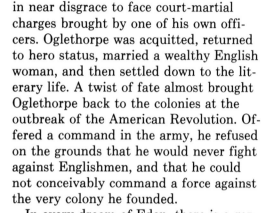

Christ Church on Johnson Square is the spiritual birthplace of Savannah. Its former ministers include John Wesley, George Whitefield, Bartholomew Zouberbuhler (the highly successful minister under the royal governors), and the revered Stephen Elliott, First Bishop of Georgia. The recently refurbished building is a virtual duplicate of the one that burned in 1897. Photo by Chan Sieg

back to Port Royal, establishing a neutral zone between the Spanish and the English. Many of the Trustees lost interest in the project and failed to attend the meetings. Even Oglethorpe became the target of adverse criticism. Military expenditures exceeded all estimates, but he would not be deterred in his efforts to defeat the Spaniards. Lacking funds from the government, Oglethorpe liberally spent his own. Following Bloody Marsh, he mounted another disastrous assault on the bastion at St. Augustine. Failure to destroy the fort sent Oglethorpe home

in near disgrace to face court-martial charges brought by one of his own officers. Oglethorpe was acquitted, returned to hero status, married a wealthy English woman, and then settled down to the literary life. A twist of fate almost brought Oglethorpe back to the colonies at the outbreak of the American Revolution. Offered a command in the army, he refused on the grounds that he would never fight against Englishmen, and that he could not conceivably command a force against the very colony he founded.

In every dream of Eden, there is a garden. The Trustees were not remiss in providing for this most apt expression of their idealism when they reserved a ten-acre plot on the eastern edge of the townsite. The Trustees' Garden was to be the fountain from which all good things would flow out to the entire colony. Here would flourish almonds, pomegranates, grapes, peaches, oranges, limes, and even coffee. The mulberry trees needed to feed the silkworms would nurse here. Lands cleared and soil turned, the presumably industrious colonists would call here for an assortment of eatables and exportables. All would thrive.

In the beginning, the word of the garden's progress was good. Samuel Eveleigh reported 1,000 mulberry trees in even rows were exhibiting new growth and estimated that in a short time there would be 100,000. There were experimental sections of herbs (cinnamon, thyme, balsam); there were figs and olives; there were Indian corn and peas, English beans, cabbage, and cucumbers. But there were also the seeds of gall and bitter wormwood. Mr. Houstoun, official botanist for the colony, died gathering the exotic plants of Jamaica; his replacement, Mr. Miller, was captured by the Spaniards, and he and his plant collection never reached the colony; Joseph Fitzwalter, gardener, was reputed to be better at gaming and fishing with his cronies than at tending the Trustees' Garden, for he lived off his wife's illegal bartending profits; Paul Amatis, silk expert from Italy, struggled with Fitzwalter

for control of the garden; and the Camuse family, successors to Amatis as silk experts, included the infamous Madame Camuse, a tantrum-ridden woman who kept her silk-spinning secrets to herself.

Savannah's climate was not conducive to tropical cultivation. The grapevines withered in summer and the citrus plants froze in winter. Animals wandered freely through the colony rooting the growing crops. People were equally destructive, plucking the fruit as it ripened, stealing plants, walking through freshly tended beds, and even cutting down the trees which served to protect the young seedlings from wind and sunburn.

The dream was ending.

In the second decade, with Oglethorpe

gone, the remaining Trustees slowly permitted reality to overcome philanthropic idealism. High expectations gave way to the bottom line of debt. One by one, the prohibitions were removed or unenforced. Restrictions on land and rum passed into history. Urged on by an impassioned plea from Whitefield, the Trustees approved the importation of slaves in 1749. In 1752, having failed to solicit further aid for their colony, the Trustees surrendered the charter to the Crown.

Of the first forty families who came on the *Anne* to found Savannah, only one head of a family remained. Captain Noble Jones survived to achieve all that the dream had promised.

Captain Noble Jones staked his claim to the land which became the famous Wormsloe, establishing a family legacy which continues to the present day. From a sketch by Christopher Murphy. Courtesy, Georgia Historical Society

CHAPTER II

The seal of the Trustees is a graphic representation of the idealism attending the birth of the thirteenth colony. The foreground figures symbolize the confluence of two rivers, Altamaha and Savannah, between which would be found a land of plenty, the New Eden. From Historical Collections of Georgia, by George White, 1855

ROYALTIES AND PROFITS

As the Trustees soothed their egos in the coffee-houses of London, a group of survivors in the colony were already pushing forward their individual designs for the future. Tempered by twenty years of vicissitude, by all the hardship that temperature, insects, disease, Indians, Spaniards, Oglethorpe, and

the Trustees could throw at them, Savannahians had developed into a new breed. Having at last gained true ownership of their lands, they were not about to let go easily. Most of them had buried parents, husbands, wives, and children on these lands; it was for these lands they had left England and neither Indian, Spaniard, nor cold of winter would drive them away now.

Ironically, these men—Jones, Habersham, Bryan, Ewen, Milledge, Parker—were the very sort the Trustees had in mind from the beginning. Acquainted too well with the enemies around them, they were strong, intelligent, and willing to work. Reasonable men, they demanded only that bargains be kept, that they be treated as free Englishmen and left unencumbered to hack out their destinies in the wilderness of the New World, and a fair share of the profits. For two decades, England was a fading memory to these families who, deposited in an alien, hostile land and denied the minimal basics of food and medicine, were obliged to develop their own resources in order to survive. In doing so, they became fiercely independent. An intense self-sufficiency was transmitted to the next generation which—despite the protests of their fathers—brought Georgia, the most loyal of the English colonies, into the Revolution as an American sovereign state.

Progress as a royal colony was phenomenal. Population and wealth increased at a rate unprecedented in the Americas. By the time of the Revolution, Savannah had reached a position of some importance.

In late October 1754, Captain John Reynolds of His Majesty's Navy barged into Savannah as the first of three royal governors to serve in Georgia. The city gave a rousing welcome to Reynolds, symbolic of the new day coming. Two-and-a-half years later, they gave an even bigger party when he was recalled. Reynolds probably was an able commander at sea, but in Savannah he managed to alienate virtually everyone.

Under the Trustees, the colonists had practically no voice in the government of the colony. Oglethorpe's presence at least allowed the settlers an authority figure to whom they could appeal grievances. As a royal colony, Georgia was organized along traditional lines. At the head, with supreme authority, was the governor and his official staff; next was the council which was an advisory board of leading citizens, usually the affluent merchants and planters; and last was the assembly of elected representatives. Trouble in the colonies usually arose in the elected assemblies and Reynolds found his assembly no exception. Starved for a voice in their own destinies, the colonists eagerly greeted the new governor. But what Reynolds expected was no more than a rubber-stamp legislature which acted on his decisions without question. Within a week, he was in trouble.

Meeting with the council in the ram-

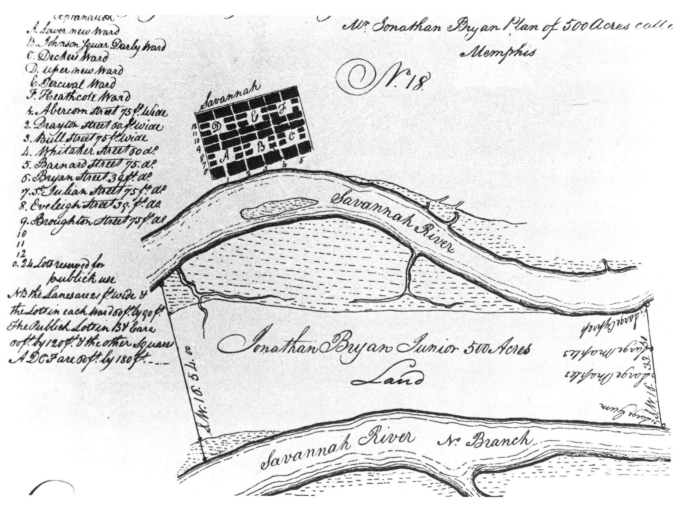

This 1752 plan depicts Jonathan Bryan, Jr.'s 500 acres on Hutchinson Island in the middle of the Savannah River. This simple sketch is the oldest known map of Savannah. Courtesy, CEL Regional Library, Gamble Collection

shackle old Council House, Reynolds presided over a discussion of the "ruinous condition" of the building. Debate concerning the erection of a "proper government house" was followed by the collapse of the roof. Fortunately for Reynolds, he escaped and ruled the colony for two-and-a-half years, but being neither politically astute nor diplomatically inclined, his career was downhill thereafter.

In 1757 the colony had survived twenty-four years and it was ready for something pleasant to happen. The happy event occurred on February 16 when Henry Ellis arrived to replace John Reynolds. Ellis, an independently wealthy man in his mid-thirties, had already distinguished himself by publishing a book which gained him entrance into the Royal Academy of Science. True to the enlightened attitude of his time, Ellis prided himself on his objective, logical observance of "all natural phenomena." His book resulted from a journey to the Hudson Bay region in search of the fabled Northwest Passage. As related by historian W.W. Abbott in his work, *The Royal Governors of Georgia,* Ellis' book detailed everything Ellis observed "in the heavens above and the earth beneath." He was particularly interested in temperature and, according to Abbott, his "deductions and conclusions are always logical, plausible, stimulating, and delivered with clarity and pungency. Unfortunately they are nearly always mistaken."

Ellis' observations of the Georgia colony were, however, accurate. His first act was to dissolve the assembly, which had been packed with Reynolds' cronies. Then he sat back and waited. As the political storms began to subside, Ellis slowly embarked on a program to bring the colony into the mainstream of the British Empire. He placed tax assessments on the elected legislature by wisely submitting an advance budget for the colony, then allowing the representatives to work it out. He issued paper currency to get the colony through a difficult time, allowing the planters sufficient credit to bring in their crops. He set about preparing a plan for the defense and security of the colony in order to attract new "persons of substance" to settle there.

The French and Indian War was underway in the north and threatened to erupt in Georgia at any time. With Mobile a strong French bastion and Indian trouble in Georgia, few new settlers chose to come.

To establish legal claims to territory already held by one European nation, the others—Britain, Spain, France, and Holland—convinced local Indian leaders to cede the desired territory to them. Elaborate papers were drawn, gifts given, and mutual admiration speeches delivered, after which the Europeans took over. Oglethorpe's first act in Georgia was to sign such a treaty with Tomochichi, chief of the "small Nation of Indians" occupying the bank of the Savannah River. Subsequent treaties with the Upper and Lower Creeks resulted in a colony that was squeezed along the coast, extending inland about thirty miles. Tomochichi, whose friendship and loyalty to Oglethorpe are legendary, visited England with trader John Musgrove as interpreter on Oglethorpe's first trip home in 1734. The rare visit of the "savages" to London was sufficient to cause great social excitement, and Tomochichi's entourage was wined and dined and presented at Court. While impressed with the might of the British Empire, the old chief did not take well to European city life. He wondered why anyone would take the trouble to build a house that would outlive him. Observing the corruption, the profligacy of the upper classes, the virtual enslavement of the poor, and the general filth, Tomochichi longed for his marshy Eden.

"I think this is a damned country, and that if you will take my advice we will be gone out of it as soon as we can."

John Musgrove, on the other hand, must have had the time of his life among the London elite. John and his wife, Mary, served Oglethorpe as interpreters and liaison with the Indians for several years. He is said to have remained so intoxicated that often the business meetings were postponed until he was sober enough to interpret the proceedings. John died of the "fevers" a few months after returning from London, leaving Mary Musgrove a healthy legacy of their trading post (called the Cowpen because of the cattle raised there), a 500-acre plantation called Grantham, a fine house, and ten indentured servants to tend stock and crops. In a few years Mary married Jacob Matthews, with whom she began—at Oglethorpe's request—a new trading post at Fort Venture on the Altamaha. In 1742, as Jacob lay sick in Savannah, Fort Venture was attacked by Indians from the Spanish territories and destroyed. Jacob's death soon after left Mary grieving over the loss of two husbands, four sons, and a large sum of money. In 1744 Mary married Thomas Bosomworth, minister of the colony, and together they formed a plan to enrich themselves.

Upon Oglethorpe's departure, Mary received his thanks and £200, with a promise of more to come. Now she planned to collect. Mary and Bosomworth marched on Savannah with a band of armed Indians. The Bosomworths' demands were not merely for money owed, which the Trustees had refused to pay. Being the niece of the Creek Emperor Brim, Mary had been declared Empress by some of the Creek chiefs who now accompanied her to Savannah for protection. By inheritance from Tomochichi, she claimed the land between Savannah and the inlet formerly occupied by the Yamacraw tribe, and the three Golden Isles of Ossabaw, Sapelo, and St. Catherines. Captain Noble Jones, young John Milledge, and a small group of rangers met them on the road and persuaded them to disarm before entering the city.

The Bosomworth plan was a major threat to the whole colony. For the first time, Savannah was faced with the possibility of warfare on its streets. Together with town leaders Stephens, Habersham, and Jones, the Bosomworths and the Indians feasted, drank, smoked the pipe, and argued for nearly a month. Mary flew into rages as she saw her cause slipping away. "A fig for your general!" she cried, "this very earth is mine."

After more than three weeks, the Indians were given provisions and boats and shipped upriver. Mary was informed she could have the islands, and a mollified Bosomworth took her to St. Catherines.

It was Ellis who finally cleared the matter once and for all. He summoned the Creek chiefs to Savannah, and there he staged an elaborate ceremony with soldiers marching, forming columns through which the chiefs were led to the royal governor's house while guns were fired and crowds cheered. At a feast, Ellis persuaded the chiefs to sign a mutual defense pact giving a measure of security to the colony against the French and Spaniards. As an afterthought he elicited from them a declaration that Mary had not been granted all the lands she claimed and that they, the chiefs, had the power to grant them to the royal governor. They agreed. Ellis chose not to lord this over Mary but persuaded the board to settle with her. Mary Musgrove Matthews Bosomworth finally received a Crown grant of the 6,200 acres of St. Catherines Island and £2,000 in return for renouncing all her other claims. Everyone was satisfied: Ellis was firmly entrenched as governor, the Indians had a British alliance, the colonists felt secure enough to return to their planting, and Mary was once again the richest, largest landholder in Georgia.

Ellis' tenure was short-lived, but effective. In three years he turned the fortunes of the colony; the population increased rapidly, and production and trade more than doubled. In 1758 a group of Congregationalists moved into Sunbury, near St. Catherines. Sunbury grew rapidly and rivaled Savannah as a trade and plantation center within a mere ten years. It also became the center of anti-British sentiment, producing many Revolutionary leaders.

Ellis resigned late in 1759, citing the "intense heats" of Savannah as the cause. The most vivid memory of this "acute observer of all natural phenomena" was of his daily stroll through the squares, protected from the sun by a large umbrella from which dangled "to the height of his nostrils" a thermometer. As published in *London Magazine* in 1759, his conclusion from these careful observations was: "It is highly possible that the people of Savannah breathe a hotter air than any other people on the face of the earth!"

Ellis was succeeded by James Wright. In mere months, Wright led the youngest colony through stages of development that had required years in the other colonies. Wright's administration was geared to accommodate the "men of substance" who began to pour into Georgia from other colonies and from the plantations of the Indies. Aided by liberal credit policies and cheap labor, they transformed the coastal plains into the great plantations of legend. Wharf facilities and warehouses appeared on the bluff as shipping demands increased almost daily. Savannah and Sunbury became ports of entry in the vast mercantile system and the new wealth brought British-manufactured goods into Georgia in prodigious quantities. A new social life developed as the wealthy found the leisure to entertain themselves, to display the new silver service, the silks and satins of London salons, and the new handcrafted carriages.

Intensely loyal to all things British, Wright had engendered a truly English city in miniature. In slightly more than a decade, he was rewarded by the Crown with a baronetcy. Wright had become the most powerful and respected of all the colonial governors of his period. In the process, he also became wealthy.

During their visit to England in 1734, Tomochichi and his nephew sat for a portrait by Willem Verelst. Though impressed with London, Tomochichi was happy to "return to nature." When the ninety-seven-year-old chief died in 1739, Oglethorpe was a pallbearer and ordered a state funeral, burying Tomochichi in the center of Wright Square. In 1899 the Colonial Dames placed a granite marker to Tomochichi in the southeast corner of the square. Courtesy, Tybee Museum

Savannah prospered under the able administration of Sir James Wright. From 1760 until the Revolution, Wright increased the size of the royal colony through acquisition of Indian territory, encouraged immigration, expanded the economic base, and raised Savannah to a position of some importance as a port. Courtesy, National Park Service, Fort Pulaski National Monument

Under the governors, the practical aspects of the Trustees' dream came to pass as Georgia entered the mainstream of the British economy and, as the southernmost extremity of British America (until the 1763 acquisition of Florida), it served well as the intended buffer. Savannah was also now an increasingly important market for British goods. The other ideal aspects of the Trustees' dream remained just that—a dream woven into the imagination of certain individuals who were already thinking of themselves as "Americans."

Despite the Trustees' ban on the im-

portation of slaves, the colonists had not hesitated to rent them from Carolina whenever need dictated or money permitted. Much of the original town is thought to have been built by black craftsmen from Charlestown. As early as 1740, a slave was sold at an auction in Savannah. He was the property of the Reverend Mr. Dyson, chaplain of Oglethorpe's regiment, who received for him twenty-three pounds and five shillings. Later that same year, a second slave brought only eight pounds and ten shillings. Contrast this with the raffle of a horse the same summer which brought twelve pounds.

Silk and wine, the anticipated money crops, had not proved successful although early signs brought great expectations. Both climate and soil mitigated against the grape harvest. The intense labor requirements and the specialized skills limited the production of silk. In 1751 a filature was erected and equipped for preparing cocoons and winding silk. Burned and rebuilt in the late 1750s, the Filature served as a center for the silk industry until the Revolution when it became a warehouse and sometime meeting place until it burned in 1839.

The big money crop was rice. The rice and indigo of Carolina had made it one of the richest colonies. Savannah longed to follow suit, but the demanding labor was not for decent Englishmen, unaccustomed to the backbreaking toil under the scorching sun in a flooded rice field. The repeal of the slavery ban solved the problem. The planters who could afford to import labor were off and running—to the bank.

James Habersham, Whitefield's assistant, had joined with Francis (sometimes referred to as Charles) Harris to form a commercial company. With offices on the waterfront, they began a small import business. In 1749 they sent the first commercial vessel loaded with deerskins, lumber, cattle, hogs, and poultry with a value of about $10,000. Prior to this sailing, all commerce in and out of Savannah had passed through Port Royal or Charlestown. With no staple commodity

Above: *James Potter's rice plantation was located a few miles upriver from Savannah. The simple frame house with long, covered porches is probably more typical of plantation homes than the more publicized "Tara." From* Historical Collections of Georgia, *by George White, 1855*

Left: *While shipping cotton brought great profits to a handful of Savannah merchants, the primary crop on the plantations was rice, which thrived from colonial days until after the Civil War. From* Harper's Weekly, *January 5, 1867. Courtesy, CEL Regional Library, Gamble Collection*

James Habersham, who came to Georgia with the Reverend George Whitefield, remained to found one of the state's most distinguished families. A trusted friend of Governor James Wright, Habersham was also a member of the royal council. Courtesy, CEL Regional Library, Gamble Collection

to attract business, Savannah languished at the mercy of the Carolina traders. Habersham and Harris' venture broke that stranglehold and others followed their lead. With rice the needed staple commodity, exports jumped to $75,000 by 1753.

The lowlands surrounding Savannah and lying along the coast were rapidly converted into rice fields as the planters took every advantage of the Trustees' allowance of land ownership and slave importation and the governor's liberal credit accommodations.

Forty-two vessels traded in Savannah in 1760 with rice exports of 3,400 pounds. A few months later, Savannah celebrated the coronation of George III. Anti-British

rumblings had periodically erupted in the northern colonies for many years, but in Savannah newly prosperous gratitude and loyalty were the expressions of the moment. In 1762 Wright was named Captain General and Commander-in-Chief, cause enough for a general holiday and gala ball at the governor's new mansion on St. James' (now Telfair) Square.

Seventeen sixty-three was a banner year for the British Empire and for Savannah in particular. Victorious over France and Spain, Britain now dominated the entire North American coast from Newfoundland to the tip of Florida. The acquisition of Florida put the seal of security on the Georgia colony after thirty years of fear. Prosperity had just begun.

Savannah has always exported more than cotton, rice, and timber products. The cupola is that of the city's first export firm, Habersham and Harris Company, established in 1744 and closed in 1899. Courtesy, Georgia Historical Society

The reverse face of the seal of the Trustees proclaimed that the colony was founded "not for themselves but for others." The hope that the Piedmontese Italians would produce a thriving silk industry is represented by the mulberry leaf, silkworm, and cocoon. Photo by Chan Sieg

In that same year, the *Georgia Gazette*—the first newspaper in the colony—began publication. Exports reached nearly $200,000. Indian treaties increased the size of the colony by millions of acres, which attracted settlers from Virginia, the Carolinas, Ireland, and Scotland. Roads and bridges were constructed to allow the easy passage of produce to the port, and public buildings and private homes increased in number and size.

In 1764 Robert Bolton accepted the task of establishing the first regular postal service, and, anticipating the future, the intrepid James Habersham shipped eight pounds of cotton to England. The shipment confounded the customs officials who confiscated it, be-lieving it was contraband because cotton "in such quantity" could not have been produced in Georgia.

Ten years as a royal colony had produced incredible changes in Savannah—and in Georgia. Reynolds ruled a colony of hardly more than 3,000 inhabitants—slaves included—who were stretched out along a narrow strip of coastline 300 miles long. Nine years later, in 1766, Wright was able to boast "... by a very careful inquiry from every part of the Province, the white people amount to 9,900, or say 10,000. ..." In addition, "My Lord, we have at least 7,800 [slaves]." Rice exports had tripled in only six years and shipping increased from "forty-two sail" to 153.

GEORGE III.

Wale delin.   Taylor Sca.

Engraved for
Russels History
of England.

George III, grandson of George II, ascended the British throne in February of 1761, making his the first coronation to be proclaimed on Georgia soil. It was also the last. While George III was respected by Savannah's loyalists, he was burned in effigy by the rebels. Courtesy, V. & J. Duncan Antique Maps & Prints

William Pitt opposed the exploitation of the colonies by Parliament, and America prospered under Pitt's leadership as prime minister. Out of office, he remained sympathetic to the American cause which demanded little more than equal treatment under British law. After the Revolution, grateful Savannahians named their county after Pitt, the Earl of Chatham. Courtesy, V. & J. Duncan Antique Maps & Prints

In 1765 Governor Wright was at the peak of his success. Everyone was happy until the news from England arrived: Parliament had passed the Stamp Act.

Passed despite William Pitt's objections, the Stamp Act was designed to refurbish the depleted treasury. In reality a small matter (a yawning Parliament had voted it in late one afternoon), the act imposed a token tax in the form of a stamp to be purchased and affixed to certain legal and commercial documents and to imported items such as playing cards and dice—popular items in the colonies. In London the colonies were represented by agents who supposedly looked out for the colonies' interests. In Savannah—the assembly and council so desiring—Wright requested James Habersham to instruct William Knox, Georgia's agent, to oppose the act. Knox refused and was fired by the assembly over Wright's veto. Wright retaliated by refusing to endorse another agent selected by the assembly. In loyalty to the king, Wright enforced the Stamp Act in Georgia—the only governor who was able to do so. Sixty ships were detained in Savannah's harbor awaiting the arrival of the stamps. The *Georgia Gazette,* one of only eight regularly printed newspapers in the colonies, ceased publication because publisher James Johnston was unable to pay the stamp tax. Urged on by radicals from South Carolina, the newly emerged "Liberty Boys" of Savannah threatened to seize and burn the stamps. Wright called out the troops and saved the stamps. His singular loyalty earned him a baronetcy. It also earned him a string of problems which resulted in his downfall.

A few months later, Pitt persuaded Parliament to repeal the Stamp Act. Wright, against the act to begin with, had used his power to enforce it, only to have the rug pulled out. His opposition had proved correct, leaving Wright's position one that henceforth would be recorded as a struggle to preserve royal power against an assembly that would no longer accept the status of "second class citizens."

Looking back on that first decade, when mere survival was the uppermost goal, one can well understand the grumblings of the Malcontents, but the decade under the royal governors produced real prosperity. This new generation of Malcontents—calling themselves "Sons of Liberty"—had little reason to grumble. The stamp tax applied to a relatively few wealthy merchants and traders in Savannah and it was not punitive to the point of stirring up a mob. In addition, the Sons of Liberty were sons of the wealthy—or at least composed the core of Savannah society. Opposition to the king's wishes seemed therefore, unreasonable, if not self-destructive.

In Savannah's early years, the arrival of a single ship might provoke a day-long celebration. There was even rejoicing when a privateer carrying smuggled goods coursed up the inland waterway, particularly if there was rum aboard. The settlers who had survived the hardships to become wealthy and respected could ill afford disloyalty to the government that made their status possible, but the next generation had other ideas.

In 1765 the Sons of Liberty distributed pamphlets, circulars, and petitions throughout the colonies. In Savannah, while the old guard discussed these "nuisances from the rabble," this new generation of malcontents was outside the door, setting up liberty poles and burning the king's image.

CHAPTER III

Sergeant William Jasper's last moments are depicted on a frieze decorating his monument in Madison Square. Jasper, a loyalist from South Carolina, is romantically credited with "saving the colors"—amid grapeshot and cannon fire—during the American attack on British-held Savannah in 1779. Photo by Beth Holland

THE AMERICAN REVOLUTION

The repeal of the Stamp Act provided justification and a sense of power to the liberty faction in all the colonies. After that victory, punitive legislation from Parliament was met with protests of public outcry—except in Tory Savannah where Noble Wimberly Jones, speaker of the assembly, quietly led the

assembly to increasing power against the governor and council. Prosperity continued as exports increased, and new settlers spread into the back country.

On Christmas Eve 1768, Dr. Jones took the step that separated him from the governor from then on. The Townshend Acts had imposed duties on numerous items imported into the colonies—glass products, paper goods, red and white lead, paint, and tea. Virginia and Massachusetts sent circulars asking other colonies to ban the importation of all listed items. Wright was faced with an assembly that included eighteen Liberty Party members out of twenty-five, and was surprised to find that Jones took no public notice of the requests for non-importation. Passing all the money bills requested by Wright, Jones asked for adjournment at 6 p.m. on Christmas Eve. The governor agreed. In the final hour Jones pushed through a bill in opposition to the Townshend Acts. Wright dissolved the assembly.

In the elections of 1770 the Liberty Party (Whigs) was virtually unopposed. Dr. Jones was again elected speaker. Wright immediately dissolved the assembly, remembering the Christmas Eve defeat and smarting from the consequent loss of an influential member of his council. Jonathan Bryan, rich merchant-planter and trusted council member, openly took sides with the Whigs, chairing public meetings to protest the "taxation without representation" poli-

cies of Parliament. Bryan was dismissed by order of the king.

While Wright was in London gathering the rewards of loyalty, the agonies of historic change touched the first families of Savannah. Acting Governor James Habersham, under orders from Wright, opposed the reelection of Jones as speaker. Jones' father, the elder Noble, was Habersham's longtime friend and co-member of the council. By using Habersham's prestige, Wright had hoped to reestablish some of the governor's authority over the assembly. Habersham rejected Jones' election. The assembly promptly elected Jones again. Habersham rejected it again. A third time, Jones was elected. This time Dr. Noble Wimberly Jones refused to serve and the name of Archibald Bulloch was presented to Habersham and approved. Learning of the third election, Habersham asked that it be stricken from the records. The assembly refused and Habersham dissolved it. The ties that bind were beginning to unravel and the inhabitants of Savannah were forced to choose sides.

The choice in Savannah was not the extreme "liberty or death," but the more temperate choice between self-rule or subservience to Parliament. Loyal subjects of the king, they refused to be subjects of Parliament. George III had replaced the pro-colony government of Pitt and had loaded Parliament with his faction. Pitt became a great hero to the colonists because of his public defense of

"'Crackers'... Emigrating to Florida" is the title of this sketch from Frank Leslie's Illustrated Newspaper, *March 26, 1870.* "Crackers"—so named for the sound of their whips—first came to Savannah as the Revolution drew near. They garnered a reputation for rude and boisterous behavior, lack of breeding, and a total disrespect for authority. The word "cracker" quickly became a term of derision and has ever since been applied to rural Georgians. Courtesy, CEL Regional Library, Gamble Collection

their position. Despite its Whig leanings, Savannah was still a Tory town at the time of the Boston Tea Party.

A new element now made its presence known in the taverns and dirt streets of Savannah. The backwoods Georgians were tough, rough-hewn, virtually illiterate, and ready to fight for the only land they had ever owned. The radical gentry, Englishmen all, referred to these rowdies as "Crackers." But from this farming group would come the heroes of the Revolution, the guerrilla fighters who harassed the British throughout the war.

Another addition to the cautious liberal element in Savannah came from St. John's Parish. In a mere fifteen years,

the Congregationalists who settled there had built a thriving community. With close ties to Massachusetts, they openly sympathized with the causes of the rebellious Northern colonies. Wright referred to them as "Oliverians," meaning Cromwell—well remembered for beheading a king.

In 1775 (the year of his death), James Habersham wrote to London: "The People on this Continent are generally almost in a State of Madness, and Desperation.... I cannot think of this event but with Horror and Grief. Father against Son, and Son against Father, and nearest relations and Friends combatting with each other...."

Habersham left Savannah that year to die a refugee in New Jersey. He was Governor Wright's best friend. That same year, Wright lost two more trusted council members—Clement Martin and Noble Jones. A few months later, Wright would be placed under arrest by Major Joseph Habersham, son of James.

Meanwhile, as the "Indians" of Boston dumped tea in the harbor, Savannah was reporting a new high in exports of $350,000, partly because it acquired the business turned away from other ports by protesting rebels. Edward Telfair, Liberty Boy and merchant, was content to sympathize with the radicals, but he and the other leading shippers of Savannah conducted "business as usual."

Britain responded to the Boston Tea Party with the Intolerable Acts, which prompted Liberty Party leaders Noble Wimberly Jones, John Houstoun, Archibald Bulloch, and George Walton to call a protest meeting at Tondee's Tavern. Wright condemned the meeting and forbade any future gatherings. Two weeks later, on August 10, 1774, Savannah was host to radicals from every parish of the colony "who did attend at the Liberty Pole in front of Tondee's Tavern."

The group passed resolutions condemning British actions against Boston, they demanded "equal rights as Englishmen," and they did *not* elect delegates to the First Continental Congress—Georgia was the only colony not represented. The group shipped a load of rice and a sum of money to aid the besieged Bostonians. (This favor would be returned almost 100 years later.)

But the Sunbury crowd was dissatisfied. Ready for revolution, they sent Dr. Lyman Hall to the Continental Congress as the official delegate from the southern parishes of Georgia. In meetings with fellow radicals from Charlestown, they even entertained notions of seceding from Georgia and joining with Carolina.

In January 1775, Jones convened a meeting of Georgia's First Provincial Congress. Wright's influence resulted in only five of the twelve parishes sending

delegates. Ever mindful of duty, Jones' group continued to meet at Government House as assembly members, informing the governor of what was occurring at their other meetings as Liberty Boys. Jones, Bulloch, and Houstoun were selected to attend the Second Continental Congress in Philadelphia on May 10. To gain lawful recognition, the Liberty Boys switched to their assembly hats and were about to endorse the delegates when Wright dissolved the assembly. This ended colonial government in Georgia.

Despite this effrontery to the will of the people, Jones reacted in typical conservative fashion. He wrote to the officials in Philadelphia that Georgia's delegates could not attend the Congress because they did not truly represent all Georgia's parishes. The Continental Congress reacted by condemning Georgia and

Joseph Habersham, son of James Habersham, boldly and singlehandedly put an end to British rule in Savannah when he arrested the shocked Sir James Wright. The young Habersham was one of many sons of Savannah's elite who rebelled and were tragically pitted against their fathers during the American Revolution. Courtesy, V. & J. Duncan Antique Maps &

Facing page, left: Lachlan McIntosh left Savannah under a cloud following the death of Button Gwinnett in their famous duel. He joined the Revolutionary Army, and by the end of the war he was a hero again. His fortunes were not to be realized in the political arena as his later years were spent in minor government posts. But McIntosh's lack of fortune did not diminish his magnanimity: he pleaded the case for the first black church in America before Savannah's city council. His influence aided blacks in establishing their right to worship in the city. Courtesy, CEL Regional Library, Gamble Collection

placing bans on trading in Savannah. The Charlestown rebels threatened to come over and "cut some throats," calling the Georgians unpatriotic cowards.

Mobs now roamed Savannah's sandy streets, stealing sugar and molasses from British ships and even tarring and feathering a Tory sympathizer. By May, Noble Wimberly Jones was less moderate.

News of the fighting at Lexington reached Savannah on May 10. The next night N.W. Jones, Joseph Habersham, Edward Telfair, and others broke into the Filature—once the hope of the silk industry, now a warehouse—and stole the gunpowder stored there, which they shipped to Boston. Tradition has it that the powder was used at the Battle of Bunker Hill. Jones' character is revealed by his insistence on leaving a receipt for the theft. Wright and the council (the elders Jones and Habersham still serving) offered a reward for the perpetrators, but no one came forward to claim the money.

On July 4 the Second Provincial Congress met and became the ruling government of the colony. This time all parishes were represented. Stung by the rebuffs of the First Continental Congress, they immediately elected delegates to the Second Congress. Led by the large Savannah constituency, the group passed resolutions emphasizing their rights under English law, their desire to find a means of reconciling differences, and their continuing view of themselves as subjects of the king.

The delegates were N.W. Jones, Archibald Bulloch, John Houstoun, the Reverend J.J. Zubly, all from Savannah, and Dr. Lyman Hall of Sunbury. In September, Houstoun, Bulloch, and Zubly sat with the great Americans in Philadelphia. John Zubly was the respected minister of the Presbyterian congregation at Savannah. A leader in the drive for rights, he preached sermons on liberty which stirred all who listened. But Zubly left the Congress when its mood changed to one of separation from England. Returning to Savannah, he was held in disgrace and his property was confiscated.

For more than a year Wright had pleaded with Parliament to send troops to Savannah but, lulled into a false security by the tempered communications of the Savannah leaders, Parliament concentrated its attention on the Northern colonies. Driven from Charlestown, British ships seeking supplies arrived at the "loyal" port of Savannah in January 1776.

Incensed, the provisional government gave orders to Major Joseph Habersham. He marched to the governor's meeting with the council and arrested his father's best friend, Sir James Wright. Promising to remain under house arrest, the governor fled a few weeks later to John Mullryne's plantation estate, and from there to the waiting ships, carrying with him the seal of the colony.

Wright's power had started to wane with the Stamp Act, where his loyalty had reached its apex only to be undercut by Parliament's repeal. His clashes with Speaker Jones finally toppled the colonial government. Wright had come to believe, with George III, that military power and some punishment to the rebels would straighten out the colonies. While the Committee of Safety ruled the colony under the Provisional Congress, Savannah was placed under the agency of the Savannah Parochial Committee, headed by Mordecai Sheftall, a prominent Jewish merchant whose family dated to that first dreadful summer of 1733. Also on the committee were Peter Tondee, whose tavern was the center of radical meetings, and a blacksmith, Mr. Lyons. Wright expressed a loyalist attitude, typical of his class, that revealed an air of smug superiority too often displayed by the British upper classes, one which would eventually cost them the Empire itself: "The Parochial Committee are a Parcel of the Lowest People, chiefly Carpenters, Shoemakers, Blacksmiths, etc. with a Jew at their Head, in the General Committee, and the Council of Safety, there are some better sort of Men, and some merchants and Planters—but many of the Inferior Class. . . ."

Savannah now prepared for war. A battalion was formed under the command of Lachlan McIntosh of Darien, son of the Scottish leader settled there by Oglethorpe in 1736. He proved to be Georgia's most able commander. There was realistic concern about the Southern frontier. Scarcely more than ten years after the Spanish threat had ended, Savannah had a new enemy in Florida—the British.

When the Declaration of Independence was approved in Philadelphia, three Georgians signed it. Two from Sunbury (St. John's Parish), Lyman Hall and Button Gwinnett, were joined by George Walton, a Savannah lawyer.

Savannah threw an all-day celebration when the news arrived. Bulloch read the proclamation publicly three times, cannons were fired, the king was burned in effigy, and the royal government of Georgia was "solemnly buried."

Savannah had returned to the position it struggled so hard to abandon. For the second time in fifty years, its only rational path was toward survival. A loyal and law-abiding British seaport, it was forced to discard its heritage and begin anew. But now there were no Trustees to bombard with gripes, no Oglethorpe to protect them. With British armies massing to the south, unpredictable Creeks to the west, and bloodthirsty Charlestownians to the north threatening to "cut some throats" and annex them, it was just like the old days.

Events proceeded quickly. Archibald Bulloch, president of the Council of Safety, died suddenly and was succeeded by Button Gwinnett. Desiring to be a "leader of men into battle," Gwinnett failed to attract troops for an attack on Florida. An earlier attempt had failed under Charles Lee (of Virginia), while

Half a century after the Revolution, Sheftall, Sheftall, of Savannah's oldest Jewish family, was granted immunity from taxation, a unique honor in Savannah history. Sheftall wore only his Revolutionary uniform until his death. When the Marquis de Lafayette visited Savannah in 1825, Sheftall was one of a few comrades-in-arms still alive to personally welcome the great general. From Historical Collections of Georgia, *by George White, 1855*

McIntosh had proved his prowess by leading successful raids that drove the British back to St. Augustine. Gwinnett then was forced to seek aid from McIntosh which caused animosity between the two leaders. In addition, McIntosh's brother had been arrested and then cleared of illegal trading charges. The bad blood grew worse when the expedition failed, neither commander allowing his troops to take orders from the other. Gwinnett's failure cost him the election as Georgia's first governor under the new state constitution, a position which went to John Adam Treutlen, much to the delight of McIntosh. Taunting remarks by McIntosh provoked a challenge from Gwinnett, who was mortally wounded in the ensuing duel. (The early death of one of the signers of the Declaration resulted in a dearth of his autographs. Collectors estimate that a Gwinnett signature is the most valuable in the world, worth perhaps a quarter of a million dollars.) Dr. Lyman Hall, Gwinnett's friend, brought a murder charge against McIntosh who was acquitted and left Savannah to join Washington's army. The incident is indicative of the division already splitting the Whigs. Bickering led to another Florida disaster early in 1778 when the new governor, John Houstoun, clashed with Colonel George Walton and General Howe, the inept Continental commander. The British threat was realized when Savannah was easily taken on December 29, 1778. While leaders argued strategy, British commander Campbell, aided by Quash Dolly, a slave, slipped into the city behind the defenders. Howe's troops panicked, and many drowned while trying to cross the marshes to Carolina. More than 400 were captured including Mordecai Sheftall. Noble W. Jones fled to Charlestown where he was captured later.

The battle itself was undoubtedly shorter and less intense than the sacking which followed. Campbell's famed Highlanders in no way diminished their fierce reputation as they pursued a course of looting and lusting such as Savannah had never experienced. When calm finally

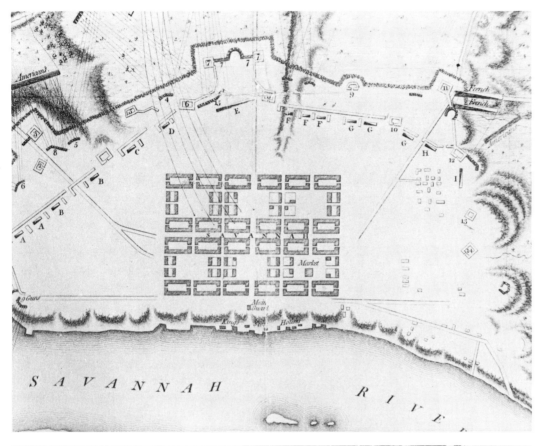

Facing page: *The Midway Church, located south of Savannah in Liberty County, was founded by Puritans in the 1750s. Though its membership never exceeded 150, many distinguished Americans are associated with this early bastion of democracy: Oliver Wendell Holmes' father, Samuel F.B. Morse's father, and two signers of the Declaration of Independence— Lyman Hall and Button Gwinnett. From Historical Collections of Georgia, by George White, 1855*

Top: *Savannah, a city walled for defense against the Spanish and Indians during the colonial era, proved invulnerable to American and French forces in the autumn of 1779. Despite the attackers' superior numbers, and days of artillery bombardment, the city remained in British hands until after Cornwallis' surrender. Shown is a detail of the "Plan of the Siege of Savannah" from History of the American War, by Charles Stedman, 1794*

Bottom: *Beaulieu was the country home of William Stephens, who served as the first president of the colony from 1743 to 1750. This bluff at Beaulieu, a few miles south of Savannah on the Vernon River, is where Comte d'Estaing and his French troops disembarked in September 1779, preceding the Siege of Savannah. From Art Work of Savannah, by Charles H. Olmstead, 1893*

General Benjamin Lincoln, Commander of the Southern Department of American forces, joined with French forces in the disastrous Siege of Savannah. The battle cost 1,000 lives, second in bloodshed only to Bunker Hill. The Americans retreated to South Carolina. Later, when the British seized Charleston, Lincoln was taken prisoner.
Courtesy, V. & J. Duncan Antique Maps & Prints

prevailed, Savannah was a British town again, ready for the return of Sir James Wright.

Sir James had just re-established his power when a French fleet under Comte d'Estaing arrived at Savannah, placing the city under siege. An American force under General Benjamin Lincoln, which included Savannah's legendary heroes Sergeant William Jasper, the dashing Polish cavalryman Pulaski, and Savannah's own Lachlan McIntosh, joined the French in what seemed an overwhelming force against a small British defense under General Prevost. But the French

leader, confident enough to be gallant, permitted "thinking time" to Prevost who thought the best thing to do was re-inforce his walls with cannon and delay long enough to allow Colonel Maitland's troops to arrive from Carolina. Two weeks into the siege, d'Estaing ordered an all-out assault which resulted in the bloodiest battle of the Revolution after Bunker Hill. Unknown to the American-French forces, Sergeant James Curry of Charlestown had informed Prevost of the attack point. Prevost concentrated his artillery batteries at that point, "pouring grape shot and chain" on the attackers. The British lost a mere fifty-five men while the American-French forces counted more than 1,000 dead, including names which now decorate Savannah's monuments and streets—Pulaski, Jasper, and Jones. Serving under the French was the largest contingent of black troops on the American side of the Revolution. Recruited in Haiti, among their number was a boy, Henri Christophe, who later helped lead the liberation of Haiti from the French. Failure to wrest Savannah from the British left the city in British hands until several months after the battle at Yorktown.

But Savannah was not the same city. Bombardment by the French siege guns had ripped gaping holes in the sandy streets and many of the wooden houses. Many civilians had fled the city. Those who remained cowered in basements under mattresses or took refuge in cattle barns on an island in the middle of the river. Whatever sympathies the population harbored were cast aside in the relief that followed the lifting of the siege. Naturally, a grand party was held to celebrate the British victory.

For the duration of the occupation, Governor Wright was saddled with a city whose population was depleted, whose commerce was virtually at a standstill, and whose loyalties were subject to question. In his one important act, he published a "hit list" of Georgia insurrectionists, 151 names that constitute a roll call of Georgia history. Jones, Habersham, Telfair, Walton, Hall, Houstoun, McIntosh—they are all there, proclaimed outlaws forever.

In July 1782, Wright and his followers evacuated the city. When James Jackson, head of the Georgia Legion, accepted the formal surrender, he liberated a town of less than 1,000 inhabitants on the verge of starvation; a town where scarcely more than 200 buildings remained intact. Even

Facing page, right: The unsuccessful attempt to retake Savannah from the British was led by Comte Jean Baptiste Charles Henri Hector d'Estaing. Twice wounded, and thoroughly defeated, d'Estaing sailed home with the French fleet. Courtesy, National Park Service, Fort Pulaski National Monument

Below: Polish hero Casimir Pulaski, escaping oppression in his native country, joined the American cause during the Revolution. Mortally wounded in an assault on Savannah's fortifications, he has been honored on many monuments including the great Fort Pulaski National Monument. Traditionally he is titled Count Pulaski, though he was actually of lesser nobility. From Historical Collections of Georgia, by George White, 1855

Nathanael Greene of Rhode Island, second in command to Washington, spent his last days in Savannah after being granted Mulberry Grove plantation as a reward for valiant service in the War for Independence. Greene's monument in Johnson Square, dating from 1830, is the oldest in Savannah. Courtesy, CEL Regional Library, Gamble Collection

a mass movement of slaves had occurred, thousands being shipped to British East Florida, others to the Indies. Once again Savannah was a frontier village saddled with debts and political rivalries. The shift of population to the interior which followed the war eventually resulted in the move of Georgia's capital away from Savannah. Slowly the city returned to what it was before the war—a center of trade. While much of America went wild with replacing all that hinted of British ties, Savannah calmly showed a sense of

proportion and taste that has earned it the accolade of "gracious" from many visitors since.

Early in the war Georgia's division into Anglican parishes had been changed to counties with appropriate names. Sunbury, hotbed of freedom in St. John's Parish, became located in Liberty County. Savannah, formerly in Christ Church Parish, chose to honor William Pitt, the Earl of Chatham, under whose Parliamentary leadership the city had enjoyed its first success. Christ Church Parish became Chatham County. In 1787 home rule was established for all towns in the state and Savannah and its hamlets were divided into seven wards, adding one along the western edge, which was named for Oglethorpe, to the original six. Incorporated as a city in December 1789, Savannah elected John Houstoun as its first mayor. With an opportunity to remake the town in their own image, the leaders exhibited a sense of history that has characterized the city ever since. Instinctively recognizing Oglethorpe's sagacity in the ground plan of the town, they simply expanded on that plan. The regular squares and streets gave—and still give—Savannah its unique ambiance. As the city grew, the plan prevailed until there was no more public land to expand upon. Thus, the Historic District of today's city was defined.

Oglethorpe had named the first four wards when he assigned building lots to the settlers in 1733. The government in 1787 retained these names which recognized members of the Trustees—Derby, Percival, Decker, and Heathcote. The remaining two were named for Admiral Anson, a British naval commander, and—in an unprecedented act of kindness—Reynolds. The three royal governors were remembered by naming squares after them. Wright received the courthouse square, once called Percival for the Earl of Egmont, while the ward name remained Percival. Ellis received the square in Decker Ward called Market Square, where his residence had been located and where he was often seen strolling with his umbrella and thermometer. Reynolds' name was placed on the square where his first government meetings were held.

Three years later the new American spirit was rewarded by expansion into Franklin, Warren, and Washington wards. Benjamin Franklin had replaced William Knox as Georgia's agent in London, and the American General Warren was killed at Bunker Hill. George Washington was acclaimed by both a ward and a square. In 1799 wards added were named Liberty, Columbia, and

James Jackson, for whom Fort Jackson is named, was a colorful figure, famous for his many duels. In his twenties, he rose to the rank of colonel and was selected by "Mad Anthony" Wayne to receive the British surrender of Savannah in 1783. Jackson later refused a chance at the governorship on grounds of his youth, but accepted his election as U.S. senator. During the 1790s, he exposed the notorious Yazoo Fraud. After that Jackson found himself old enough to be governor. He died in Washington in 1806, reportedly "as a consequence of the accumulated wounds of many duels." Courtesy, CEL Regional Library, Gamble Collection

Greene, the latter for war hero, Nathanael Greene, who spent his last years near Savannah at Mulberry Grove plantation which was granted to him in gratitude for his wartime leadership. In 1803 names left from the old days were changed and Duke, Prince, and King streets became Congress, State, and President.

In 1791 George Washington was lavishly entertained by a thriving community of nearly 2,500. While other early settlements declined and passed into the historical record (Abercorn, Ebenezer, Highgate, Frederica, and even Sunbury in the nineteenth century), Savannah had survived threats by Indians, Spaniards, Britons, Americans, Charlestown renegades, and Crackers. The little town had withstood absentee landlords, wind and weather, fires, famines and fevers, poverty, and Parliament. It was ready for the rebirth of affluence. It was ready for universal freedom as its citizens seriously pondered the ways of ending slavery.

But a visitor from Yale was residing at Mulberry Grove plantation in 1793. At the suggestion of a friend, he conceived an incredible machine and, with this touch of technology, Eli Whitney changed the course of Savannah's history—and that of the nation.

CHAPTER IV

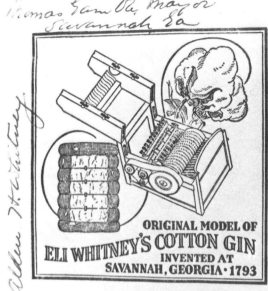

Thomas Gamble, Mayor
Savannah, Ga

Eli Whitney

ORIGINAL MODEL OF
ELI WHITNEY'S COTTON GIN
INVENTED AT
SAVANNAH, GEORGIA · 1793

ELI WHITNEY DAY

Savannah, Georgia, October 7, 1940

Walter P. Marshall, Chairman

SAVANNAH
OCT 7
9-AM
1940
GA.

FIRST DAY OF ISS

UNITED STATES POSTAGE

Mayor Thomas Gamble
City Hall
Savannah, Georgia.

As late as 1940 Savannah took time off to commemorate the machine that nearly built an Eden. With remarkable selectivity, Savannah's historians usually omit references to Eli Whitney's later inventions which were instrumental in the downfall of the Confederacy. Courtesy, CEL Regional Library, Gamble Collection

THE INCREDIBLE MACHINE AND THE PECULIAR INSTITUTION

While America was suffering the agonies of separation from the mother country, England passed from an intellectual state of enlightened inquiry to one of practical engineering. Accompanied by the banging of new machinery and the whimpering of child laborers, the Industrial Revolution conquered the

British Empire. The British philosophy of manufacture was to produce quality products for the people who could afford them. It was left to the Americans to produce quality products for people who could *not* afford them.

The new technology in England had drawn the peasants from the countryside to the cities. In America the opposite was true—people left the populated coast and moved westward where, it was said, the topsoil was three feet deep.

Throughout the colonial period, Britain had zealously prevented the development of manufacturing in the Americas. The few items produced in the colonies were handmade by individual artisans. As a result, there were few men on the entire continent who had even a basic knowledge of machinery, mechanical engineering principles, or manufacturing methods. Difficulties of transportation forced containment of all but raw products to nearby markets. Almost everything was one of a kind.

Eli Whitney was a Yankee from Massachusetts adamantly opposed to slavery. In his teens he was already making spare money from the manufacture of nails—a scarce commodity in those days. At the insistence of his father, Whitney went to Yale law school and after completing a year, accepted an offer to tutor down South where he presumed he could study

for the bar in his spare time. On the ship, Whitney became friends with Nathanael Greene's widow. As a guest at her plantation, Whitney learned of the plight of the landowners from Phineas Miller, manager of Mulberry Grove.

The problem was one of a production bottleneck. England's new textile factories were using cotton at an incredible rate and the demand for raw cotton was driving prices sky high. New territory in Georgia was ready for exploitation and cotton was the perfect crop. Before shipping, however, the seeds had to be removed from the cotton bolls, a tedious hand process that required a day's labor to produce a single pound for export. What was needed, Miller explained, was a machine to do the job quicker. In one of those rare moments in history, Whitney replied that he would think about it.

A variety of ginning machines swept across the South like wildfire. They might have been copies of copies of copies, but they ginned cotton. Usually honest planters felt no compunction at stealing the idea and immediately putting it to use. In one year, cotton production increased from five to eight million pounds. When Whitney gave up the struggle to maintain the rights to his invention after five frustrating years, production had reached thirty-five million pounds. In 1825, when Whitney died, the

Eli Whitney realized none of the wealth that his invention of the cotton gin created in cotton production. Virtually bankrupt, he managed to secure a government contract to produce firearms, and by the time of his death in 1825 his mass-manufacturing techniques were leading the North toward industrialization, just as his gin helped induce the South to remain agrarian.

for all Arkwright's machinery to New York—in his head. There he joined Moses Brown and set up the first American textile factory in Pawtucket, Rhode Island. The mill exceeded all expectations. In 1793, the year Whitney invented the gin, production exceeded supply when the mill used up all the available cotton. In that same year demand increased even more when Slater's wife invented cotton sewing thread. This combination of events triggered a symbiosis of success, bonding the industrial North with the agrarian South in a pursuit of profit which resulted in the most romantic—and tragic—era in American history.

Savannah was not, however, a cotton producing area; rice was its natural money crop. The coastal tidelands had been conquered by clever Savannah planters who perfected techniques for planting, cultivating, and harvesting the labor-intensive crop. Georgia, at the end of the Revolution, was still a narrow strip of land along the coast, existing as no more than a border to the Creek and Cherokee territories. There followed a series of land-grabbing schemes, broken treaties, and outright butchery as the Indians slowly were pushed back to the interior while planters moved slaves in to girdle the trees and burn the brush where the Indians once hunted. Under governors Troup and Lumpkin, Georgia gradually moved the Indians far west—an idea that originated with Thomas Jefferson, but was hardly carried out in the manner he proposed. In 1837 the "Trail of Tears" left Georgia free of Indians forever. They were replaced by the ecological nightmare that the pursuit of cotton profits eventually produced. Savannah contented itself with becoming the trading center of the cotton empire—which was where the large profits were to be made.

Cotton demanded transportation, so roads were opened from Savannah in all directions. A few years of "canal fever" followed, but the canal system was soon replaced by railroads. In the 1830s W.W. Gordon spearheaded the development of the Central of Georgia Rail-Road which

United States cotton figure was 225 million pounds. Thousands of people, from planters to retailers, had made fortunes—but not Whitney.

King-to-be cotton had lingered on the edge of greatness for many years, delayed by a dependency on linen as the "warp" to strengthen it. Cotton spun on the standard spinning wheel was simply not strong enough to take the battering of the loom. Hargreaves' Spinning Jenny changed all that. With William Arkwright's modifications, 100 percent pure cotton material became a reality. But England jealously guarded its monopoly on textile production, forbidding anyone with manufacturing skills or experience from leaving England.

Samuel Slater worked in Arkwright's mills in England. Escaping the country disguised as a farmer, he took the plans

As much as any machine has changed the course of history, the cotton gin set the South on a collision course with destiny. Cheap land, slave labor, and a worldwide market led to the development of social distinctions which still persist. This gin is on display at the Ships of the Sea Museum. Photo by Chan Sieg

Savannah's branch of the United States Bank, designed by William Jay, introduced a new look to the city's public buildings. Henry McAlpin was influenced by this design when he built a new courthouse on Wright Square in the 1830s. Courtesy, CEL Regional Library, Gamble Collection

eventually connected with other systems, providing rail service with a major intersection at a small settlement called Marthasville (later Atlanta). The importance of this rail system is underscored by the monument to Gordon in Wright Square on the very location where a pyramid of stones had marked the grave of Tomochichi, Oglethorpe's friend. As early as 1819, steam had made Savannah the center of world attention. The S.S. *Savannah,* conceived and financed by Savannah businessmen led by William Scarbrough, sailed from Savannah across the Atlantic, the first steam-powered vessel to do so. President Monroe was present for the launching, took a ride on the boat, was wined and dined lavishly, and attended the dedication of the new Independent Presbyterian Church, one of the city's architectural masterpieces. Though a financial failure, the experimental ship had made its point. In a few years, technical improvements brought steam tugs to Georgia's rivers and canals. They hauled barges loaded with cotton bales and pulled sailing vessels up the difficult channel to the cotton wharves below Fac-

tor's Walk, next door to Savannah's City Hall.

Savannah was still a city of a mere 7,000 residents, but the evidence of cotton wealth was obvious. Young William Jay was designing and constructing buildings that are the equal of any in the land in beauty and craftsmanship; warehouses and docks now lined the once sandy bluff; and banking became a major enterprise. The recipients of all this bounty strolled the squares under delicate umbrellas and traveled the dirt streets in horse-drawn carriages and chairs; in the heat of summer the gentry retired to country places near the sea. It all rested on the foundation of white cotton—and black labor.

Relief from the summer heat first came to Savannah in 1818 when ice was imported. It was advertised at 6-1/4 cents per pound and touted as "highly desirable to cool water, milk and wine." That December the new Savannah Theatre had a gala opening, beginning a history that earned it the present title of one of "the oldest continuously operating theatres in America." Exports now exceeded fourteen million dollars; no less than fifty inns and taverns were licensed for pouring; the unsalaried mayor and aldermen were finding ways of adding city improvements which included oil lamps for street lighting, a police department, and an increased fire fighting capacity. Savannah could indeed find time to celebrate during 1819.

The year 1820 was one of utter disaster. Less than two months after the S.S. *Savannah* returned from its triumphal European tour, fire devastated the entire city north of Broughton Street destroying 463 buildings. Only a few brick structures remained, including Christ Church and the Planters' Bank, formerly the home of the Habershams and now known as the Pink House. It was one of the worst fires in American history.

Savannah was now repaid for past generosities as relief came from all over the country—Pennsylvania, Virginia, Maine, New Orleans, Massachusetts, and Maryland. Mr. P. Brasch advertised: "Bread Gratis to all persons burnt out, who have not means to purchase." But one incident serves to illustrate the temper of the times: "The Mayor of New York sent a check for $10,238.29 and goods by sea." But there was attached to the donation a condition that in the distribution there should be no "discrimination on account of color." The implications chagrined the Savannah City Council, who politely refused the check and returned the goods. The final report on the fire included a very pointed statement: " ... No discrimination had been shown in the distribution of aid funds. As a matter of fact the negroes who had suffered from the fire were among the first provided for."

On September 5 of that same year, as Savannah still worked at rebuilding the devastation, a ship arrived from the Indies "with yellow fever on board." In a few days the fever had spread through the city with worse effect than the fire. Within a month more than 700 were dead and the city of 7,523 was reduced to a mere 1,494—so great was the panic.

The yellow fever began a decline in

rice cultivation in the immediate Savannah area. "Dry culture" required draining the low-lying rice paddies and swamps. On January 21, 1821, Alderman Dr. Waring delivered the official report on the causes of fever epidemics. While revealing the state of scientific inquiry at the time, it also paints a picture of what Savannah was really like. In summary, Dr. Waring concluded that epidemics were caused by climate and atmosphere—an "uncommon deficiency of the electric

The museum at Old Fort Jackson contains a number of examples of military garb from the various wars of American history. This shako is from the 1812 period, when Fort Jackson was constructed. Photo by Chan Sieg

During the War of 1812 builder Isaiah Davenport was commanded by the federal government to construct a fortification at the mouth of the Savannah River on Tybee Island. The Martello Tower, shown here in an 1879 illustration from Harper's Weekly, *was once believed to be of Spanish origin. Historian William Harden clarified the matter in his 1913* History of Savannah and South Georgia. *Courtesy, CEL Regional Library, Gamble Collection*

fluid", the trees, "Internal putridity"—caused by the growth of population and foreign visitors, and the high position of the city itself led to the attraction of all the "unwholesome vapor and miasmata" of the surrounding wet lowlands.

While it was not until eighty years later that Walter Reed established the mosquito as carrier of yellow fever, Savannah commenced the long process of cleaning up. After these disasters of 1820, city government records show an increasing concern with the appearance and conditions of the city. Appropriations begin to appear for better water systems, sewage and garbage removal, street maintenance, police and fire protection, city lighting, and even aesthetic landscaping. Savannah was becoming a real city. But ahead were other fires, other plagues.

Savannah had hardly recovered from the 1796 fire when a new threat came with the declaration of war against Britain, its best customer. As early as 1808, President Jefferson had begun urging preparation for what seemed an inevitable conflict. With the British in possession of East Florida, Savannah's vulnerability required that it be fortified against attack. Fort Jackson, now the headquarters of the Coastal Heritage Society, was begun in 1808 and was ready for gun mounting by the middle of 1812. Mayor George Jones and the council at a public meeting passed resolutions supporting the war read by Alderman T.U.P. Charlton, distinguished civic leader, poet, and orator. The city spent three anxious years preparing for an invasion that was threatened but never came. In addition to Fort Jackson, the mouth of the river was fortified by the construction of the Martello Tower by Isaiah Davenport, most famous of Savannah's master builders, and a wall of trenches was dug around the city in which even political leaders set an example by assisting in the manual labor, though most of the heavy work was accomplished by slaves. Terrified by rumors that British Admiral Cockburn was sailing toward Savannah with orders to "burn or ransom the city," Savannah spent the entire war period watchful, digging in, mobilizing.

Fortunately, a treaty was signed before war actually came to Savannah, though the British ship *Epervier,* captured off the coast, was impounded in the Savannah harbor. A great celebration was held when the war's end was announced. A grateful city commemorated the War of 1812 by naming city divisions for Hull, McDonough, and Perry, for Andrew Jackson, and for the great victory at Chippewa. (Another faraway war was remembered by an intensely patriotic citizenry when the Mexican War brought the

Left: *Savannah's proud military unit, the Republican Blues, made a widely heralded visit to New York City in 1860 where they were featured in Harper's Weekly. Courtesy, CEL Regional Library, Gamble Collection*

Below: *The Chatham Artillery, dating from the funeral of Nathanael Greene in 1786, lists on its roll call many of Savannah's most distinguished citizens. M. Edward Wilson photographed the artillery's banquet in 1907. Courtesy, Georgia Historical Society*

Right: *Resplendent in their full-dress uniforms, the Georgia Hussars await the signal to parade down Bull Street circa 1895. Courtesy, Georgia Historical Society*
Below: *Fanny Kemble, celebrated English actress, was briefly married to Pierce Butler, a wealthy planter-merchant. Her experiences on the Butler plantation, south of Savannah, made her a confirmed abolitionist. After dissolving the marriage, she returned to England and wrote a book about her stay in Georgia. The book helped cast some doubts on British sympathies for the Southern cause. In 1859 Pierce Butler held one of the largest slave auctions in Savannah history, selling 460 human beings in a single mass marketing. Courtesy, V. & J. Duncan Antique Maps & Prints*

names of Zachary Taylor and Monterey to Savannah's Historic District.)

From its birth, Savannah has enjoyed a close relationship with all things military. The pioneer settlers had served as farmers and soldiers throughout the Trustee period. Rangers and militia roamed the coast defending against Indians and Spaniards, protecting the city from raids by privateers and pirates. Oglethorpe's zeal for building forts established a tradition that has not yet ended. From Bloody Marsh to Granada, every major American conflict has felt the presence of Savannah.

The many military units which sprung to being through the years also served as social clubs. Every holiday, every parade, every official funeral, and every distinguished visitor was treated to a colorful display of precision drill and rifle salute. Even the names are colorful: Irish Jasper Greens (for Sergeant Jasper, felled in the Siege of Savannah), Republican Blues, Phoenix Riflemen, Oglethorpe Light Infantry, German Volunteers, Chatham Artillery, Georgia Hussars. (The Chatham Artillery is justly famous for its punch, guaranteed to defeat all enemies.)

The smaller units also expressed their pride of identity in their names: Blue Caps, Banks Rangers, Irish Volunteers, Mounted Partisan Rangers, Chatham Guerrillas, Telfair Irish Grays, Warsaw Rifles—to name a few.

From the disasters of 1820 to the degradation of 1864, Savannah experienced the halcyon days of the antebellum period. Much of its present look dates from this time as architects like Jay, Norris, and Cluskey replaced the wooden tenements with elegant homes and public buildings of brick, stucco, granite, and marble. The simple elegance of the Davenport House, peak achievement of the Georgian style, gave way to the massive and often ornate Greek Revival as columns began to appear all over town. With a plantation house and a Regency townhouse, the affluent planter could confidently while away the hours at the plush Pulaski Hotel where the wine cellar was of the finest and fortunes changed hands at the flip of a card as charming ladies smiled provocatively through the smoke of hand-rolled Havanas. Imported crystal, china, and silver adorned the tables of many homes as the Savannah style of gracious entertaining emerged to equal that of Charleston and New Orleans.

Distinguished visitors provided ample excuse for leading citizens to show off their finery and manners: the Marquis de Lafayette, Daniel Webster, William Makepeace Thackeray, former Presidents Polk and Fillmore, the actress Fanny Kemble. John James Audubon visited Savannah in 1831 soliciting subscriptions to his *Birds of America* series—at $1,000 per copy. Savannahians William Gaston, Alexander Telfair, James Potter, Thomas Young, John Mongin, Thomas King, and Thomas Metcalf subscribed. Two of the founders of the Georgia Historical Society were putting together collections of inestimable value—Israel Teft's autograph collection was world famous, containing many letters from the best-known persons of the time, and Alexander Smets' library included medieval illuminations, Hogarth originals, and rare volumes from all over the world.

Savannah reached its antebellum zenith after the 1847 completion of the Central of Georgia Rail-Road, in which the city itself was a shareholder and Mayor Gordon the first president. The 190 miles of track made the Central the longest rail system owned by a single company in the United States. Now profits really soared and Savannah enjoyed a period of unprecedented growth. In addition to cotton, other sources of income were tobacco, rice, corn, lumber, and naval stores. Small manufacturing concerns developed in support of the railroad system and the shipping demands; Henry McAlpin, an ironmonger, made his fortune in manufacturing bricks—the famous Savannah Grey—at his plantation called the Hermitage where he had laid the first rail tracks in the United States. On Factors' Walk along the river's edge, fortunes were made as the gentlemen played Wall Street Savannah-style.

The population tripled, the city limits were extended, gas lighting made its appearance. Hospitals, churches, and orphanages grew in number for blacks and whites as excess wealth permitted the emergence of the charity traditions which were Savannah's birthright. Cathedral and synagogue stood side by side with Baptist and Methodist structures. The Laurel Grove Cemetery, built upon the drained fields of the Spring Hill plantation, replaced the old Colonial Cemetery which had overflowed with bodies following the fevers of 1820. The new burial ground was rapidly employed as the fever returned in 1854, causing more than 1,000 deaths including ten doctors, three medical students, and three ministers. Two-thirds of the people fled the city until the fever ended in November. During the peak of the epidemic in September, a hurricane flooded the town and many people drowned.

A city in mourning pulled itself together and soon returned to the business of moving cotton. In the last exciting years before the Civil War, Savannah toasted

freedom and liberty while its lawyers argued states' rights in the government houses and a Savannah ship, the *Wanderer,* delivered its awful cargo. It was the last of the slave ships.

In 1763 the British acquired all slave trading rights from the Spanish. From that point until the Revolution, British slavers poured their cargoes into the colonies. From New York to Florida, wherever there was a market, the ships unloaded, advertised, and held their ghastly auctions. With the coming of the Revolution, led by Pennsylvania and Massachusetts, the states began to legislate against the "peculiar institution." Congress passed acts banishing the importation and trading in slaves. In 1798 Georgia by law abolished the slave trade. Despite the ideals behind its passage, the

law was about as effective as Prohibition. The incredible machine conceived on Greene's plantation provided the impetus for a total change of direction, the costs of which have far exceeded the sum of profits from cotton plantations of the South or the factories of the North.

In 1766 Governor Wright had boasted of the colony's phenomenal growth during his tenure—10,000 whites and 7,800 slaves. This population was concentrated around Savannah and the Sunbury-Midway district. Twenty-five years later, the first United States census placed Georgia's population at 82,000. Savannah was not large enough to be considered a city, but local records show a town of less than 3,000 plus about 2,000 blacks when Washington visited in 1791. Ten years later the census reported 162,000 in the state, and 5,100 in Savannah. By 1810 Georgia had reached more than 250,000, an increase of nearly 90 percent, with approximately 100,000 slaves. Savannah in the same ten-year period had increased by an actual count of forty-nine individuals. Savannah would reach a population figure of 10,000 only after celebrating its 100th birthday.

Once more, Savannah was going its own way. Cotton and slaves in vast quantities simply passed through in opposite directions, leaving enormous profits in their wake. Exports for the year 1800 exceeded two million dollars.

A stable population coupled with increasing wealth equals luxury. In the early decades of the nineteenth century Savannah laid the foundation for the reputation enjoyed today—gracious living, a leisurely lifestyle, and elegant homes inhabited by people who just "love to party."

Under the royal governors, social stratification had developed along customary British lines, a condition that held in all the royal colonies. After the Revolution, any hint of royalty or aristocracy was anathema, so the landed gentry replaced the topmost class, assuming the role without the title. This planter-merchant ruling class determined Savannah's destiny from then on. Supported by the church, less than 100 families controlled all the means of production and distribution, the social life, and the politics of Savannah. The same men whose sense of duty and responsibility urged them to public service at various levels of government—often without salary—who could sincerely support the national cause of banning the slave trade, could just as sincerely succumb to the lure of the enormous cotton profits and continue, illegally, the awful institution they had voted to abolish.

The human commerce of Savannah was conducted a few yards from where Oglethorpe had pitched his damask tent; where the proud city fathers had erected the Exchange, a building that dominated the landscape and was the center of po-

litical and commerical life for 100 years. But the slaves did not remain long in Savannah where only the servants of the gentry and the few freedmen were permitted housing. The majority were shipped inland to the rice and cotton plantations that surrounded the city, or were traded to landowners in the north and west. Those who lived in the city enjoyed privileges far greater than their counterparts on the plantations. As city-dwellers, some became craftsmen, some city workers, a few even learned to read. The house servants not only cleaned, cooked, and tended the house, they shopped the markets and babysat the children.

The effects of the French Revolution were far-reaching. In Haiti, black patriots Toussaint L'Ouverture and Henri Christophe revolted against French rule, eventually defeating Napoleon's army and massacring nearly 40,000 whites who were unable to flee.

Reports of atrocities reached Savannah and fear gripped the city. Thereafter, restrictions were placed on importing blacks from the Indies, with or without their masters. Curfews, identity passes, and strict adherence to regulations were imposed on city-dwelling blacks. No large gatherings were permitted and even religious services had to be supervised to prevent sermons which might "stir up rebellious instincts."

The great revival of religious fever that swept America after the Revolution reached walking distance of Savannah at Brampton Hall, Jonathan Bryan's plantation. Slaves there were permitted contact with Christian doctrine through the preaching of Jonathan's slave, Andrew Bryan, who had been baptized by George Leile, a freed slave who left Savannah when the British pulled out in 1782. Andrew was arrested for preaching in Yamacraw, Savannah's ghetto, and was soundly whipped. True to his Christian teaching, he prayed forgiveness for his tormentors who subsequently permitted him to establish the first black church in America in 1788. Lachlan McIntosh, the

Facing page: Andrew Bryan, slave of Jonathan Bryan, became one of the great figures of American religious history. He established the first black church in America in 1788. In 1790 the city granted Andrew Bryan a lot for construction of a meetinghouse. Within three years the Reverend Bryan managed to secure another site, 575 West Bryan Street, where a larger church was built—today occupied by the First Bryan Baptist Church. Courtesy, First African Baptist Church

The First African Baptist Church, constructed in 1859 by the congregation, was the first black-owned brick building in Georgia. In the foreground, restoration of Franklin Square is in progress. Photo by Beth Holland

war hero who outduelled Button Gwinnett, helped Bryan obtain a lot in the city where the First Colored Baptist Church was organized.

Slavery developed its own social strata. The freedman who actually was paid for his labors—often a carpenter, cobbler, or blacksmith—was the envy of his race. A handful of the most industrious slaves earned their freedom, joining this elite group. Next came the household servants who lived in close association with white families; common field hands supported the whole system and were by far the majority. Treatment of these people ranged from the reported kindness of such masters as Henry McAlpin at the Hermitage to the brutal lashings behind the walls of the city jail. The field hands were deprived of the charities granted to the city slaves who at least could attend church and receive treatment at the Georgia Infirmary, opened in 1832 as the first black hospital. Neither could they experience the gay social life of the city where horse racing, boat racing, sports events, parties and balls, and celebrations were regularly serviced by the city blacks.

The price of slaves increased rapidly after laws against trade were passed. Many Savannahians began to question a system that required an investment of nearly $2,000 per slave. These liberals privately voiced their opinion that perhaps the whole system wasn't worth it. The fear of insurrection increased though none ever occurred in Savannah, and talk of social equality from Yankee liberals only increased the restrictions and rhetoric against change.

Bull Street, the first street laid out by Oglethorpe and Colonel Bull of Charlestown, is—and was—Savannah's most important street. The finest squares and most impressive buildings lay along its wide path. In antebellum Savannah, Bull Street was completely segregated. The white elite strolled the west side and, by common law, slaves and poor whites were forced to walk on the other side. Any breech of this tradition might result in severe punishment. To perpetuate tradi-

tions like this, Savannah committed the lives of an entire generation, the fortunes it had struggled so long to attain, and the sacred honor it—tragically—held so dear.

Historians are fond of assigning causes to great events. The Civil War—or War Between the States, or War to Free the Slaves, or War of Rebellion, or War for Southern Independence—was *caused* by slavery, or states' rights, or the Industrial Revolution, or "Southern nationalism." It is undoubtedly more circumspect to reject such simplistic conclusions and favor the ideas of recent revisionist historians—James Randall and Avery Craven, for example—who support the idea that the war resulted from "a blundering generation" that permitted fanatical leaders, "short-sighted politicians and zealous editors" to control the destiny of both sides. Whatever the causes, the results speak for themselves: 618,000 dead, a wasted South, and more than three million slaves freed in a world that delivered neither forty acres nor a mule.

When South Carolina seceded, Savannah rejoiced, raising in Johnson Square—birthplace of the New Eden and later of the American state—a rattlesnake flag with the motto: "Don't tread on me!" It was hoisted upon the monument to Nathanael Greene. Before Georgia officially left the Union, Colonel Lawton was dispatched with troops to secure forts Pulaski and Jackson, virtually unguarded federal installations. The city mobilized thirty-nine companies to serve the cause, this from a population of only 23,000 of

Facing page, left: *Henry McAlpin's Hermitage reportedly had the finest slave quarters. In addition to neat rooms in brick cottages with fireplaces, McAlpin maintained a hospital for his slaves. They were slave cabins nonetheless. From* Art Work of Savannah, *by Charles H. Olmstead, 1893*

Facing page, right: *The Hermitage was famous, too, for the uniquely designed mansion, with identical front and rear entrances. The structure was razed in 1935 by Henry Ford. Photo by Emil Hoppe. Courtesy, Georgia Historical Society*

Facing page, bottom: *From 1815 to 1851 the Hermitage served as a preeminent example of plantation management and land usage, encompassing rice cultivation, livestock, cotton, lumber, brick making, and iron casting. Courtesy, Manuscript Department, William R. Perkins Library, Duke University*

Above: *When the Union navy captured nearby Port Royal in November 1861, the news was met with panic by many Savannahians. This scene in Johnson Square was titled "Indiscriminate Flight of Inhabitants to the Interior." Courtesy, Georgia Historical Society*

which nearly 40 percent were blacks. On May 21, 1861, Captain Francis Bartow led the Oglethorpe Light Infantry to Richmond. Two months later, on July 27, the remains of Colonel Bartow were returned and buried in Savannah, a casualty of the First Battle of Bull Run (Manassas).

The Union's blockade of ports reached Port Royal, South Carolina, in November. Savannahians reacted by sinking ships "laden with stone" in the river channel and increasing fortifications at Pulaski. General Robert E. Lee arrived on November 11, inspected the fort and pronounced "that it could withstand all the attacks of the enemy." Had the war been fought a decade earlier, Lee might have been correct, but his remarks underline the Confederacy's tragically outdated concepts of warfare and military technology. On April 11, 1862, Fort Pulaski surrendered after a mere thirty-hour bombardment. The fort's massive walls simply could not withstand the Union's newly developed rifled artillery pieces. Eli Whitney's early production methods had developed into a large-scale factory system in the North which, at the outbreak of the war, produced 97 percent of the weapons manufactured in the United States. Seventy years of cotton profits resulting from the gin were lost before the war was over.

After the fall of Pulaski, the war around Savannah settled into a series of tactical moves in which each side observed the other across Eden's marshes. Realizing the impracticality of concentrating Savannah's defense around Fort Pulaski, Lee advised an inner defense ring around the city. Centered on the river at Fort Jackson, several batteries made the city secure from a naval attack while other positions along the inland waterway prevented anything more than occasional probes from Union forces. The Yankees controlled the outer islands with a naval blockade and a concentration of troops at nearby Hilton Head, while the Confederates held the mainland and the inland water passages. The great railroad system became a kind of shuttle for Confederate reactions to Yankee steamers moving up and down the coast.

Blockaded from its lifeline to the sea,

Despite the privations of war, there was still time for occasional festivity including a grand ball for the Union officers at Fort Pulaski on Thanksgiving 1863. Sketched by W.T. Crane for Frank Leslie's Illustrated Newspaper. *Courtesy, National Park Service, Fort Pulaski National Monument,*

Savannah declined rapidly. Crowded conditions led to scarcity; scarcity to inflation. Without trade revenue, the city was forced to procure loans from the banks in order to set up its own store to fight the black market. The daring Rebel blockade runners too often profited from the war effort. In the three years from the fall of Pulaski to the coming of Sherman, Savannah gradually starved.

Less than twenty miles south of the city, Fort McAllister guarded the railroad crossing at the mouth of the Ogeechee River. Behind a series of earthen mounds, less than 200 defenders successfully repelled six major assaults by the Union navy. The sixth attempt occurred on March 3, 1863, when "four ironclads, five gunboats, and two mortar schooners" slipped in on the morning tide and launched a terrible bombardment on the little fort. Captain George Anderson was well prepared, and only three men were wounded. The attack was abandoned after a day and night of shelling. The determination of the defenders placed Fort McAllister at the front of military objectives as Sherman marched to the sea.

On March 9, 1864, Lincoln appointed U.S. Grant to head the army; Grant quickly named William Sherman as commander in the west. With these appointments, the warfare objective changed from winning battles to destroying the enemy. Sherman's initial moves into Georgia were frustrated by Confederate General Joseph Johnston's delaying tac-

tics. Outmanned, outgunned, and undersupplied, Johnston had little choice; but Jefferson Davis, in a move that characterized the confusion of Confederate leadership, replaced Johnston with General John Hood. Hearing of this, Sherman was moved to remark sardonically: "Before this, the fighting has been as Johnston pleased, but hereafter it shall be as I please." And so it was.

At this juncture in the war, Georgia had supplied more troops and suffered more casualties than any of the Confederate states. The "real war" was still ahead.

True to his word, Sherman defeated Hood in little more than a month. News of Atlanta's fall cast a pall over the Confederacy, and in Savannah church attendance rose dramatically. Sherman then offered to negotiate a separate peace for the state with Governor Brown, but was refused. Sherman then rendered Atlanta incapable of bellicose posturing and started for the sea. It was an object lesson not wasted on Savannahians.

For the next month news of the destruction spread terror as the legends of Sherman grew more monstrous. Georgia's magnificent rail system was ripped up, heated, and left wrapped around trees; everything usable was destroyed—crops, cattle, cotton gins, mills. Refugees poured into a Savannah that was already starving. Personal valuables were hidden in every conceivable place or shipped away or buried. Mayor Richard Arnold called for every man capable of bearing arms to prepare the defense.

Fort McAllister finally fell to General Hazen's advance force, the Second Division of the Fifteenth Army Corps. George Anderson, now a major, commanded a force of 150 against this division. With seventeen men dead and thirty-one wounded, the little fort was overwhelmed. To his surprise, Anderson discovered that General Hazen was an old comrade-in-arms. With typical Southern panache, Anderson then refused to surrender unless Hazen agreed to have dinner with him at Lebanon plantation. It was De-

cember 13, 1864. Nearly 70,000 Union troops were drawing the noose tightly around Savannah. In addition, the presence of the Union forces on Hilton Head and the Union navy made the military situation impossible.

The terrified city was now overrun with black and white refugees seeking escape from the certain doom which Sherman would impose on one of the most important slave centers of America. The remnants of the Confederate forces—which were supposed to defend the city—numbered a mere 10,000 plus militia and reserves. By December 17 Sherman's main force was in position and demanded an unconditional surrender. General Hardee refused, but after orders from General Beauregard, he abandoned Savannah on the night of December 20 and crossed the river on hastily constructed pontoon bridges, taking his entire army and what equipment he could transport into South Carolina. Savannah was left totally at the mercy of Sherman's vengeance.

With the military withdrawn, Savannah's city government had to take charge of the situation. Mayor Richard Arnold and the aldermen took to their carriages and went out to meet the advance led by General Geary, Sherman's representative. They offered the hospitality of the city and requested that the general protect the citizens and private property from destruction. Geary accepted and immedi-

ately entered with an advance battalion which stopped the looting mobs already gathering in the streets. On Christmas Day, Sherman arrived and went to the Pulaski Hotel where he was informed that his headquarters was to be in Savannah's finest mansion, the recently completed Green House—so new it had gas lights and a real bathtub.

Charles Green was a wealthy Savannah businessman who still retained his British citizenship. His vested interests included 25,000 bales of cotton still in his warehouse. Accepting the invitation,

Above: *Black labor was used extensively to prepare the defense of Savannah. This view by an English artist shows a crew at work near Fort Jackson and a portion of the extensive rice fields at the edge of the city. From* Illustrated London News, *April 18, 1863. Courtesy, V. & J. Duncan Antique Maps & Prints*

Left: *Lieutenant General Hardee, learning that the valiant outpost at Fort McAllister had fallen, saw that his 10,000 Confederates had little chance against Sherman's forces. Hardee organized a stealthy retreat across the Savannah River at night. Reenactment of this occasion is regularly performed at historic Fort Jackson. Courtesy, CEL Regional Library, Gamble Collection*

The home of British merchant Charles Green was one of Savannah's newest showplaces when Sherman made it his headquarters. It remains beautifully preserved today having passed through the ownership of Judge Peter Meldrim, Savannah's mayor at the turn of the century, to its present ownership by the St. John's Episcopal Church. From Harper's Weekly, *January 21, 1865. Courtesy, CEL Regional Library, Gamble Collection*

Sherman quartered at the Green mansion, where he notified Mr. Lincoln: "I beg to present you as a Christmas Gift, the City of Savannah. . . ." Sherman took the cotton despite the gracious hospitality but, because Green was British, the general was forced to pay rent during his occupation of Savannah.

The Yankee army prevented looting and black marketeering and the dreaded slave riots. What food remained in the city was placed at the disposal of the civilian population. Though many of Savannah's ladies refused to come out of their homes, there must have been many who did, for one of Sherman's troops observed that there were more "ladies of the pavement" in Savannah than in any city they'd ever visited: "There is the most hoars here that I saw in my life

both black and white; I thought Washington had enough, but this beats that."

On December 28, Mayor Arnold called a public meeting at Masonic Hall where it was agreed to "lay aside all differences" and "bring back prosperity and commerce." Savannah had rejoined the Union.

News of Savannah's capture had been publicized widely in the Northern press. To South and North it signaled the early end of the war. But when Savannah's eagerness to cooperate became known, it was brutally castigated by other Southern cities. The Augusta newspaper called Savannah a city of "miserable sycophants. . . . lower than any other in the abyss of degradation. . . ."

Noble Jones, John Milledge, and William Stephens earlier had disarmed

the Indians and, with diplomacy and hospitality, had saved the colony. Traditional history has it that Mayor Arnold accomplished the same feat by tricking Sherman's advance guard, thus preventing the sure burning of Savannah. But Sherman has probably suffered more from bad press than any other American general. The torching of specific military objectives in Atlanta—public buildings, railroad yards, warehouses—was calculated to remove Atlanta from further participation in the war. Sherman did not occupy Atlanta, but abandoned it. His campaign to split the Confederacy was not aimed necessarily at Savannah, just at some point on the coast where the Union land and sea forces could connect. With no intention of abandoning Savannah, there was no reason to destroy any part of it, not even ammunition dumps and arsenals. Instead the city was humiliated by the presence of the 33rd U.S. Colored Troops, one of the first black regiments in the army, made up of ex-slaves from Georgia and South Carolina. In her unusual book, *Reminiscences of My Life in Camp,* Susie King Taylor, an ex-slave employed by the Union army, wrote in detail of this period. She had become literate in secret, as those blacks who learned to read and write were forced to do. One can only imagine the chagrin of Savannah's proud populace, forced to take orders from former slaves who walked wherever they pleased—on either side of Bull Street. A few weeks after departing Savannah, Sherman burned Columbia, the capital of South Carolina.

A Savannah garrison fought Sherman's army throughout the Carolinas until the very end. In April the Savannah Volunteer Guards, under General John Gordon, led the last rebel attack at a farm near Appomattox.

A grizzled Sherman sat for this portrait upon his retirement in November 1883. Courtesy, CEL Regional Library, Gamble Collection

CHAPTER V

A view of Savannah's harbor in 1883, from Harper's Weekly, *shows the city's thriving commerce. Courtesy, CEL Regional Library, Gamble Collection*

RECONSTRUCTION AND RETRENCHMENT

Six years of combat between the vindictive Reconstruction leader, Thaddeus Stevens, and the recalcitrant Georgia legislators, interwoven with carpetbagger governments and military rule, finally resulted in the ratification of the Thirteenth, Fourteenth, and Fifteenth amendments and the restoration of civil authority in Georgia.

The Civil War and Reconstruction are delightful periods for historians to tackle. The available data, records, and anecdotal material provide a gold mine upon which one may easily justify any number of viewpoints. Certainly it was a tragic era for the conquered South; certainly it was a time of exploitation of both ex-slaves and masters; certainly it was a time when bravery in war was replaced by corruption in politics. The embryonic attempts at political self-expression by Southern blacks resulted in what W.E.B. Du Bois called "a splendid failure." White supremacy was restored through Ku Klux Klan intimidation and political dealing, but this retrenchment was as much a failure as Thaddeus Stevens' reconstruction policies. It would take another century to establish the full rights of all Americans, but fundamental changes brought about during Reconstruction laid the groundwork for today's society. The decade after the war saw the rise of the cities, the formation of labor unions, the great surge in manufacturing, the beginning of scientific farming, and a new national emphasis on education.

Two years before secession, Darwin published his *Origin of Species*, causing an intellectual war that still rages. Nowhere were the principles of survival more evident than in Savannah where those who adjusted to change, survived and prospered; those who would not, or could not, adjust to the new order, quietly and sadly passed into history.

Sherman did not burn Savannah, but the city did burn when, a month after its surrender, a fire broke out in the stable behind the Confederate ammunition dump in Granite Hall. Amidst explosions and flying debris, 100 downtown buildings were lost.

The radical Northern press had cast slurs on the great general's character in reference to his disinterested treatment of and attitude toward the newly freed slaves. Sherman faced a "dressing down" from Secretary of War Stanton. His defense was that he was fighting to restore the Union, not for personal politics. While he was ignominiously forced to wait outside his own office in the Green mansion, twenty black ministers of Savannah's churches—led by Garrison Frazier—cleared him of all racist charges. As a result, Sherman issued Special Field Order No. 15, setting aside the coastal islands for exclusive use by ex-slaves. The forty acres per family granted to applicants temporarily assuaged hostilities. With relief, Sherman headed north.

Leadership in the starving and occupied city was divided between moderates who could face the realities of the new order and those who, enslaved by their own lack of flexibility, insisted on a return to the status quo. When relief ships suddenly appeared in Savannah with "Welcome Back to the Fold" messages from Boston and New York, citizens were happy to accept the charity, but in a

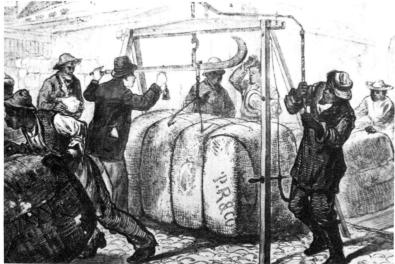

there were men who spent the rest of their lives on park benches, "muttering to themselves."

Savannahians now set about the arduous task of repairing a decimated economic system. The rails were virtually destroyed, currency was practically nonexistent, and the plantations were definitely a thing of the past. While the plantation system changed from feudal practices to those of sharecropping, hiring workers, and land renting, the railroads were rapidly rebuilt and expanded—often through the politically backed expedient of impressed black labor. Bankers acquired the needed currency through whatever deals they could make with Northern capitalists. Within a year after the war, Savannah was rolling again. Exports for the year 1867 exceeded fifty million dollars! The predictors of doom following the loss of slave labor were proved wrong as a rising market pushed cotton production to levels never realized under slave labor.

The return of King Cotton was a mixed blessing, however. The easy profits undermined any incentive for experimentation with new agricultural methods and were largely responsible for the long delay in modernization which characterized the South for the next 100 years. Combined with a new political order that maintained control over the black population, cotton money helped establish a caste system that replaced slavery. Although attempts to establish a black power base failed as the ex-slaves slowly were forced to accept a "separate but equal" society, the decades following emancipation produced many positive results. The militant leadership of black men like Aaron Bradley gave way to moderation from church leaders like James Simms and James Porter. Following the "splendid failure" of these legislators, blacks entered a long period of gradual assimilation. As a result, they developed their own culture, built their own institutions, formed their own business associations, created their own art, music, and literature—and in the process, devel-

paradigm of the Confederate tragic flaw, many of Savannah's "gentlemen of substance" felt it beneath them to labor with their hands at unloading the needed food. Instead they requested that the Union army furnish the necessary labor. Refusal followed, and many ex-slaves were treated to the sight of "Savannah's finest" unloading cargoes while the women distributed the goods.

But there were women in black who never came out on the street again, and

oped a black elite that led the march into the twentieth century. The first newspapers to be published by black journalists were the *Savannah Tribune,* the *Savannah Weekly Echo,* and the *Daily News and Herald.* Social clubs and literary organizations became the glue that held the displaced freedmen together as they sought means of belonging in the new order. In addition to Masonic organizations, secret societies, and lodges, the Georgia Volunteers was an all-black infantry battalion commanded by Major John Deveaux. Marching bands and drill teams became an integral and popular part of holiday celebrations and parades. The most foresighted of the black leaders realized that education was essential for progress, and their efforts resulted in the early establishment of all-black schools and a black college, the Georgia State Industrial College (now Savannah State College). In one of the most ironic results of the war, blacks were allowed to establish a school in the home of William Scarbrough, who first sent a steamship across the Atlantic. The home built for him by William Jay is a Savannah landmark and was acquired by the city for

school purposes from Wymberley Jones DeRenne, descendant of Noble Jones. The mansion today is headquarters for the Historic Savannah Foundation, Inc.

Though cotton remained the major money crop for years to come, Savannah businessmen were discovering another source of real profit in a native product—the pine tree. The growth of naval stores in the latter half of the nineteenth century eventually led to Savannah's position as the world leader. In the 1880s the Cotton Exchange building made Savannah the "Wall Street of the South" as a million bales were shipped all over the world, more than twice any pre-war level.

The influx of refugees after the war prompted the city government to establish a strong police force. By 1870, Savannah spent more money on police protection than any city comparable in size. Chief Robert Anderson's summary in 1871 showed 114 policemen on a payroll of nearly $120,000, consisting of "Irish 57, American 36, German 4, English 2, and Hungarian 1." Anderson carried out his duty to maintain the public morals, reporting information "not given prior to or afterwards." He conscientiously detailed

Facing page, top: *Soon after the Union army occupied the city, a fire broke out in a stable on Savannah's west side, quickly spreading to Granite Hall and setting off explosives stored there. The eighty-foot water tower in nearby Franklin Square was damaged, as depicted in* Harper's Weekly, *but remained in use until the city adopted the artesian well system in 1892. Courtesy CEL Regional Library, Gamble Collection*

Facing page, bottom: *After the war King Cotton returned stronger than ever, bringing an illusion of perpetual wealth to a South which felt secure in having weathered Reconstruction. Courtesy, V. & J. Duncan Antique Maps & Prints*

Above: *Bay Street, crowded daily with carts moving cotton, required regular watering down. From* Frank Leslie's Illustrated Newspaper, *September 21, 1867. Courtesy, CEL Regional Library, Gamble Collection*

Top: *The original buildings of the Georgia State Industrial College for Colored Youths, where black education in Savannah first began to achieve credibility, were located in the suburb of Thunderbolt. The school formally opened in October 1891. Its growth through the twentieth century has brought this institution to its present status as Savannah State College.* From Art Work of Savannah, *by Charles H. Olmstead, 1893*

Bottom: *The great fire of 1889 gutted the Independent Presbyterian Church—Savannah's most distinctive house of worship—which was dedicated in 1819 with President Monroe attending. The church was rebuilt from the original plans of Rhode Island architect John H. Greene. Iron railings were evident throughout the city until the 1890s, when most of them were removed, only to be rediscovered half a century later. Courtesy, Georgia Historical Society*

" ... 11 houses of ill-fame in the city, containing 65 women, 50 streetwalkers, and 150 kept women, a total of 265 prostitutes." Six years later the police force was cut to fifty-five men, attesting to the calming of post-war hostility and the feeling of security that accompanied the reestablishment of traditional authority.

From the end of the war to the end of the century, Savannah was visited regularly by natural disasters: in 1876 yellow fever returned—killing more than 1,000; the same year a fire starting at Kelly's Wharf destroyed "all the buildings north of Bay Street between Drayton and Bull"; the Yamacraw ghetto was hit by a fire in 1883 which destroyed 300 buildings and left 1,200 homeless; the earthquake of 1886 damaged numerous homes and left a terrified populace—many of whom slept in the open squares for weeks afterward; the "Great Fire" of 1889 began at Hogan's store and consumed several blocks of buildings, including the beautiful Independent Presbyterian Church, the Odd Fellows' Hall, and the Guards' Armory. It was followed by two more the same year—one on the docks, another at A.J. Miller's store where falling walls killed and injured several firefighters; the hurricane of 1893 killed fifteen persons, wrecked thirty ships in the harbor, and caused the Park and Tree Commission much grief; another hurricane in 1896 lasted only fifty minutes but killed sixteen and damaged 1,000 buildings; and on August 30, 1896, a cyclone sucked away hundreds of roofs, damaged nine ships, and caused flooding fifty miles inland. Such disasters hastened the demise of the already weakened rice industry. Always dependent on slave labor, Savannah rice planters faced increasing labor costs and competition from the Mississippi delta fields where mule labor could produce a cheaper product. Gradually the great plantations went out of business, as they were drained and sold for industrial development.

Accustomed to disasters and debts from its earliest years, Savannah embarked on a twenty-five-year period of returning to solvency while vastly increasing the services and facilities of a modern city. Concern for public health following the fever of 1876 led to the founding of the Department of Sanitation. The subsequent draining of lowlands still existing around the city was accompanied by rapid development of an entirely new sewer system, updated methods of garbage and waste disposal, and an expensive system of artesian wells that provided Savannah with "the purest water of any city."

The banner year of 1883, Savannah's 150th birthday, was celebrated by pageants, parades, and balls attended by Governor Alexander Stephens, vice president of the Confederacy. Unfortunately Stephens caught cold "from the fatigue and exposure" and died soon afterward. President Chester Arthur visited his kinsman, Henry Botts, in April of 1883, and in August the Brush Electric Light and Power Company treated a delighted populace to electric lighting. Topping off the year, the monument to W.W. Gordon, mayor and railroad man, was unveiled in Wright Square where it still stands.

New homes and buildings replaced the old and the burned as construction raced forward. Victorian gingerbread adorned the stoops of row houses that spanned

This familiar sketch of old houses along Savannah's waterfront gives an indication of the construction along the upper and lower bluffs. From Picturesque America, *circa 1872. Courtesy, CEL Regional Library, Gamble Collection*

entire blocks; cast and wrought iron "equal to any in New Orleans" enclosed balcony windows and small gardens and provided hand railings up the steep stairs and around parks. A new City Market with its elegant multiple arches was erected on the very square where Governor Ellis checked the temperature on his daily stroll. The security of marble and granite housed new financial institutions—Savannah Bank and Trust Company, Citizens Bank, and Southern Bank of Georgia, among numerous others. The post office, the new (now old) courthouse, and the elegant DeSoto Hotel were showplaces. The city acquired its present museum, the Telfair Academy of Arts and Sciences, from the estate of Mary Telfair. Another outstanding new building, Hodgson Hall, became the permanent home of the Georgia Historical Society.

Electric streetcars and paved streets made life easier in town while the railroad to the beach offered the populace a respite from the summer heat—a luxury heretofore reserved for the elite. Band concerts in the park on Sundays, picnics and boatrides, "star performers" at the Savannah Theatre, yacht races and horse races—all these and a host of Saturday night socials contributed to an essentially happy Victorian period in Savannah. In keeping with its earliest tradition, Savannah unleashed 1,000 thirsty citizens for the opening of the Savannah Brewing Company in 1889 where they enjoyed free samples of home brew.

Perhaps the major engineering accomplishment of the period was the dredging of the river channel to a depth of twenty-six feet; it had been only fourteen feet at the end of the war. The channel had been blocked by the Confederates to prevent Union ships from approaching the city. A number of ships, including the ironclad *Georgia,* were scuttled and timber "cribs" loaded with tons of ballast were sunk. First with the city's funds, then with federal help from the United

Facing page, left: *Georgia's Governor Alexander H. Stephens was royally entertained at Savannah's 1883 celebration of the founding of Georgia.*
Facing page, right: *"The Peanut Seller" is typical of Savannah's famous Old City Market. Courtesy, CEL Regional Library, Gamble Collection*
Facing page, bottom: *The Telfair Academy of Arts and Sciences, one of the oldest public art museums in the South, was designed originally as a residence by architect William Jay circa 1820. The museum formally opened in 1886 following extensive remodeling and an addition by architect Detlef Lienau. Photo by Beth Holland*
Above: *The Savannah Brewing Company, opening in 1889, thrived until Prohibition. From* Art Work of Savannah, *by Charles H. Olmstead, 1893*

States Engineers, the muddy old river was carved to accommodate larger vessels. Savannah was ready to become a truly international city, connected to the world by land, sea, and telephone.

As port of embarkation for the Spanish-American War, Savannah was visited by thousands of soldiers. President McKinley passed through town and General Fitzhugh Lee was made commander of the Seventh Army Corps which treated Savannah to a dazzling grand review of 16,000 troops! The name Lee was still magic in Savannah and the women of the town turned out to provide a Thanksgiving feast for him and his troops.

King Cotton was now ensconced on a throne higher than any of the slavery days. Savannah had been devastated in a losing war, occupied by Union troops, suffered calamity after calamity and lost its number one ranking to a hustling Atlanta, but in the final quarter of the nineteenth century it shipped out more than twenty-one million bales of cotton. The dollar value amounted to $946,306,271. Kingly indeed, when one discovers that highly paid public officials such as judges and engineers were salaried at less than $3,000 per annum.

At the close of the century, a proud city eagerly prepared for the good years ahead and its next important guest— Admiral Dewey.

Facing page, top: *The ironclad C.S.S. Georgia, scuttled in the Savannah River, remains a silt-preserved museum, awaiting only sufficient funds to restore it. Courtesy, CEL Regional Library, Gamble Collection*
Facing page, bottom: *In 1893 one-fifth of Savannah's bustling streets were paved. From* Art Work of Savannah, *by Charles H. Olmstead, 1893*
Above: *Propelled by sail and steam, the proud flagship of the Ocean Steam Ship Company of Savannah plied the waters between New York and Savannah in the late nineteenth century. Courtesy, Ships of the Sea Museum*

CHAPTER VI

Savannah gained international prominence as host city for the Gran Prix auto racing events of 1908, 1910, and 1911. Here three teams of drivers await the start of the 1911 race, the last to be held in Savannah because many citizens found the engines noisy and the crowd unruly. Courtesy, Dr. Julian Killen Quattlebaum, Sr.

THE PROGRESSIVE ERA AND WORLD WAR I

Savannah's history abounds in symbolic events. The closing of Savannah's oldest firm, Habersham and Harris Company, in 1899 marked the end of the rice era. After a century and a half, the cultivation of rice was no longer economically feasible and thereafter the plantations along the river fell into the

hands of industrial developers. Appropriately, one of the oldest buildings standing in Savannah, the Habersham House (now called the Pink House), was built shortly after the Revolution at least partly from rice profits. Mayor Herman Meyers' 1903 annual report signaled the end of another symbol from another era. "In Savannah no one carries a visitor to the city hall without an apology for its appearance," he stated, referring to the decrepit condition of Savannah's first great public building, the City Exchange, center of the city's political and economic life for a century. Shortly after, the Exchange was razed despite protests by historians like Thomas Gamble who pleaded for its restoration.

But Savannah was too important to be without a showpiece of its modernity. President McKinley and his cabinet had visited in December 1898 while Savannah was enjoying the notoriety of being the port of embarkation for the Spanish-American War. And Admiral Dewey had kept his promise to visit the city in 1900. The Old Exchange was found unsuitable for a city that ruled the cotton market, entertained foreign dignitaries, and was exposed to the scrutiny of the world as a major American port. By 1906 the present City Hall had replaced the Exchange. Today there is again talk of the need for a modern facility.

The energy which characterized the 1890s in Savannah continued through the first two decades of the new century. Af-

ter 150 years of being Georgia's "First City," Savannah had lost that position to Atlanta's incredible post-Civil War growth. In addition, Savannah was being challenged by industrial growth around Columbus and Augusta, but these newcomers were of little threat to a city which was justifiably proud of its position as the leading cotton city of the eastern seaboard. Not even Boston or Philadelphia could boast Savannah's 200-million-dollar shipping income. Savannah's long-term family and business connections with Liverpool, trade center for the entire British Empire, gave the little marsh city a strong position in the world's markets. Meeting the challenge of declining cotton prices, Savannah simply increased its output by expanding rail connections and shipping facilities. During this period railroad service to Savannah reached out thousands of miles to the West and Midwest. The approaching completion of the Panama Canal was seen as the gateway to an Asian market which would propel Savannah to ever new heights.

When Thomas Gamble published his *History of the City Government* in 1901, he chronicled the story of a city which had overcome seemingly insurmountable obstacles, emerging in the twentieth century as a positive, energetic, and progressive leader among Southern cities. Civil War hero Charles Olmstead and Adelaide Wilson had produced brief but glowing accounts of Savannah a decade before

At the turn of the twentieth century cotton bales by the million were shipped from Savannah to all parts of the world, making Savannah the principal cotton port of the nation. Courtesy, Manuscript Department, William R. Perkins Library, Duke University

Left: *Half a century after the war the Confederacy was very much alive in Savannah as veterans proudly displayed their old uniforms in a Memorial Day parade. Courtesy, Manuscript Department, William R. Perkins Library, Duke University*

Below: *The City Hall, built between 1904 and 1906 to replace the old City Exchange, stands on almost the same spot where Oglethorpe commanded the view of his settlement. Photo by Chan Sieg*

Gamble's detailed work. Olmstead's *Art Work of Savannah* is interesting for its early use of photography and for its unusual frame of reference in regard to illustration: the "art work" pictured is not of paintings, sculptures, crafts, and the like, but of elegant homes, business buildings, public buildings, and large industrial structures. Wilson's book, *Historic and Picturesque Savannah,* is an intensely emotional account of Savannah's story, written in the florid prose of late Victorianism. Together these works illustrate the attitude of a city proud of its British origins, its American patriotism, its Confederate loyalty, and its business acumen.

The first two decades of the twentieth century gave rise to numerous social reforms which lent the period its popular designation as the Progressive Era. While some progress was made in education, health care, services for the handicapped, prison reform, and child labor, the Deep South states expended their small resources in re-establishing the antebellum caste system. With slavery outlawed, "separate but equal" seemed progressive indeed.

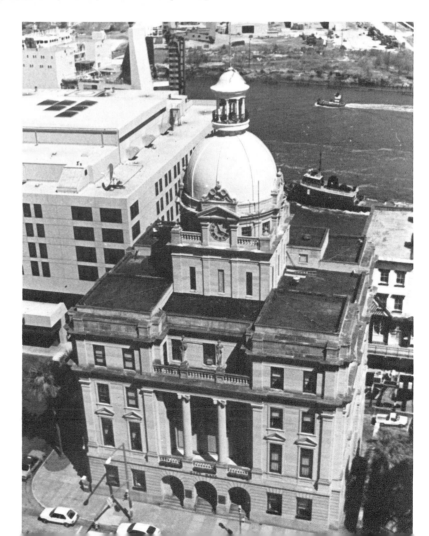

In 1915 members of the Savannah fire department proudly posed with the city's latest acquisition of modern firefighting equipment. Courtesy, Manuscript Department, William R. Perkins Library, Duke University

The Supreme Court's upholding of segregation laws virtually put an end to all the progress America's blacks had made for forty years. On the other hand, the restricted options forced the black man on his own resources. Black leaders Booker T. Washington and Bishop Henry Turner both died in 1915. Turner's idea of establishing a free nation of blacks in Africa never reached fruition, but Washington's great influence prevailed in the South. The death of the two leaders left W.E.B. Du Bois and Monroe Trotter as America's foremost black voices. Du Bois left Atlanta University to exert his influence on the now famous Niagara Movement which led to the founding of the NAACP, and the long struggle for black rights ensued.

Savannah's black community had made a number of important strides in the post-Reconstruction years. Led by newspapermen like Sol Johnson and John Deveaux, important ministers such as E.K. Love and Henry Turner spearheaded the struggle for education, jobs, and fair treatment. Under President McKinley, John Deveaux was appointed to the important position of Customs Collector of Savannah, which caused great concern among the princes of the cotton exchange. But Deveaux followed the precepts of his patron, Booker Washington, and when his reappointment came up there was little protest.

Jobs for black Savannahians were limited mostly to menial or heavy labor activities. Skilled workers who had prospered during the early years after the war were confronted with competition from whites in the job markets, forcing more and more blacks away from white patronage and into business within the black community. One of the centers of black business was begun on a modest $102 by L.E. Williams and friends. That enterprise was the Wage Earner's Bank, which by 1915 was able to build new quarters and commanded an entire block of downtown Savannah.

While the state was torn by political strife, such as the Atlanta riots in 1906, Savannah could boast that no such incidents took place within the city limits, nor did any of the more than 500 lynchings that occurred in Georgia.

Two of the progressive black groups functioning in Savannah in the early part of the century were the Savannah Urban League, which made strides in care for the aged, and the Negro Civic Improvement League which spearheaded a movement to clean up the growing slums of Savannah's overcrowded black neighborhoods. Years of protest and litigation finally led to reformation of two major problem areas: child labor and convict-leasing. These two sources of cheap labor had been the foundation of post-Reconstruction growth in the South. Leaders saw no wrong in placing a child in a factory for twelve hours a day as soon as he was old enough to learn a simple skill. Old enough meant ten years old—indeed, Georgia's manufacturing work force, largely employed in textile mills, consisted of a million workers of which nearly 30 percent were age fifteen or under. The convict-leasing system was more than a source of cheap labor for rebuilding the state's transportation and industrial system after the war; it was also a means of controlling the black population since approximately 90 percent of the convicts were black, arrested on minor charges, and given major sentences to increase the labor supply. In 1888, for example, 1,388 blacks and 149 whites were leased to private companies, according to figures compiled in 1933 by E. Merton Coulter. Coulter attributes the great rise in the black prison population which followed the war to blacks being "unadapted to their new freedom." Two of the men who

benefited most from the leasing system were Joseph Brown and John Gordon. Gordon, from a prominent Savannah family, formed one of three companies in 1876 which promised the state half-a-million dollars in revenue over twenty years in return for rights to lease prisoners. Thus the railroad system was rebuilt, mining developed, and lumber was cut and hauled. To his credit, it must be said that despite his reputation as one of the early Klan leaders, Gordon would not tolerate the cruel treatment which so many convicts suffered at the hands of what Coulter refers to as "poor white trash" overseers. In 1887, after much hue and cry from irate citizens about the brutality of the prison camps, Governor Gordon imposed what was considered an excessive punishment on two companies where flagrant violations had occurred: he fined them each $2,500.

Perhaps the most illuminating example of the bad conditions under convict-leasing can be found in the solution finally arrived at by the state government in 1908 when the system was abolished. The

The Savannah Public Library was established in 1903 and shared space with the Georgia Historical Society until 1916, when the library moved to its own building on Bull Street. At present, the Chatham-Effingham-Liberty Regional Library serves as center for fifteen branches in Chatham County as well as one each in Effingham and Liberty counties. Photo by Beth Holland

Above: *By 1915 recent construction along Bull Street was giving Savannah its characteristic skyline. Courtesy, Manuscript Department, William R. Perkins Library, Duke University*

Right: *The Savannah chapter of the Georgia Society of the Colonial Dames of America restored and maintains the historically important Andrew Low House. Built by architect John Norris circa 1849 for British Consul Andrew Low, the house later was the home of Juliette Gordon Low who resided in it until her death in 1927. It was here in 1912 that she founded the Girl Scouts of America. Photo by Beth Holland*

"progressive" spirit of the time led to the formation of what became popularly known as the "Georgia Chain Gang." Until 1938, anyone growing up in Savannah regularly saw men in striped suits and leg irons.

For those Savannahians whose family lore still retained a vestige of the dream of Eden, there was considerable progress during the first decades of the new century. Not only was a new City Hall constructed, but large buildings sprang up all over the old city. The present skyline is little changed from that of the pre-war period. The city expanded southward and eastward with the construction of fashionable suburbs; industry was encouraged to locate in Savannah, and names like Dixie Crystals and Wesson Oil became nationally known. In November 1903, the first truly public library was established. Conservative Savannah, having refused a Carnegie grant in 1901, established its own library in 1903 and joined the great national library craze with Carnegie help

a few years later. Since antebellum days, any interest in books had been vested with the Georgia Historical Society which had generously shared space with the Savannah Library Society. For twelve years the Savannah Public Library was located in Hodgson Hall, home of the historical society.

The years before World War I changed Savannah in many ways. In 1909 Chippewa Square was decorated with the busts of two Confederate heroes, Lafayette McLaws and Francis Bartow. The following year these heroes were moved to Forsyth Park and replaced by Daniel Chester French's statue of Oglethorpe. The erection of Oglethorpe's great bronze image completed the major decoration of Bull Street. Bull was now the "Avenue of Heroes," the "Monument Street," the street of the great squares. In 1912 Juliette Gordon Low founded the Girl Scouts of America in her home on Lafayette Square. During this same period, and particularly during the war years,

The thrill of the electric automobile appealed to a number of Savannah's daring ladies who did not hesitate to take a turn along one of the city's dirt roads early in the twentieth century. Courtesy, CEL Regional Library, Gamble Collection

The dapper Felice Nazzaro was one of the favorites in the 1910 Gran Prix. With curled moustache and sun goggles, he was a dashing figure to the unsophisticated Savannah populace. An estimated 200,000 spectators were thrilled by the spectacle of speed along the 415-mile course on Savannah's southside. Courtesy, Dr. Julian Killen Quattlebaum, Sr.

Florence Martus, Savannah's famed "Waving Girl," was establishing the city's reputation internationally as a place of hospitality and warmth.

Perhaps the most far-reaching event was the introduction of the automobile. In 1908 enterprising Savannah took advantage of New York's injunctions against automobile racing, built a road track on its southern extremes, and was host city for *Gran Prix* and Vanderbilt Cup racing that year and again in 1910 and 1911. The *Savannah Morning News* reported that an estimated crowd of 200,000 thrilled to the spectacle of speed which exceeded seventy miles an hour. The jet set of the time converged on Savannah during race week, including in their number famous drivers of France,

Italy, and Germany who pushed their sleek Fiats, Ferraris, and Mercedes to the limit along Savannah's scraped dirt perimeter. One American car buff who attended almost unnoticed but who played an important role in later Savannah history was Henry Ford of Dearborn, Michigan.

"The Peak Year of Human Felicity," as commentator Elmer Davis called 1913, marked a turning point in world history. The war that followed changed the entire established order. Savannah was riding a crest that not only boasted close to two million bales of cotton a year, but of the thriving growth in timber, naval stores, and agricultural products. Some of Savannah's leading women were shocking their peers as they espoused social causes

By World War I, movies and vaudeville were becoming the most popular entertainment in Savannah. The Odeon Theatre, located at Broughton and Abercorn streets, continued in operation until after World War II. Courtesy, Manuscript Department, William R. Perkins Library, Duke University

like temperance, suffrage, prison reform, education, and the end of child labor. It was an age where the affluent could afford to be charitable and the poor could afford to be hopeful. Pride in the city was summed up in the publication of William Harden's long-awaited *History of Savannah and South Georgia* which chronicles the tragedies and triumphs, the advances and setbacks, the heroism and heartbreak of a little settlement on the marsh through its growth to a city. Describing Savannah in the year before the "war to end all wars," Harden wrote:

... a city which today counts its population up to a figure beyond 70,000; a city with streets and houses of beauty, comfort, and adequate proportions; a city with everything in the way of conveniences and utility that may be looked for in the wealthiest metropolis on the globe; a city that is admired by everyone who has ever entered its gates; a city where may be found all that may be called for or heart may desire; a city that is all which its beautiful name of Spanish origin implies; ... Savannah is today on a steady and constant upward move which seems to be destined to continue without cessation or interruption.

For a few, it *was* Eden. They traveled the city's half-paved streets in the most fashionable hand-wrought carriages powered with or without horses; their homes

were furnished with excellent Northern and European craftsmanship; their cotillions were gay and elegantly fashionable; their manners still essentially British and essentially nineteenth century. Most importantly, their power was unchallenged.

A single shot in Sarajevo plunged the world into war the year after Harden's great work was published. Starkly symbolic of the end of an era, Harden's homage to his home town would never be duplicated and from that time forward historians would be forced to look at Savannah from a twentieth-century viewpoint which takes into account technology, social reform, cultural achievement, and the health and welfare of *all* its citizens.

In 1910 the blows Jack Johnson delivered to the Great White Hope Jim Jeffries spawned a war of nerves that trembled through America. Jim Crow laid a heavy hand of protection into every corner he could reach. In 1914 the fear led to the renewal of the Ku Klux Klan in Atlanta. Scarcely two years later, D.W. Griffith's *Birth of a Nation* broke all box office records and polarized a racially tense nation. During this same period, industry in the North began a search for cheap labor in the South, sending agents to lure blacks away. Savannah became the scene of what John Dittmer calls the "Great Emigration" when seven trains of the Pennsylvania Railroad "packed full of black laborers" left Savannah for the North. "The most important event in black America since emancipation," the northern migration would see half-a-million blacks leave the South during the war years, resulting in a shortage of labor and producing measures of conciliation in the form of better education and higher wages for the blacks who remained.

The war also raised prices, particularly on farm items, and Savannah benefited from a rise in the price of cotton from seven to thirty-five cents per pound between 1914 and 1919. As a major war port, Savannah prospered during the war years and for a short period thereafter, continuing its program of expansion to the suburbs. Business was good as the great ships of war steamed in and out of the little harbor, and the trains moved men and goods through Savannah at a hectic pace. But the seeds that would bring decades of decay had already been planted.

CHAPTER VII

In 1938 the children of workers at the Lebanon plantation, a few miles south of Savannah, look out on a world of depression and poverty. Photo by Mrs. H.J. Morrison. Courtesy, Georgia Historical Society

THE KING IS DEAD

Despite the great influenza epidemic which took more lives than the war and was sorely felt in Savannah, the city entered the 1920s with much optimism, assured that its position atop the cotton kingdom would last forever. The Panama Canal opened Savannah to a whole new world of possibilities. But

few people, in Savannah or elsewhere, realized that the world had undergone vast changes; that the Roaring Twenties in America muffled the quiet rise of Hitler, Stalin, and the Japanese military oligarchy.

The Cotton Exchange had closed in 1916, ending thirty years of Savannah's power. But the war brought its usual profits to the city's businessmen as thousands of troops moved in and out on the great ships, and shipbuilding even flourished as long as the war effort required more transport. Conservative Savannah returned to its former posture after the war, seemingly assured that cotton would continue its dominance.

Instead, the King—like other monarchs of the twentieth century—was dead. A number of factors contributed to the demise: the war produced a changed world market which increased competition while it reduced prices; industrialization, with its promise of decent wages, continued to draw the rural laborer away from the South (Georgia's population figures showed an increase of less than one percent from 1920 to 1930), which raised the cost of production; as land became used up, the center of the cotton belt moved steadily westward, away from the Atlantic coast which aided the competitive position of shippers on the Gulf of Mexico; finally, the "cross between a termite and a tank"—the description many farmers gave to the boll weevil— devastated the Georgia cotton fields in 1921 and 1922,

reducing production by more than 50 percent. Despite the emergency infusion of pesticides which aided in restoring production, Georgia never regained its prominent position. A century of misuse had stripped the forests and leeched the land; Eden was on the verge of becoming a desert, the victim of negligence and greed and a stubborn resistance to change even in the face of disaster. Long before the Civil War, planters had been warned by agronomists in such publications as the *Southern Agriculturist* that continued replanting of cotton would eventually destroy the soil. But land was so plentiful that a leeched field was simply abandoned, another forest cleared, and more cotton planted. Not until the ravages of the Great Depression and the intervention of the federal government would modern agriculture make an impact on Georgia.

While Northern industry pulled Georgia's labor force in one direction, the Florida boom of the 1920s lured rural farm workers and poor city dwellers in the other. The promise of the good life and easy money drew thousands of Americans to Florida in a migration that took many of them through Georgia. The influx of vehicles in a virtually unpaved state provoked a political reaction that has never diminished. Georgia's legislature entered a highway building program that at times engulfed half of the entire state budget, produced a new era of convict labor, and gave Georgia the reputa-

Right: *Despite its importance as a port, Savannah's shipbuilding enterprises have been largely sporadic. During both world wars, federal funding launched many ships on the old river. Courtesy, Georgia Historical Society*

Below: *Until after World War II, Georgia was predominantly a rural state. Near Savannah poor farmers, black and white, lived in whatever they could fashion—often without power or water, or even glass windows. This photo is titled "Sweet Potato Cottage." Courtesy, Georgia Historical Society*

tion which even loyal historian E. Merton Coulter recalled in 1933: "Georgia might have been one of the last states in education, but it was first in highways!" By 1928 it was possible for a motorist to journey from South Carolina to Florida on a paved highway.

But not even massive road-building could stem the decline of an already poor Southern economy. Savannah—proud, traditional, and ultra conservative—virtually stood still while the storms of major change were sweeping America. Led and owned by social and political forces which held fast to post-Reconstruction attitudes, Savannah watched its once-burgeoning riverfront slowly deteriorate, its little palaces gradually decay, and its most important citizens move away to fashionable, newer dwellings.

The twenties roared into a Savannah whose leadership was not quite prepared for radical change. While the privations of Prohibition were successfully side-stepped by private clubs, night boats from Cuba, hip flasks, and good old Georgia corn, the behavior of some Savannah women caused many heads to shake. The Georgia League of Women Voters was organized in 1920; Savannah's women began to appear downtown in short hair and shorter skirts, participated in physical education classes, and brazenly wore form-fitting suits to the beach. Worst of all, they danced the Charleston and Black Bottom to the wild rhythms of jazz. Attempts to outlaw such activities met with little success as staid old Savannah succumbed to the fever of the twenties. Sons and daughters of the affluent

When Prohibition ended, Savannah businessmen were prepared to satisfy the needs of a deprived population. Courtesy, Georgia Historical Society

In the middle of the Depression Savannah's resourceful children were delighted to earn a quarter by walking miles through the city drumming up business for Clark Gable and Claudette Colbert's latest movie, It Happened One Night. *Courtesy, Georgia Historical Society*

found refuge in rumble seats until Henry Ford's manufacturing genius made movement available to everyone. Movies drove live actors from the stage while Valentino and Clara Bow were seen everywhere.

In 1923 a number of Savannah's women, with the help of poet Edwin Markham, founded the Poetry Society of Georgia. In doing so, they began a tradition of literary leadership that still remains today. With the exception of the Georgia Historical Society, Savannah never developed a tradition of culture, either in literature, music, or the visual arts. Artistic activities generally had been restricted to special-interest clubs. There were a number of musical and literary-forensic societies which met regularly to enjoy programs of local talent or to dis-

cuss books and topics of contemporary interest. While vaudeville troupes continued to play the city, live professional theatre gave way to cinema, and Savannah lost its position as a regular stop for the professional acting companies. Theatre had been the one mainstay of Savannah's culture for more than a century as Edwin Booth, Tyrone Power, and Joseph Jefferson played the classics to crowded houses. Construction of the City Auditorium in 1916 permitted at least a portion of the public to experience symphony, opera, and ballet performances a few times each year. But impresarios like Lawrence Alnutt found that investing in such events was not always profitable in Savannah. The arts offered no competition to carnivals and circuses and nightclubs, while the nearby beach enjoyed a popularity that made it the party spot of the Coastal Empire.

One of the major effects of World War I was construction of Ardsley Park, Savannah's first residential subdivision. The development of this large tract set the tone for the entire future of Savannah's growth which has remained essentially southward and eastward along the coastal streams for prime residential areas, and westward for industrialization. But until after World War II, Savannah's center of government, economics, and business remained within a few blocks of City Hall.

As the city moved south, Oglethorpe's gridwork of streets and squares became increasingly crowded with those escaping the wretched life of tenant farming and sharecropping. But scarcely anyone protested as the once elegant little palaces metamorphosed into boarding houses and rental units. The last great mansion in the Historic District was built in 1920 when the Armstrong family constructed the imposing home which still stands on Bull Street at Forsyth Park. The Italianate house, of marble-dusted brick and elaborate ironwork, was short-lived as a residence. In 1935 it became the administration building of Armstrong Junior

For many families, owning an ox and a cart was not only a means of transportation but a source of a little extra income during hard times. Courtesy, Georgia Historical Society

The building of railroad tracks across the marshes, an engineering accomplishment, opened Tybee Island as Savannah's first public resort. The Tybee Hotel was a favorite gathering place during the first half of this century. Courtesy, Manuscript Department, William R. Perkins Library, Duke University

College, Savannah's only institution of higher education for whites.

For eighty years Savannah's major industrial effort was construction and expansion of the Central of Georgia Rail-Road. The company had survived war, competition, and even receivership. In the twenties, under the leadership of Dr. Craig Barrow, the Central established the first full-service medical facility for railroad employees in the United States. The hospital served not only the railroad, but many of the general population for many years. The Central of Georgia Hospital augured the social responsibility that characterized the period following the Depression and World War I.

The effects of the 1929 stock market crash gradually filtered to a comparatively isolated Savannah in the form of lost fortunes, lower real estate values, less economic activity, and an influx of a new and poorer population which added to the decline of the downtown area. The Depression was a time when enormous amounts of land changed hands, when the last of the rice plantations along the river were parceled and sold to industrial interests. In the Historic District, venerable townhouses rented for a mere twenty dollars a month; one- or two-bedroom apartments were had for eight or ten dollars. City improvements came to a virtual halt in the face of declining tax revenues. For the first time since Sherman, Savannah was visited by the sight of hungry citizens lining up for charity food distributions.

Despite privation and hardship, Savannah found the means to celebrate its 200th birthday in 1933. With pageants and balls and historic gatherings, the celebration lasted for nearly the entire year, culminating with the visit of President Franklin Roosevelt. The "Warm Springs Connection" would serve Georgia and Savannah very well indeed in the years ahead.

Roosevelt's first administration was less than well-received by his adopted state, however. Governor Eugene Talmadge bitterly opposed all attempts to impose the New Deal in Georgia. In a state that was starving, ill-educated, and disease-ridden, the leaders proudly re-

fused any idea that the federal government could serve their needs better than they could. But Roosevelt's reelection brought a new governor to Georgia, Ed Rivers, who immediately set about accepting the programs of major economic and social change proffered from Washington.

Savannah's pride and insistence on doing things its own way had earned it the nickname of "State of Chatham," but its business acumen quickly adjusted to the New Deal. As World War II approached, Savannah reaped the benefits of federal aid in education, libraries, health services, vocational training, harbor improvements, housing construction, and a

Free lunch for poor schoolchildren was one of the many blessings of the Roosevelt years in Savannah. Serious nutrition deficiencies and childhood diseases were commonplace in the Deep South until federal intervention. Courtesy, Georgia Historical Society

growing military presence. Of particular importance were the Corps of Engineers, the Civilian Conservation Corps (which labored for the U.S. Park Service on the restoration of Fort Pulaski among other projects), and the Works Progress Administration (WPA) which provided hundreds of jobs in a variety of areas. One WPA project may be pinpointed as the beginning of the historic revival period. The Writers' Project conducted several years of intensive research into Savannah's past, producing volumes of inestimable value and reviving an interest in

history which had become the province of the wealthy few. Archeological teams explored the region and excavated the Irene Mound complex, the burial place of Tomochichi's Yamacraw tribe and site of the first school for Indians in Georgia—established by the Moravians in 1736.

Savannah scientist Dr. Charles Herty had experimented with pine tree products for years. His discoveries led to the establishment of Savannah's largest company, the Union Bag and Paper Corporation (now Union Camp Corporation), on the site of the famous Hermitage planta-

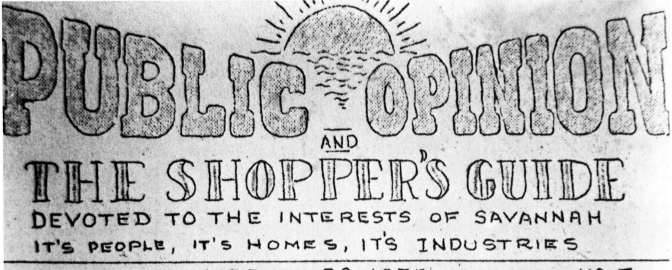

PUBLIC OPINION

AND THE SHOPPER'S GUIDE

DEVOTED TO THE INTERESTS OF SAVANNAH
IT'S PEOPLE, IT'S HOMES, IT'S INDUSTRIES

| VOL 1 | MARCH 22, 1935 | NO. 5 |

EDITOR OF PUBLIC OPINION ON SPOT!

WHO IS THE OCTOPUS OF THE COASTAL EMPIRE?

tion. The buildings of the Hermitage had been sold to Henry Ford who moved two of the slave cabins to Dearborn for restoration and display in the Ford Museum. Ford's hope of establishing a plant here was not a popular one, even in the Depression, because of his radical business practices (like high minimum wages), but Ford invested heavily in land south of Savannah and for a time developed the Ford Plantation where he erected a home using some of the original material of the Hermitage mansion.

One of the great moments in Savannah history was the opening of Armstrong Junior College by Mayor Thomas Gamble in 1935. The first institute of higher learning for whites in the city, Armstrong quickly established a reputation for ex-

cellence under president Foreman Hawes. Students who graduated from Armstrong could transfer credits to the most prestigious colleges in the land. It was most unfortunate for Savannah that growth following World War II saw Armstrong swallowed up by the state university system.

By the time war came, Savannah was well on the way to recovery from the horrors of the Depression. An expanding military presence boosted the economy, raised rents, and opened hundreds of associated businesses both desirable and tawdry.

Facing page: *Before Dr. Charles Herty developed his method of using clay cups to collect resin from pine trees, many trees died from the older practice of girdling. Courtesy, Georgia Historical Society*

Above: *Tradition has it that the Depression years were not so hard in Savannah, but for many the early thirties were enough to spawn an underground press. Printed on a hand-cranked mimeograph machine in a basement of Madison Square,* Public Opinion *for a time raised the consciousness of the public. Courtesy, Mrs. E.A. Sieg*

CHAPTER VIII

In Chippewa Square, Oglethorpe continues to watch over his city in the modern era. Photo by Beth Holland

THE MARCH TO A NEW EDEN

Throughout its history Savannah has been concerned with trees. The first settlers not only had to clear the native flora, but were required to furnish food for the silkworms in the form of mulberry trees by the hundred. After the smoke of the Revolution cleared and Savannah had its first modern edifice,

the Exchange, tree planting for decoration was rewarded with a cash bonus for careful cultivation. Its nickname became the "Forest City." Mulberry and chinaberry trees have virtually disappeared into history, replaced by moss-laden oaks, a plethora of groundcovers, azalea varieties, and a veritable botanical dictionary of ivies. When the weather cooperates, March can indeed turn Savannah into a blazing Eden.

When America moved quickly from the Depression to economic resurgence after Pearl Harbor, Savannah almost overnight shucked off its forest image and became a fortress. As in every crisis in American history, its patriotism was undeniable.

In the multi-volume *Georgia in World War II,* Lamar Q. Ball details the impact of "Roosevelt's War." The acceptance of federal aid for land reform, roads and highways, housing construction, agriculture, and mining under Governor Rivers prepared Georgia for entry into the war. Without the improvements of the late thirties, the military presence in Georgia—and Savannah—might have been far less. As it turned out, Savannah became a major center in the war effort: south of the city Fort Stewart was hastily constructed for the army while the Army Air Corps established a major facility nearer to the city at Hunter Field. A city in which an airplane with two engines was a rare sight soon grew accustomed to the heavy bombers of the Eighth Air Force which were ferried from Hunter Field to points across the Atlantic.

Shipbuilding, long a sore spot in Savannah's development, reached a peak with the Southeastern Shipbuilding Corporation which employed 15,000 people in the rapid construction of the famed Liberty Ships. (The first one launched was christened *Oglethorpe,* served briefly, and was cut down by one of the many German submarines that prowled the waters close to the mouth of the Savannah River.) War brought the usual privations in the form of rationing, and a particular irony was sugar rationing in Savannah where Dixie Crystals sugar was a prime industry. Gasoline stamps were as good as gold, often bartered and sold at many times their face value. By law, auto headlights were half-covered to conceal the coastal defense area from enemy aircraft and submarines. Tenant farmers and sharecroppers, lured by the promise of fifty dollars a week, streamed into Savannah from rural Georgia. Every available space was filled; mansions and townhouses, once the pride of the city, often were partitioned into one-room apartments by absentee landlords who reaped enormous profits. The blacks continued to struggle, a few into the professions, many into the armed forces, most into the same frustration which had lasted nearly a century since emancipation.

The war turned Savannah from a sleepy, traditional, backward-looking town on a muddy river into a full-fledged, twentieth-century American city. Savan-

Above: *One of Savannah's many nicknames is the "Forest City." Preservation advocates exert great influence on developers in the matter of removing valuable trees. A view from the Savannah Bank and Trust Company, the city's tallest building, shows the dark foliage of thousands of oaks, magnolias, and other trees. Photo by Chan Sieg*

Right: *In 1940 Savannah native Wing Jung became the first Asian-American to graduate from West Point. His sister Mary posed for this photo and performed other public relations service to symbolize the friendship between the United States and China. Courtesy, Georgia Historical Society*

nahians gave what they had to the war effort, burying another generation of their youth and generously entertaining the youth of other cities. As their mothers and grandmothers had before them, Savannah's women worked tirelessly to make a home-away-from-home for the boys who were passing through the city. Savannah became a favorite off-duty town for thousands of soldiers, sailors, and marines from bases many miles distant. While officers were entertained by ladies at posh hotels and nightclubs, the troops found their own brand of relaxation at honky-tonks, jive joints, and red-light clubs where blue laws were forgotten.

But the war ended almost as suddenly

Left: *During World War II, the post office was the site of regular patriotic activities, particularly the selling of war bonds and stamps. Visiting heroes and celebrities urged citizens to "buy bonds." Courtesy, Georgia Historical Society*

Below: *The Southeastern Shipbuilding Corporation was Savannah's largest war industry during the early forties. The public relations division issued a pocket-sized magazine called the Sou'Easter, which encouraged harder work, tighter lips, and appropriate wartime prejudices. The irony of using a quote from Sherman to inspire Savannahians is obvious. From Sou'Easter, May 1, 1945. Courtesy, Old Fort Jackson*

Right: *Soldiers, sailors, and marines were "always welcome" at the Recreation Center for Colored Service Men, who were no less segregated during war than they were during peace. Courtesy, Georgia Historical Society.*

Below: *The Savannah Volunteer Guards' Armory was built as headquarters for the military groups of the city. It served for fifty years as home base for 700 Volunteers and as a social center. During World War II the armory became the Savannah U.S.O., providing a home-away-from-home for troops stationed in or near the city. In the seventies, the armory was renovated and became the Savannah College of Art and Design. Courtesy, Georgia Historical Society*

as it began. The Southeastern Shipyard closed, and the massive troop enclaves became deserted as soldiers were mustered out and returned from whence they had come. Suddenly an entire population was unemployed, and they left the city.

What remained was a partially deserted, once-fashionable Historic District. Savannah had moved south to low-roofed suburbia, abandoning hundreds of high-ceilinged townhouses to the dereliction of uncaring tenants, little or no maintenance, and, worst of all, unprofitable values. No wonder that the post-war business leaders reached the conclusion that if Savannah were to survive and flourish, the old city must make way for progress. But the preservationist attitude had found its way into the lives of a handful of influential residents who became dedicated to the principle that demolition was not the only answer to

Top: *In 1940 Tuten's Tasty Tavern, located on Bull Street Extension (now White Bluff Road), offered the very latest in nightclub decor and bands to party-going Savannah. Courtesy, Georgia Historical Society.*

Middle: *From boogie-woogie taverns to Arthur Murray ballrooms, Savannah's favorite recreation in the 1930s and 1940s was dancing, and its favorite band was the Merrymakers. Courtesy, Sandor Chan*

Bottom: *Family enterprise was not lacking in Savannah in 1943. In a custom-made, horse-powered vehicle, happy customers were transported to an evening of Southern comfort. Courtesy, Georgia Historical Society*

decay. In 1946, when the International Monetary Conference was held at the Oglethorpe Hotel on nearby Wilmington Island pursuant to the founding of the United Nations, Lady Astor piquantly referred to Savannah as having a "dirty face" and the city responded first with outrage, then with the shame of reality.

Despite Lady Astor's cogent observation, Savannah was fortunate that the remark included only the visage and not the entity. Savannah had prepared hard for the influx of international VIPs. The Historic District was dusted lightly, bedecked with flags of many nations, and strewn with "Welcome to Savannah" signs in a dozen languages. The celebrities came, went immediately to the privacy of their island retreats, and left as quickly as they had come. Lady Astor's quip was their main legacy.

Conditions in Savannah following World War II are not remembered with great pride. Essentially a nineteenth-century city in terms of social structure, class distinction, industrial development, and architecture, Savannah's major concession to the twentieth century was the automobile. Air-conditioning was still considered an unnecessary luxury by many—as long as the old ceiling fan worked. The harbor was literally rotting away—its wharves and pilings encrusted with age and infested with rats. The river, the lifeblood of the city, was itself a testament to greed, ignorance, and sloth.

Stripped of its wooded banks by settlers, then by plantation owners, and then by industrial developers, the once-clear waters were forever reddened with wasted land while generations of residents regularly added their own waste to the aqueous disaster through the ducts of an antiquated sewer system that emptied directly into the river near City Hall.

In virtually every aspect of modern life, Savannah had resisted change. A city which had begun serious street paving and sanitation measures after the Civil War had never completed the job. Even the downtown district, site of all the glory of the past, was not fully paved, nor cleaned, nor maintained in any but the least costly way. The stench of the harbor and the nearby factories poured a constant atmosphere of sulfurous putrefaction over the once-neat squares and homes. Traffic lanes still cut through many of the squares, preventing any real landscaping effort. A proliferation of low-cost housing projects accompanied the

late thirties and forties and were guaranteed to become slums within a decade. Savannah, which prided itself on being a cultural center, had a population whose average educational accomplishment was little more than seventh-grade level. The oldest city in Georgia had led the fight to establish education as early as 1785 when Abraham Baldwin and the legislature created the University of Georgia at a meeting in Savannah. The university was built on land given in 1801 by Savannah native John Milledge. In 1788 the Chatham Academy was established as part of a public school system. But the school was not erected until 1815 with funds supplied by the Union Society, Savannah's oldest benevolent organization. An elitist leadership which considered itself cultured actually did little to foster the growth of education for other than its own members.

Chatham Academy is praised in the historic record as a major advance in Savannah's interest in education, but the

What began in the 1920s as the posh General Oglethorpe Hotel has come full circle, through hard times and several owners, to emerge as the posh Sheraton Savannah Resort, located a few miles east of the city on Wilmington Island. World attention was focused on Savannah in 1946 when the General Oglethorpe Hotel hosted the International Monetary Conference, prior to the founding of the United Nations. Photo by Chan Sieg

113

Until the 1850s Chatham Academy, chartered in 1788, was Savannah's only representative in the field of public education. The building, extensively modified, now houses the Savannah-Chatham County Board of Education. Courtesy, Manuscript Department, William R. Perkins Library, Duke University

academy was a tuition-charging institution. Were it not for the power of the Union Society, the few poor students who were educated there would not have been accepted. Education had, in fact, been a sore point in Savannah's story since its beginning. Not until Reconstruction was a public school system established in Georgia. Ironically, the city leaders, believing that higher education was the restricted province of those who could afford it, were faced with the reality of a new order of things when Savannah's first college was built in 1891—the Georgia State Industrial College, an all-black school. The traditional city fathers did not push for higher education until the mid-1930s when Savannah at last established the Armstrong Junior College where, for the first time in more than 200

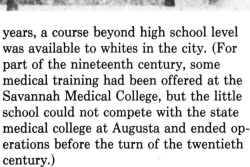

of war veterans suddenly found themselves with a hope never dreamed of. For the first time in world history, the average man had a real opportunity to rise above the social and economic conditions of his birth. With no degree programs available to its white population, male or female, Savannah had for years seen the emigration of its best talents to cities of better opportunity. In its first century of existence, before it reached a population of 10,000, Savannah had provided an extraordinary number of nationally important figures: governors, senators, cabinet members, and diplomats had sprung from the vigorous little city on the marsh. After secession, only John Gordon had made it to the governor's mansion. The most famous figures from Savannah in the first half of the twentieth century were Juliette Gordon Low, founder of the Girl Scouts, and three men in the arts whose careers had been made far from Savannah: actor Charles Coburn; lyricist Johnny Mercer; and Conrad Aiken, one of the most important figures in American literature. But where energy and innovation had once been the hallmark of the city, the twentieth century, until the

By the end of World War II the Old City Market was more interesting to local artists than local merchants who eagerly embraced the suburban exodus. Until the market was demolished in 1954, only a handful of citizens appreciated its historic value. "Market Scene" was painted by Hugh Tallart in 1946. Courtesy, Georgia Historical Society

years, a course beyond high school level was available to whites in the city. (For part of the nineteenth century, some medical training had been offered at the Savannah Medical College, but the little school could not compete with the state medical college at Augusta and ended operations before the turn of the twentieth century.)

Enter the G.I. Bill of Rights. Millions

Juxtaposition of old and new is one of many anomalies seen during restoration. In 1983 an eighteenth-century-style clapboard cottage was moved to a site adjacent to a row of richly restored mid-nineteenth-century townhouses on East Charlton Street. Protests from townhouse owners resulted in removal of the cottage. Photo by Chan Sieg

present boom, had been a scene of lassitude and decay.

Popular folklore pinpoints the beginning of Savannah's renaissance to that night in 1953 when the Old City Market, scheduled to be razed, hosted a farewell Halloween Party. Nostalgia tinged with anger and fear led to the formation of the Historic Savannah Foundation, Inc. Composed of old and new social leaders and businessmen, the foundation soon established itself as the arbiter of all things historic in Savannah. The advent of federal programs antedating the national bicentennial provided funding that expanded the small organization to the influential position it enjoys today. Early leaders—Anna Hunter, Raiford Wood, Walter Hartridge—all long associated with Savannah's small cultural element, gained the assistance of financier Lee Adler and other businessmen. In 1955 sufficient funds were raised to purchase the Davenport House, a brick home of the Williamsburg tradition constructed in

1820-1821 by Isaiah Davenport, master builder and alderman. With the assistance of groups like Savannah's Junior League, further fund-raising resulted in the excellent restoration of the Davenport House. The razing of the traditional marketplace of Savannah and the saving of the Davenport House are generally recognized as the beginning of the new era in Savannah's history.

But there are other factors which undoubtedly played a part in the return to historic pride. Late in the Depression, many federal programs instituted by the Roosevelt administration had a profound effect on Savannah. The Federal Writers' Project, the National Park Service, the Irene Mound Archeological Project— these and similar undertakings represented the first concentrated effort to research and catalogue many aspects of the region's history.

The National Park Service began the arduous restoration of the Fort Pulaski National Monument; the Irene Mound

Project not only revealed much of the Indian heritage of the area, but also uncovered long-forgotten knowledge about the Oglethorpe years; and the Writers' Project compiled mountains of notes on various aspects of Savannah's history—architecture, commerce and industry, the plantations, the black heritage. Much of their material is the souce of contemporary writing about the Georgia coast.

Shortly after the war ended, the first real attempt at restoration occurred when Mrs. Hansell Hillyer, wife of the Savannah Gas Company chief executive, decided to renovate part of the dilapidated area near the gas works. Many thought her quite foolish to modernize old clapboard cabins and small houses when any good businessman knew it was cheaper to

start over. But the charm of the freshly painted and air-conditioned little buildings soon made it a very popular rental area, and the return on that initial investment has been realized many times since. In the center of the district, just a block from the river, there had existed for years a small tea room, gift shop, and museum—the Pirates' House. Ancient in appearance and presumed to be as old as it looked, the Pirates' House was touted as the inspiration for Robert Louis Stevenson's *Treasure Island*. It sported a small upstairs room with an old bed containing a waxen body with coins on its eyes—Captain Flint himself. Rumor also had it that the trap door in the floor led to a secret tunnel where unsuspecting sailors, "come in for a swig of rum," were

The Pirates' House exudes legend and myth. Robert Louis Stevenson was inspired to write Treasure Island *while staying there. The ghost of Captain Flint still inhabits the old eaves, and the Jolly Roger recalls the days when unsuspecting sailors were plied with rum, clobbered, and spirited away through an underground tunnel. Photo by Chan Sieg*

The Talmadge Bridge, named for one of Georgia's most powerful senators, connects Savannah with South Carolina. Growth of the Savannah harbor has already made this post-World War II symbol of progress obsolete. Current plans call for its replacement by a taller structure compatible with the increased capacity of container ships. Photo by Chan Sieg

belayed and shanghaied, to awaken hours later at sea on their way to China. For years, the "oldest building in Georgia" stood next door to the little tea room. Called the Herb House, it was traditionally dated 1734 and was unequivocally believed to be the first building constructed in the original Trustees' Garden. The 1853 Herb House remains a good example of what Savannah looked like way back when.

The success of this project led restaurateur Herb Traub, who with partner Jim Casey had operated Our House, Savannah's most popular drive-in, to purchase the Pirates' House and open it as Savannah's most unique eatery. Excellent service and food combined with the quaintness of old decor made the Pirates' House an early attraction as Savannah's tourist industry began to grow. In that first decade after the market was turned into a parking garage and the restoration move was gaining momentum, the Pirates' House played a major part in Savannah's new image.

Other events affecting the city include the massive change in the national method of transporting goods and people from railroad to airplane and truck. A city which had given its life for states' rights (and still preached them loudly) began to enjoy the fruits of federal funding as the Eugene Talmadge Memorial Bridge opened the path to South Carolina, spawning a host of motels, while the U.S. Engineers and the state combined to establish the Georgia Ports Authority hardly a mile upstream from the old City Hall. The Korean War initiated a revival of the military presence in the South—thanks largely to the long tenure of Georgia politicians who had achieved seniority on House and Senate committees. From a strictly historical standpoint, the acquisition of the Richardson-Owens-Thomas House by the Telfair Academy, to whom it was willed, preserved the first of the famous William Jay buildings constructed in Savannah. Built between 1816 and 1819, the Richardson House brought Jay to Savannah where he implanted the Regency style.

Every remaining project of Jay's is now

Historic fever has some unusual side effects, as a three-story house is relocated in preparation for its restoration. After the foundation has been removed, the house must be carefully balanced. Tandem flatbed trucks then carry the house to its new address. Photo by Beth Holland

considered a historic treasure. Juliette
Gordon Low's birthplace, a Jay design,
was purchased by the Girl Scouts of
America and restored as a mecca for girls
the world over. Even before its purchase
by the famous Gordon family, the house
had an elegant history, having been the
home of James Wayne, Savannah's ap-
pointee to the Supreme Court. Wayne
not only tried the infamous case of the
last slave ship, the *Wanderer,* in 1858 at
Savannah's Custom House, but he remained on the court through the war
while his son fought for the South.

The decade of the fifties can be sum-
marized as a learning period for Savannah; it was learning new ways of business
and new technologies. It was learning
how to write grants, how to take advantage of federal programs. It was even
learning how important Oglethorpe's plan
was, not only to its past, but for its future. The most momentous event of the
fifties was *Brown* v. *Board of Education.*
Shocked, fearful, and resistant, Savannah's leaders held back the tide of change
for another decade before learning that
integration was more profitable than resistance.

Blacks returning to Savannah after the
war found themselves in the same ghet-
tos, the same caste system, the same
hopelessness. As with the whites, there
were a few who prospered, maintained
fine homes, and educated their children
far from Savannah. In a totally segregated society, they had developed their
own social strata. Well over 100,000 in
population, Savannah was more than 40
percent black. To correct one glaring
flaw, the city agreed to train a carefully
selected group of black men to become
the South's first black policemen. After
careful indoctrination, they were placed
on duty in the black areas of the city.
Though not permitted to enforce the law
upon whites, they were a hopeful symbol
of change.

The leader of the local NAACP, W.W.
Law, a much venerated man today, ex-
erted rational influence on one volatile
situation after another. Under Law's ca-

pable leadership, the inevitable kept
coming. In no small measure, credit must
go to men like Law and women like
Esther Garrison, the first black woman to
be elected to a board of education in the
South. Savannah did not suffer the
horrors of other cities where confrontation between races was more militant
than rational. While no one can claim it
was a comfortable period for blacks and
sympathetic whites, there were no incidents of dogs set loose on freedom riders
or hoses turned on demonstrators. The

pacifying effect of the many churches, social organizations, and charitable groups helped produce dialogue—heated to be sure—but preferable to violent confrontation.

While much energy was spent in the struggle to maintain a civilized image, progress was inexorably invading Savannah in the form of new business, increased shipping, a construction boom, and a new spirit that had not been felt for generations. From the highway programs of Eisenhower, through Kennedy's

New Frontier and Johnson's Great Society, to the debacle of Nixon, Savannah prospered, paralleling a southward urban sprawl with an intensive revitalization of the old city. Beneath the cracked stucco and gnarled vines of antiquated townhouses, a forgotten city was discovered.

Savannah was pleased but not completely satisfied when Juliette Gordon Low's birthplace made it to the social register of American history by being named Savannah's first national historic landmark in 1965. The next year the His-

Memorial Medical Center is the region's largest health-care institution, serving more than thirty-five counties. Begun after World War II and dedicated to the memory of the war dead, the center is constantly expanding in size and upgrading to the very latest in medical technology. Photo by Chan Sieg

toric District was designated the "largest Historic Urban Landmark in America." The city went to work writing grants, making rules for restoration, hiring whatever laborers it could find, and restoring, within a few years, more than 1,000 old buildings.

Restoration was only a small part of what has become virtually a complete rebuilding of the city. In the three decades since the fall of the old City Market, Savannah has changed its form of government to a modern management system, built the Civic Center to replace the fifty-year-old auditorium, established new water and sewer systems, and landscaped and re-lighted the old squares. Major efforts in health care began with the establishment of Memorial Medical Center which has grown into a high-tech, full-service facility providing the latest in care for a growing population that reaches far beyond the limits of Chatham

County. Other recent developments in the health field include a regular program of insect control (always a problem in the marsh country), extensive programs in prenatal and parent-and-child care, and a hospice service for the terminally ill. Other traditional hospital institutions have in the past few years opened new facilities—Candler and St. Joseph's being the largest.

The city has felt the impact of the ecology movement also. Rekindled interest in the preservation of the marshes has led to strict regulations regarding the development of any wild areas; groups like the Georgia Conservancy, the Sierra Club, the Oatland Island Education Center, and the Skidaway Institute of Oceanography exert their influence on any project threatening the delicate balance of the coastal area. Ralph Nader castigated the city for the poor condition of the Savannah River and water supply

Savannah's well-deserved reputation as a "party town" is enhanced by the monthly festival known as First Saturday on the River. Before its restoration in the mid-seventies, River Street was a rotten-wharved, rat-infested eyesore—the refuse of the cotton era. With today's boutiques, bars, and restaurants, it is now the center of Savannah's nightlife and a favorite tourist attraction. Photo by Chan Sieg

early on, leading to the expenditure of hundreds of millions of dollars by river-based industries long accustomed to low taxes, cheap water supplies, and the dumping of chemical waste into the old river.

Throughout its long history, Savannah has drawn its lifeblood from the river, and along the riverfront is where the most impressive changes have been made. The Georgia Ports Authority and the U.S. Army Corps of Engineers have combined to make the harbor a deep-channel port where the ships of the whole world visit regularly. The modern development of "containerization" is best exemplified at the Savannah docks which now collect more money in customs revenue than any port from Baltimore to New Orleans. The old facilities which had long served the cotton kingdom and which had become ragged shadows of their former selves were completely renovated in the seventies under Savannah's high-profile Mayor John "the Greek" Rousakis. Retaining the basic historical qualities of the old warehouses, Savannah architects Bobby Gunn and Eric Meyerhoff rebuilt the entire 2,000-foot front of the old harbor, creating a landscaped mall of modern de-

A regular schedule of activities and re-enactments makes Fort Jackson the true "living history" museum of Savannah. The ritual cannon-firing is conducted late every afternoon. Photos by Chan Sieg

sign and lighting with historic atmosphere. The warehouses bloomed into a fantasy world of boutiques, restaurants, and cabarets, becoming the center of the city's night life. Before restoration, the riverfront (like the squares) was a war zone of abandoned buildings and abandoned people. Today the city's new look and the nightlife along River Street attract many visitors annually.

For most of the twentieth century, Fort Jackson lay overgrown and abandoned just two miles downriver from City Hall. The Coastal Heritage Society now manages the restored landmark and presents a regular program of "living history" demonstrations at Old Fort Jackson in addition to its facilities and museum.

Recreation being the great business stimulator that it is, Savannah and its suburbs have spent vast sums to provide facilities that attract visitors. Marinas, fishing camps, golf courses, bicycle paths, jogging trails—all the appurtenances of

the new lifestyle are available. At Tybee Island, Savannah's beach, the problem of erosion which plagues much of the Atlantic coast is being corrected by the U.S. Engineers. No effort is being spared to make Savannah attractive.

For most of its history Savannah traditionally left cultural matters to those educated few. But a new population of ethnic diversity and backgrounds not traditionally of the Savannah mold are exerting an influence in a city where a paucity of available artistic experience was not considered a problem. But this new mixture of people believes that no city can attain importance without some real concern for the artistic experiences available within its borders. The result is that a strained city budget now finds some means of helping support a symphony orchestra, ballet companies, theatre groups, and an art association. The Savannah College of Art and Design is the newest addition to the city's educa-

In 1818 William Jay designed the playhouse which was the center of Savannah's fashionable nightlife for many years. The theatre was widely praised for its small but elegant interior. Courtesy, Georgia Historical Society

tional institutions while public radio station WSVH-FM 91 airs a variety of musical programming including classical, folk, jazz, and country.

For Savannah natives whose ancestors hacked the city out of marshes, underbrush, and pine trees, the past thirty years and the accompanying changes have passed quickly. The relaxed country life now is reserved mostly for weekends when people take to the beach or the gay life of the riverfront clubs or to private gardens on nearby islands where wine and wisteria mix perfectly with japonica and gin.

The real problem in downtown Savannah is finding a parking space. Saturated with automobiles years ago, the city has sought the help of several imported traffic experts, but no solution has been found. For a period of time the move of businesses and population to the sprawling southside threatened to vacate the Historic District. Broughton Street, the traditional main street of fine businesses, lost many of its oldest firms that had been there for generations. One man is often mentioned as helping keep the street from total decay—Jake Fine, owner of Savannah's most prestigious women's store, refused either to close his Broughton Street store or to open another outlet in the southside malls. Such faith helped to raise the city's consciousness to the point at which it cleaned up the street with planters and new lighting. But the parking problem vexes all downtown merchants who shake their heads when the Chamber of Commerce announces that tourism is bringing hundreds of thousands of visitors to the city.

Surpassing 200 million dollars a year in tourist revenue, Savannah looks forward to doubling that figure in the eighties. History has become Savannah's big business. With its dirty face now cleaned up, except around the edges, Savannah loves to be in the movies. Not only is Hollywood a frequent visitor, but television companies, public broadcasting programs, documentaries, commercials, and magazines all have discovered the visual ex-

The Savannah Theatre building today retains none of Jay's original design. However, its function has been completely recycled: from playhouse to movie house and back to playhouse. It has been the home of the Savannah Theatre Company since 1983. Photo by Chan Sieg

citement in the new-old city.

But the most welcome of all visitors is the military, whose economic impact on the community is enormous. The Hunter-Stewart complex, which begins in the city limits and extends miles southwest through Bryan and Liberty counties, is one of the nation's largest and most advanced training sites. A little farther south at Kings Bay, the base for nuclear-powered Trident submarines is under construction. Estimated at more than 600 million dollars in 1983, the economic importance of the military is still growing.

It is commonplace to speak of life to-

day as fast-paced, the rate of change constantly increasing; but one of Savannah's most recent undertakings underlines that view more graphically than any other example. At the close of 1984 the Great Savannah Exposition opened in a completely restored section of the old Central Rail-Road terminal building, which also houses the Savannah Visitors Center and Chamber of Commerce. The Expo is a more than ten-million-dollar effort to create a major tourist attraction that not only incorporates history, but is entertaining and profitable. Featuring a life-sized, animated, pneumatic Oglethorpe

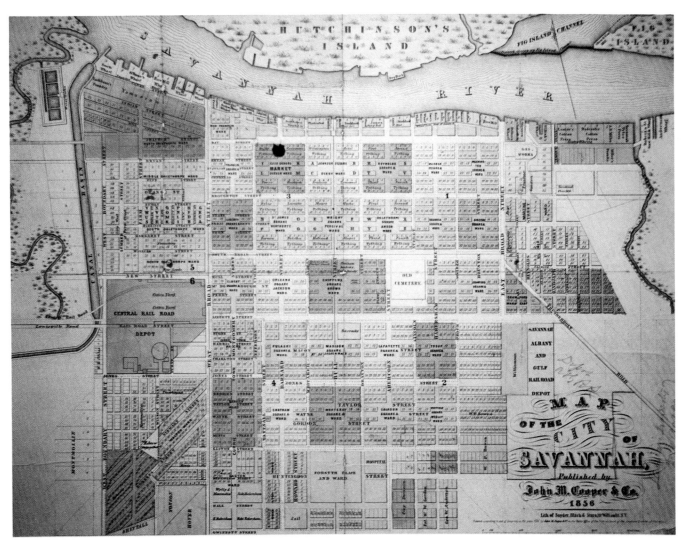

Surveyor John M. Cooper prepared this map of the city of Savannah in 1856, revealing a town which had grown beyond the original 5,000 acres allotted the colony. The twenty-four squares were laid out by 1851 and, from that point on, Oglethorpe's original plan was discarded. Courtesy, CEL Regional Library, Gamble Collection

*During the spring of
1861, Confederate troops
prepared in Monterey
Square to march to Vir-
ginia. Led by Francis
Bartow, the Savannah
contingent distinguished
itself at the first battle of
Bull Run where Bartow
was killed. Courtesy, CEL
Regional Library, Gamble
Collection*

Near the end of the Civil War, a Confederate fleet steamed down the Savannah River under a flag of truce on its way to meet Union ships for an exchange of prisoners. From Harpers Weekly, *December 3, 1864. Courtesy, CEL Regional Library, Gamble Collection*

Right: *Erected in 1910, the Oglethorpe statue by Daniel Chester French was the last of the great monuments placed in the squares on Bull Street.* © Grant Compton, 1985

Facing page, top: *Like thousands of tourists, winter visits Savannah on a regular basis. Despite its location on the edge of the sunbelt, Savannah enjoys the variety of the changing seasons. For more than a century, the magnificent fountain in Forsyth Park has provided Savannahians a welcome respite from the tribulations of the work-a-day world. Photo by Beth Holland*

Facing page, bottom: *The statue of John Wesley, Savannah's most famous minister, stands in Reynolds Square (named for John Reynolds, the first royal governor). West of the statue is the late-eighteenth-century Habersham House, built for James Habersham, Jr. Known today as the Pink House, it is a popular restaurant and tavern. Photo by Beth Holland*

As a permanent reminder of Savannah's dependence on both the salt water of the ocean and the fresh water of the river, "old Triton blows his wreathed horn" in Forsyth Park. Photo by Chan Sieg

Under President Jefferson, Congress authorized construction of coastal defenses for the young United States. Savannah brick-making facilities were insufficient to provide the hundreds of thousands needed for Fort Jackson's construction. (Henry McAlpin's "modern" production methods at the Hermitage were still a decade away.) The fort walls clearly indicate an array of varied brick shipped to Savannah from Charleston and other cities. The three lower layers of brick were laid between 1808 and 1812; the uppermost was added between 1845 and 1860 when the moat and brick barracks were constructed. Photo by Chan Sieg

Right: *Once located outside the palisaded walls of the city, the "Old Burial Ground" is now maintained in the very heart of Savannah's Historic District as Colonial Park. Along with the vault of Revolutionary War hero Lachlan McIntosh, visitors can see the gravesites of many of Georgia's most famous early citizens including the Habershams, Archibald Bulloch, Button Gwinnett, and Nathanael Greene. Photo by Chan Sieg*

Below: *Today the home of Solomon's Lodge, the Cotton Exchange, built in 1886, symbolizes the thirty-year period during which the merchants of the world paid tribute to Savannah's business acumen. Photo by Chan Sieg*

The home of the Georgia Historical Society was a gift from Margaret Telfair Hodgson in memory of her husband. Hodgson Hall was built in 1875 by New York architect Detlef Lienau who also remodeled the Telfair Academy of Arts and Sciences. Photo by Chan Sieg

Top left: *The Isaiah Davenport House, dating from 1820, was scheduled for demolition in 1955 but was saved by the Historic Savannah Foundation. A concerted fund-raising effort resulted in its restoration, and to many people the Daven-port House is the symbol of Savannah's historic reawakening. Photo by Chan Sieg*

Bottom left: *A horse-drawn carriage provides a leisurely view of historic Savannah. © Grant Compton, 1985*

138

Facing page, top right: *The recently restored 1896 King-Tisdell Cottage, operated by the Savannah-Yamacraw Branch Association for the Study of Afro-American Life and History, functions as a community center and museum for Savannah's rich African past. Photo by Beth Holland*

Facing page, bottom right: *From the unique side balcony of the Richardson House, the Marquis de Lafayette greeted cheering citizens during his visit to Savannah in 1825. Photo by Chan Sieg*

Above: *Rice fields and plantations have given way to harbor development and industrial expansion, which anchor the present growth of the city. Photo by Chan Sieg*

Left: *Tourism, too, thrives on the waterway.* © Grant Compton, 1985

139

Left: *Dating from 1799
"Laura's Cottage" is
prized as the earliest
work of the renowned
Isaiah Davenport.*

Right: *The Scottish Rite
Temple on Madison
Square attests to the long
tradition of Masonry in
Savannah, going back to
Oglethorpe's membership
in Solomon's Lodge, the
third oldest in the U.S.
Photos by Chan Sieg*

Along the Intracoastal Waterway at Isle of Hope near Savannah stands the mansion traditionally known as White Hall. With its tabby foundation dating from the 1750s, White Hall has endured fire, flood, and war. Many owners rebuilt, expanded, and improved the original—the most recent being the elegant restoration by its present owner, Linda Bedingfield-Kelly, and the author and the photo researcher of this book. More than any other location, White Hall represents to the author the fulfillment of the dream inherent in the title of the book. Photo by Chan Sieg

The Independent Presbyterian Church is prominent among the more than 200 places of worship in the Savannah area. © Grant Compton, 1985

The 1889 Court House and the Lutheran Church of the Ascension stand on adjacent trust lots on Wright Square. The Salzburgers built a wooden church on this site in 1771. After a fire, the present edifice was begun in 1843 and completed in the late 1870s. Photo by Chan Sieg

Left: *After the disastrous yellow fever epidemic of 1820, the remains of Captain Noble Jones were moved from the city cemetery to the Bonaventure Cemetery.*
Right: *St. John's Episcopal Church emerges from the morning fog, a symbol of Savannah's historic tradition of religious freedom.*
Below: *The Mickve Israel Temple, designed by Henry Harrison, has stood on Montgomery Square since 1878. In addition to the original Torah brought to Savannah in 1733, the temple contains interesting historical documents such as letters from Presidents Washington, Jefferson, and Madison. Photos by Chan Sieg*

Top: *St. Patrick's Day was once the biggest day of the year in Savannah, rivaling the holiday's celebrations in New York and Boston. Then it became the biggest weekend; now it is the biggest week, drawing more than 300,000 guests to the city in 1984. Hotels are booked a year in advance, food and drink are stocked in enormous quantities, and anything that can be colored green is—including the river, fountains, hair, eggs, and even grits. Held annually since 1824, rain or shine, the parade brings out politicians, movie stars, and a population that mysteriously consists of nothing but children of Old Erin. Photo by Beth Holland*

Middle and bottom right: *On Georgia Day, children don patriotic costumes for a traditional parade. © Grant Compton, 1985*

Bottom left: *The Annual Scottish Games attract hordes of visitors for a week of celebration. A festooned Fort Jackson is the center of all the activity, where "bonnie lassies" compete for honors in traditional dances. Photo by Beth Holland*

Pulaski Square lent a turn-of-the-century atmosphere to the movie East of Eden, *starring Jane Seymour and Timothy Bottoms. Photo by Chan Sieg*

that talks, the Expo's museum displays the kind of historic memorabilia that is sure to please the casual visitor—the actual cars which competed in the Vanderbilt Cup Races at Savannah seventy years ago, for example. The Expo proudly advertises that Savannah's 253-year-old history repeats itself every twenty minutes. If the Expo smacks of commercialism to some people, it must be emphasized that making money for the city—and its investors—is the whole idea. Whatever else one may say in criticism of Savannah's history, one is forced to admit that at no time has Savannah been incapable of calculating the bottom line in any venture. If Expo reaches its goals, it will soon sit at the center of a

major convention facility with all that is implied for the continued growth of the downtown area.

When Sir Robert Mountgomery was huckstering the promise of a New Eden, he could hardly have thought that people would believe what he was selling, that they would actually pursue such a dream, and that some of them would come to realize it. Albert Scardino, son of a Savannah doctor, realized his dream for one brief moment. In the late seventies, he raised enough money to publish a small weekly newspaper which he called the *Georgia Gazette*, after the first paper published in the colony in 1763, the eighth such undertaking in America. The new *Gazette* dedicated itself to "responsi-

THE
GEORGIA GAZETTE

Incorporating the Savannah Journal-Record   The Georgia Gazette *is the official legal newspaper for Chatham County*

8 Pages

In Short
Commissioner wants county committees

The committee system previously used by the Chatham County Commission to analyze community problems and recommend solutions to the commission is in danger of extinction when the incoming county administrator assumes his duties in mid-March, according to Robert McCorkle.

The 4th District commissioner, speaking on "personal privelege" following completion of the commission's regular agenda Friday ("It's the only time I can speak on anything anymore.") said he feared losing touch with his constituents if, when they come to him about a problem, he has to tell them to take it to the county administrator.

The new administrator, a post mandated by the state General Assembly last year when it legislated changes in county governments, will be Volusia County, Fla., assistant manager Patrick Salerno, chosen by Chairman Charles Brooks and informally confirmed by the full commission last week. He takes over the day-to-day operations of the Chatham County government March 11 following a planned formal commission vote on his choice.

"I've talked to the chairman three or four times about this and

Shipping

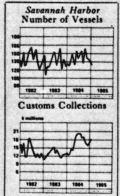

Savannah Harbor
Number of Vessels

Customs Collections

The number of vessels calling on the port of Savannah dropped to 130 in January, compared to 137 the previous month. Customs collections, however, rose to $18.1 million in January from a revised $16.0 million the previous month. During the same time period last year 133 vessels called on the port and $13.1 million in customs fees were collected.

Source: GEOSTATS from U.S. Customs and City of Savannah

Adler, who turns 60 this summer, said he always expected to retire by the time he reached that age.

Gazette bids farewell

Over its seven-ye
Georgia Gazet
blockbuster sto
after week and
tolerance for dif
opinion. Edit
publisher Albert
jorie Scardino (c
ed the venture a

The Georgia Gazette *was Savannah's first newspaper, published by James Johnston from 1763 to 1802. Revived in the 1970s, it went out of business in 1985, a year after being awarded a Pulitzer Prize. From* The Georgia Gazette, *February 28, 1985*

ble journalism" in an atmosphere where the traditional function of newspapers, radio, and television is to advertise and entertain, not criticize or complain. Savannah's journalistic tradition was established by none other than James Johnston, first publisher-editor of the old *Georgia Gazette.* Knowing full well the attitude of Governor Wright toward the Liberty Boys' meetings, Johnston nevertheless published the announcement leading to the outbreak of the Revolution. He must have had some thoughts about personal freedom for he had ceased publication in protest of the Stamp Act. But he was typical of Savannah's practical businessmen when Colonel Campbell's forces ran the Americans out of Savannah and sacked the city. He started publication of a new journal which he called the *Royal Georgia Gazette.* It was as short-lived as Scardino's revival. But the little weekly made an impact on the Savannah of the 1980s which will never be forgotten. Scardino, for his editorials, was awarded the Pulitzer Prize in 1984, bringing to Savannah's historical record the highest honor in its life. A year later the paper went out of business, having lost its contract to publish legal notices.

The national press has been good to Savannah, giving it mostly rave notices, calling it the "most restored city in America" and a "city of European atmosphere, with charming manners." The old town has been sucked into the twentieth century by the tornadoes of change. Despite conservatism, tradition, and a reluctance to completely let go of the old ways, a city which lay sleeping and almost unconcerned with national and world affairs now finds itself affected by such matters as Japanese import quotas, the devaluation of the pound sterling, or the odds on the Georgia game. An ethnically diverse population which is increasingly non-native is reviving the international flavor first evidenced in the days of Oglethorpe when John Wesley is said to have learned several languages in order to preach the gospel. Savannah is leaving behind its old reputation for insu-

larity and xenophobia, abandoning at last the hollow smugness of its "State of Chatham" image.

Savannah is a new city raised on an old foundation. Oglethorpe's design has passed the test of time and, like the old river, has withstood all that more than ten generations could throw at it. But Oglethorpe gave Savannah more than a plan of streets and squares; he imbued his city with a fountain of ideals unique to America. Cast aside and forgotten after his departure, these principles have again come to the front with the recognition of Oglethorpe's skill as city-planner. In an age of greed, Oglethorpe taught charity—Savannah is famed for its charitable institutions. In an age of cheap land and vast wilderness, he advocated proper use and distribution of the land—today Savannah holds the oak tree sacred and woe to him who would build a motel on the marsh. In an age of bigotry and persecution, Oglethorpe insisted on religious tolerance—Savannah probably has more churches per capita than any city in America. In an age of oppression and slavery, he advocated equality of opportunity and banned slaves in his colony—the Supreme Court has seen to that. In an age of drunkenness, he espoused moderation—Savannah permits no public drinking from bottles or cans on St. Patrick's Day, only Dixie cups.

Having proceeded from beginning to middle to beginning again, Savannah entered the eighties with its birthright intact and its ideals legalized. The child of Oglethorpe and February, the old city still engenders dreams of Eden as a new age dawns.

CHAPTER IX

Factors' Walk, a row of offices and warehouses, was the very center of Savannah's cotton empire. Dealers in the cotton trade, called "factors," could easily stroll from their offices to the Cotton Exchange (dark building on the far right) where the price of cotton was determined each business day. Photo by Chan Sieg

PARTNERS IN PROGRESS

To that tart-tongued grande dame, Lady Astor, Savannah was "a pretty lady with a dirty face." That stinging characterization was delivered in 1946, for Astor was appalled by the shabby neglect that disfigured the harmonious beauty of the city's eighteenth- and nineteenth-century squares and townhouses. To John P. Rousakis, making the 1970 inaugural speech marking his first term as mayor, it was under a spell that caused him to plead: "All around us, an enchanted city lies dreaming . . . I ask you to help awaken her."

In the waning years of its third century Savannah has never been more vibrant, more blessed by successful endeavor, more amenable to the myriad prospects and challenges of a world in technological flux— a world that would have been wildly incomprehensible to the "First Forty," who, with James Edward Oglethorpe, climbed the steep riverside bluffs on a raw February day in 1733.

The smudges have been removed by the Herculean task of renovation and restoration that created the largest National Historic Landmark District in the United States. And the economic consequences have been as staggering as the historic ones: Savannah is some $182 million richer, yearly, thanks to tens of thousands of visitors from around the nation and the world, who come to savor the palpable delights of this colonial and antebellum gem of a town.

The "awakening" gains impressive momentum with each passing year. The cornucopia of raw materials and finished goods that move through its port have long since contributed to the eclipse of the city's nineteenth-century days of glory when cotton was king. In 1984 alone, some 3.5 million tons of cargo, representing over $100 million, came from or were dispersed to every quadrant of the globe.

Military installations close to Savannah contribute, in various ways, more than $100 million to its coffers, while Savannah International Airport, with its Foreign Trade Zone facilities, swells local revenues by some $50 million. Savannah's economic vitality is favorably out of balance with the mere numerical weight of population figures which, at the beginning of 1984, showed the city proper at 143,708, while the combined Savannah-Chatham County total stood at 210,266.

If, traditionally, the Savannah River has been the city's conduit both to the sea and to the world's markets, that continuing source of economic well-being has been broadly augmented by the diverse goods and services offered by local businesses. Finally, the simple fact of this book is tied to the resourcefulness, encouragement, and devotion to an idea of a man who is the quintessential gentleman, Southern and otherwise: Charles H. Wessels.

The organizations whose stories are detailed on the following pages have chosen to support this important literary and civic project. They illustrate the variety of ways in which individuals and their businesses have contributed to the city's growth and development. The civic involvement of Savannah's businesses, institutions of learning, and local government, in cooperation with its citizens, has made the community an excellent place to live and work.

COASTAL HERITAGE SOCIETY

For an uninitiated observer, it would have been a mind-wrenching vision: a military panoply, compressing notable periods of the eighteenth and nineteenth centuries' history of men at arms into the dazzle of a single day late in the twentieth century. The onlooker would have watched, in parade-ground display, proud elements of such units as the South Carolina King's Company (1725); Savannah's Regiment de Foix (1779); les Chaussers Volontaires des Sainte Domingue (1770s); the Chatham Artillery (1812); the Eighth U.S. Infantry (1813); and the Twenty-second Battalion, Georgia Heavy Artillery (1864).

This was to be seen—in an impressive reenactment by smartly uniformed and crisply drilled volunteers—at Old Fort Jackson, during celebrations commemorating Memorial Day in 1983. Most important, this display—and the continuing existence of the 177-year-old fort itself—was, and is, due to the passionate dedication and involvement, from the most arcane scholarship and research to backbreaking manual labor, of those who have breathed continuing life into the Coastal Heritage Society.

Founded in September 1974 by William C. "Rusty" Fleetwood, Jr.,

The Twenty-second Battalion, Georgia Heavy Artillery, is a volunteer group that participates in many of the Coastal Heritage Society's programs.

Frances Wilson Smith, and John Hall, the Savannah-based organization was created to: "engage in the preservation of Coastal Georgia's cultural and national heritage, and the development of a sense of awareness and pride in that heritage, through programs of active involvement promoting cultural and national heritage."

The organization's goals have been eloquently elaborated in the book *Tidecraft,* written by Rusty Fleetwood and researched by Coastal Heritage's Antoinette Goodrich. Published in 1982 it was the issue of the Georgia Watercraft Research Project, which received generous financial support from the National Trust for Historic Preservation. Yet, since its inception, much of the society's energy and efforts have, of necessity, focused on the fort.

Begun in 1808 as Savannah's defense against seaborne incursions, the nine-acre site was named for the Revolutionary War hero, General James Jackson. The oldest remaining Georgia fort, it was closed following state budget cuts in 1975. Its new life, which finds some 75,000 people gathering annually for more than 200 days of activities per year, has made it virtually a self-sustaining operation, al-

though the City of Savannah provides vital, continuing funding for special projects and exhibits.

At present some 150 volunteers annually add dedicated muscle and wit to ongoing reconstruction and maintenance, as well as a broad variety of special programs, under the experienced guidance of Scott Smith, fort curator and Coastal Heritage's executive director. Society president for five of its first years was Savannah budget director Robert McAlister, who oversaw development based on sound fiscal principles. The current president is Gail Alexander.

Major projects engaging the society's demonstrated talents are reclamation and preservation of the CSS *Georgia,* the Confederate ironclad vessel sunk in the Savannah River; construction of a boat shed to house the plantation-type dugout donated by South Carolina's Mitchell family; and the restoration of the 1850s Smith and Porter portable steam engine, oldest in the United States, and typical of those used to drive the pilings for the fort.

The preservation of Old Fort Jackson, the oldest remaining Georgia fort, is at the forefront of the Coastal Heritage Society's activities. Shown is the fort's west wall.

D.J. POWERS COMPANY, INC.

The principal artery feeding the commercial life of Georgia's "Queen City" is the Savannah River. The restless parade of great vessels that ply its waters come from Bangladesh and go on to Brazil, bring cargo from Calais and take stores to Calcutta.

Savannah is firmly established as the number one South Atlantic port; containerized cargo alone, during the most recent fiscal year, exceeded 2.25 million tons. Sitting in the busy offices of D.J. Powers Company, Inc., a major customs brokerage and international freight-forwarding firm, the visitor is keenly aware of the global quality of business transacted here. Employees move purposefully, checking teletype machines and computer printouts that track the international whereabouts of cargo for a broad spectrum of clients.

One of the major responsibilities of the firm is to thread its customers' goods through the maze of customs regulations, and the same meticulous attention accorded gargantuan pieces of machinery such as printing presses is also given to a consignment of tiny ball bearings.

The customs broker is an avid student of literature most of us never hear of: several pounds' worth of U.S. Customs regulations, several more pounds of fine print, the "Tariff Rate Code Annotated," and, every week, a 50- to 100-page publication, *Treasury Decisions,* of which each word is significant to the broker, and to his clients. He also must be thoroughly conversant with the functions and specialized idiom of a host of other federal, state, and local regulatory agencies involved in the movement of cargo across the nation—and the world.

For a substantial number of its clients, D.J. Powers Company also serves as a freight forwarder, or cargo agent, ready with expert advice on the best rates, routes, and mode of equipment, be that air, land, sea, or intricate combinations thereof.

The firm, which currently has sixty employees and branches in Atlanta and Charleston, South Carolina, had its beginnings in August 1930. D.J. Powers, then with Savannah's Strachan Shipping Company, began representing

D.J. Powers, founder and first president.

a few clients as a customhouse broker; he continued this practice, as a sideline, for the next twenty-four years. By 1954 the accelerating growth of the Port of Savannah convinced him that he should focus exclusively on developing his brokerage business.

The Powers Company's principal import commodities, initially, were burlap bagging and carpet backing. Today international shipments handled run the gamut from petroleum to sporting goods, electronic equipment to heavy machinery, and almost everything in between.

In January 1963 Powers established a partnership with W. Earnest Carter, a former U.S. Customs official with twenty years' experience in virtually every phase of that agency's operations. With Powers' retirement in February 1968, Carter became president and sole owner.

Now well past the half-century

W. Earnest Carter (1917-1985) became sole owner of the firm in 1968.

mark, D.J. Powers Company, Inc., has always maintained offices on East Bay Street. Originally, four employees staffed an office in the American Building, which continues to provide space for the steady, successful growth of the firm, which is now principally housed next door. As Earnest Carter pointed out, "When cotton was king, Savannah was queen; she remains a queen, and we're proud to contribute to her healthy longevity."

ATLANTIC WOOD INDUSTRIES, INC.

The Savannah plant of Atlantic Wood Industries, Inc., located in bustling Port Wentworth, an eight-mile drive from the city's National Historic Landmark District, is also corporate headquarters for one of the nation's foremost producers of quality treated wood products for a variety of customers who span the country—and the globe. The firm has seven major wood-treatment plants in five East Coast states, from Georgia to New York. The two largest plants—Savannah and Portsmouth, Virginia—have deep-water terminal sites, giving them direct access to oceangoing vessels and facilitating both export shipments and domestic coastal deliveries. Some 120 of the firm's 300 employees are in Savannah.

Savannah is also the headquarters of Atlantic Wood International Sales Corporation, the organization's export arm. And, while there is no mention of it in the firm's promotional materials, the Savannah plant is a site typical of company activities that would have dumbfounded the legendary Paul Bunyan and his mighty blue ox, "Babe."

That Herculean figure, storied among Minnesota's lumberjacks, would have had his work cut out for him, amidst the enormous marine pilings, utility poles, and other huge timbers, some of them more than 100 feet in length. All are part of Atlantic Wood's stock-in-trade, and both Paul and his mighty ox would have been flabbergasted by the ease with which mammoth, thirty-ton diesel cranes deftly load and unload railroad cars, and perform other tasks no race of brawny giants could have attempted unaided.

Founded in 1919 as the Savannah Creosoting Company, the firm's wood-treating enterprise was limited to railroad cross ties, most

Atlantic Wood Industries' Savannah complex is not only corporate headquarters but the firm's major deep-water terminal site. Courtesy, William Cornelia

of which were shipped to fruit companies in Central America. Creosote, the oldest, best-known wood preservative, remains a popular, proven treatment.

However, the growth in product development, production capacity, and distribution points, characterized by the change in name to Atlantic Wood Industries, also saw the intensive research that led to the formulation of additional specialized and highly effective treatment processes. And there has been a corollary product growth: the range of pressure-treated wood products has expanded from the original cross ties to embrace utility poles, bridge timbers, foundation and marine pilings, and structural lumber.

Each of Atlantic Wood's seven plants has a modern quality-control and research laboratory. This is augmented, at a national level, by the firm's active support of supplemental research conducted at many of the country's leading engineering schools. Company-owned or -managed timberlands not only provide a standing inventory, but are a vital, renewable resource.

From the banana-train cross ties of sixty-five years ago to the pres-

ent, a strong international flavor has marked Atlantic Wood's operations. Charles B. Compton, executive vice-president, spoke with obvious pride of the role he was called upon to fill, as company representative, in a 1984 international trade mission sponsored by the United States Department of Commerce. Eight differing companies, of recognized national and international standing, were chosen by the government for a mission entitled "U.S. Electric Power Generation, Transmission, and Distribution Equipment," which paid visits to Syria, Egypt, Morocco, and Algeria.

Corporate direction for Atlantic Wood Industries is provided by a management team consisting of Andrew G. Labrot, chairman and president, and executive vice-presidents Compton and Charles H. Slinghoff, Jr. Under their guidance, the firm is currently generating an annual sales volume of $35-40 million, as it continues to put firm timber foundations under the enterprises of others.

FOLEY HOUSE INN

Savannah's Foley House Inn offers guests historic authenticity and luxurious accommodations on a grand scale.

Hollywood has done much to create memories that tend to become woven into the sense of history of moviegoers worldwide. For three generations of film enthusiasts, when the Deep South of the War Between the States era is the topic, what is often envisaged is the sweep and flash of *Gone With The Wind.*

Not surprisingly, then, guests arriving for the first time at Savannah's elegant historic hostelry, the Foley House Inn, often comment that "something seems familiar" about the graciously appointed parlor-floor area. It's not unlikely that they are recalling the glittering candelabra, topped with Waterford crystal, that surmounts the turn of the staircase. It was part of the lush background in the town house shared by Scarlett O'Hara and Rhett Butler, in the beleagured Atlanta of the 1860s.

According to manager Suzanne Davis, it is this kind of meticulous attention to capturing the form and feel of that "lavish gentility of the bygone South" that characterized the restoration and refurbishing of the Foley House Inn. The house, which commands a pleasing prospect of Chippewa Square, one of Savannah's most imposing downtown parks, was originally completed in 1896 for the then-sizable sum of $9,500.

Honoria Kirby Foley, widow of Owen Foley, an eminent merchant and community figure, had commissioned the noted architect, Henry C. Urban, to create for her "a grand, four-story brick home." And so he did. In its first bloom, Mrs. Foley's home would have afforded an excellent vantage point from which to watch the town's gentry make its way across the square for an evening's entertainment provided perhaps by Sarah Bernhardt or Lillian Russell, both

great favorites at the palatial old Savannah Theatre.

In the full flower of its restitution, the inn is a tribute to the dedication of its owners, the Foley House Partnership, and the master craftsmen who redeemed its late Victorian elegance. Partnership principals Richard W. Botnick and David W. Allen, together with other limited partners, poured well over $1.5 million into renovation work and furnishings.

The first segment, at 14 West Hull Street, opened in the fall of 1982, offering eleven luxe bedrooms. In January 1984 the adjoining three-story house opened, as did the two-story carriage house directly behind it, offering, respectively, five and four equally majestic rooms.

Interior designer Barbara B. Rushing, one of the eight limited partners, oversaw what she terms

the "renewal" of Foley House. She discovered the *Gone With The Wind* candelabra at an Atlanta auction, emphasizing that appropriateness was the key to selection of antiques. Furniture, silver, china, Oriental rugs, and hand-colored engravings were chosen from the most select sources worldwide.

The ambience breathes "pampered," from fireplaces in each room and oversized jacuzzis in many of the private baths, to a well-stocked movie library for tele-viewing in each room. Complimentary wine and evening cordials are available upon request. Inn guests find chocolate mints on their evening pillow, shoes left outside the door at night gleam with new polish in the morning, and the inn's private town car whisks guests to and from travel connections.

Savannah's magic resides in the full dimensionality of its cherished history—and Foley House Inn has become a graceful part of that magic.

HUSSEY, GAY & BELL, INC., CONSULTING ENGINEERS

Hussey, Gay & Bell has done extensive work for the Georgia Ports Authority.

It began, in the spring of 1958, in 500 square feet of office space, renting at thirty-five dollars per month, in Savannah's old Arcade building on Bay Street, with the two original partners. Today the organization numbers over 100 professionals and support staff, operating from its own $2.3-million, 38,000-square-foot building. The signature of the firm's engineering specialties is in evidence from Australia to Arabia, from Ecuador to the United Arab Emirates; closer to home, the firm's seal is on a myriad of major projects along or close to the southeast Atlantic Coast, stretching from North Carolina to Florida. In all, it has worked in over fifteen states and seven foreign countries.

What is presently Hussey, Gay & Bell—and its subsidiaries, Metroplan, responsible for all planning and landscape architecture activities, and Hussey, Gay & Bell International, which handles all commercial building design in addition to international projects— originated as Hadsell & Gay, Inc., Consulting Engineers.

Benjamin E. Gay, founder and president of HGB, holds a bachelor's degree in civil engineering from North Carolina State University. He initially came to Savannah in the spring of 1951 to join Union Camp Corporation, and was subsequently associated with a local firm of consulting engineers before entering his own practice with William V. Hadsell. At the end of 1960 Hadsell withdrew from the firm, and early the following year Roy Hussey, a Georgia Institute of Technology graduate with ten years of professional experience locally, became associated with Gay, and the firm was renamed Hussey & Gay, Inc.

When Gustavous H. Bell III became associated with the firm in 1966, the management structure as reflected in the current name was achieved. Bell, who holds a BSCE degree from The Citadel, had been employed by the U.S. Army Corps of Engineers, and a private firm of consulting engineers, from 1959 to 1966.

The fourth of HGB's current principals is Richard B. DeYoung, another Citadel graduate who holds an MSCE degree from Oklahoma State University. DeYoung had been chief of the Soils Section, Savannah District, for the Army Corps of Engineers prior to joining HGB in 1973. He was named a principal of the firm in 1980. Hussey, Bell, and DeYoung are vice-presidents of the organization, while Hussey also serves as secretary and Bell as assistant secretary.

In addition to its headquarters in the HGB Building, at 329 Commercial Drive, the firm has branch offices in Statesboro, Georgia, and on Hilton Head Island, South Carolina, and a fully staffed office in Columbia, South Carolina. It is a multidiscipline company, providing a full range of civil, environmental, and structural engineering services and architectural consultation to its clients. HGB staff members hold professional registration in Georgia, North and South Carolina, Florida, Tennessee, Alabama, Virginia, California, Nebraska, and Minnesota, as well as in the Kingdom of Saudi Arabia and the United Arab Emirates.

Many of the land development projects in Chatham County and on Hilton Head Island were provided engineering services for land planning and site development by HGB. The firm provides a broad range of engineering services for well over twenty cities, counties, and public service districts. Municipal projects have included the design of paving, storm drainage, sanitary sewerage systems, wastewater treatment facilities, water systems, and varied studies and reports having to do with such projects. Essentially, HGB's areas of professional expertise fall into these categories: water and sewer; marine and ports; geotechnical and coastal; commercial and industrial; streets, highways, and railroads;

The principals of the engineering firm are (left to right) Richard B. DeYoung, Benjamin E. Gay, Gustavous H. Bell III, and Roy Hussey. Courtesy, The Savannah News-Press

and land planning and site development.

Provision of services in a relatively new area has taken place under the aegis of Hussey, Gay & Bell International. Industrial waste treatment facilities in Ecuador, Venezuela, and Australia, and a fertilizer blending plant in Guatemala have been among such projects. Intensification of operations in the Middle East is reflected in design work performed for both an office/apartment building and a recreation complex in Dubai, United Arab Emirates. HGB International has designed a public library and four neighborhood centers in Jubail, Saudi Arabia. In addition, the firm's design activities have transformed a relatively undeveloped 8,000-acre island, Al Batinah, which lies off the coast of Saudi Arabia, into an elegant and extensive recreation complex.

What combination of factors lent authority to HGB International's successful pursuit of world-class engineering projects on the Arabian Peninsula? "Interestingly enough," says Benjamin Gay, "it was the firm's extensive experience with and knowledge of the geographic and geologic peculiarities of the coastal Low Country of Georgia and South Carolina, where so much of HGB's work has taken place. Basically, that part of the world is the peninsular equivalent of our Low Country, for one works in, and with, sand and a high water table."

Among the more publicly visible

One of the many projects undertaken by the firm was the 5.0 MGD Wastewater Treatment Plant in Statesboro.

feathers in the firm's professional cap are the respective developer-clients responsible for three of the Southeastern Seaboard's most exclusive island resort-residential enclaves: Palmetto Dunes and Indigo Run on Hilton Head Island, and The Landings on Skidaway Island, southeast of Savannah.

In addition to several score municipal, industrial, and private clients, HGB has completed extensive projects for an alphabet of federal agencies, including the U.S. Army Corps of Engineers, Federal Housing Administration, Department of Housing and Urban Development, Environmental Protection Agency, Economic Development Administration, Federal Aviation Administration, the U.S. Navy, the U.S. Coast Guard, and the Farmers Home Administration. And, not surprisingly, HGB has long served the Georgia Ports Authority and various port-related industries and organizations not only in Savannah, but in Bainbridge, Brunswick, and Colonel's Island to the south.

Much of the fundamental work performed by skilled seasoned engineers such as those of Hussey, Gay & Bell is not publicly visible

Shelter Cove Marina, with the Harborside I and II Condominiums at the Palmetto Dunes Resort, on Hilton Head Island, South Carolina.

and does not dramatically impinge upon the consciousness of the citizenry. And this despite the incontestable fact that such work—the streets and highways, the railroads, the water and sewage systems and their related treatment plants, the cargo buildings, and packing and processing plants—represents elements that tie together and make our contemporary civilization workable. For the planners and builders, the drama and excitement are implicit in the challenge of each new, and varied project.

If one were compelled to single out *the* Savannah project that, having garnered local, state, and national admiration and official acclaim, manifests the engineering expertise of Hussey, Gay & Bell, it would be the Savannah Riverfront Restoration. Designed as a joint venture of HGB, and Gunn & Meyerhoff A.I.A. Architects, P.C., this massive urban-renewal project was launched in 1975 as part of a $7-million HUD grant, initiated through the City of Savannah. The restoration was completed in 1977, subsequently receiving the U.S. Department of the Interior's highest award for the conservation and preservation of the nation's cultural heritage. Accolades of this sort add to the enthusiasm of the people at Hussey, Gay & Bell, Inc., as they build upon the bedrock of nearly thirty years of solid achievements.

GUNN & MEYERHOFF
A.I.A. ARCHITECTS, P.C.

The Savannah riverfront.

Donegal tweeds, handwoven in the Irish county of that name, are prized the world over for their distinctive good looks and extraordinary durability; they are also known as "salt-and-pepper" tweeds, thanks to their unique colors and patternings. To spend an hour or two in the company of Bob Gunn and Eric Meyerhoff, long-term partners and friends, is to witness the components of this readily arrived-at simile for several reasons, in a variety of ways.

Physically, the two men who founded Gunn & Meyerhoff A.I.A. Architects, P.C., are as salt and pepper. Bob Gunn, a rangy man whose coloring suggests his Scot's heritage, accents much of what he says with a twinkle; his partner, Eric Meyerhoff, is compact and dark complexioned, his earnestness often illuminated by a winning flash of smile. And, like a well-woven suit of good tweeds, the two obviously work and wear well together. In terms of a complementary creativity, enthusiasm, and agreement upon objectives and their attainment, all interwoven with an infectious sense of humor, these men are surely cut from the same bolt of cloth.

To look around Savannah—the old, history-burnished core of the city and, as well, the new life and accompanying growth that's wedging itself into the historic architectural fabric—is to see, at virtually every turn, examples of the architecture conceived in the minds and articulated at the drawing boards of the firm of Gunn & Meyerhoff, an architecture both creatively original and sensitive to its surrounding heritage. From the nationally acclaimed Savannah Riverfront Project to the Fine Arts and Paramedical buildings at Armstrong State College, the firm's work extends from the city's

historic and physical beginning, north, at the river's edge, to the burgeoning south side that is the high-water mark of community expansion in that direction. Nor have Savannah's other quadrants been neglected.

To the east, on Skidaway Island, are the Shellfish Mariculture Building and the Marine Extension Building, with its beautiful seawater aquarium, that Gunn & Meyerhoff designed for the Skidaway Institute of Oceanography; westward, there is the corporate headquarters building of Chatham Steel Corporation, and at nearby Kings Bay, Georgia, is the new Trident Submarine Base, where each building has been influenced by the Architectural Design Guide for the entire base, created by this firm at the request of the Secretary of the Navy.

The firm of Gunn & Meyerhoff had its formal beginnings in January 1957, but that partnership figuratively had been struck almost a decade earlier, when the two met at the outset of their architectural studies at the University of Florida. As undergraduates, both were active students, and quickly recognized a community of aspirations, talents, and life goals, and agreed

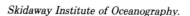

Skidaway Institute of Oceanography.

that, ultimately, they wanted to practice architecture together.

Meyerhoff, who graduated in 1952, served in the military with a European-based Army topographic engineering unit, sandwiching in a year of advanced architectural studies in Stuttgart, Germany. Gunn, who took his architectural degree, with honors, in 1953 (having served two years with the Army's 82nd Airborne Division prior to entering college), is the firm's in-house interior designer, having studied interior architecture at Norway's University of Oslo as part of his undergraduate course work.

Professionally, Gunn and Meyerhoff followed separate paths, in Florida, Georgia, and South Carolina, before founding their firm.

Gunn gained what he considers invaluable early experience under the tutelage of his father, Errett, a civil engineer who had started his own firm in the mid-1950s, following a long period with the Army Corps of Engineers. Meanwhile, Meyerhoff worked for several firms on both coasts of Florida, designing hotels and resorts, before they reunited with the advent of the firm in 1957.

It has been said that the city plan of Savannah is a crown, and its buildings are the jewels in that crown. Gunn & Meyerhoff has certainly had a hand in the improving of this rare tiara, considering its works of restoration; and certainly in its compatible new buildings. Gunn is quick to point out that "you really can't specialize in our city." Thus, Gunn & Meyerhoff conceptions have moved, with equal ease and grace, from nineteenth-century restorations to an array of arresting contemporary structures, including churches, college and medical buildings, office complexes, corporate headquarters, and parks and squares.

The firm prides itself in being designers of unique project types requiring research, creative design, and functional coordination. The seawater aquarium for the Skidaway Institute of Oceanography; Firefighting Training Facilities, both for the City of Savannah and the Mayport Naval Base, in which spaces were designed to withstand extreme temperatures; and a Flight Simulator Building for the Air Force were all challenges to Gunn & Meyerhoff's creative innovation.

At the same time, the firm has been deeply involved in the historic preservation movement. This is evidenced by its American Institute of Architects award for Gunn & Meyerhoff's restoration of the

Oglethorpe Office Building.

Sturges House, circa 1818 (now headquarters for Morris Newspaper Corporation); its renovation of the 1920 eleven-story Savannah Financial Center on Johnson Square; its consultation and restoration work on the Massie School (1845), the state's oldest school; and being the architects for the reconstitution of Franklin Square, one of Savannah's squares that was desecrated in the mid-1930s.

The company is housed in its own gracious building at 128 Habersham (circa 1850), another renovation deep in one of the oldest sections of the National Historic Landmark District. That is as it should be, since Gunn & Meyerhoff was the first architectural firm to contribute its talents to that same historic preservation movement in Savannah. It is interesting that neither of the company's principals was born in Savannah, yet in their expanding years of practice they have both been deeply involved in the retention of Savannah's heritage.

Gunn, who became a member of the board of Historic Savannah Foundation the year after its founding, later serving as its president and chairman, chaired the committee that wrote Savannah's historic zoning ordinance. Complementing that, Meyerhoff was the first architect to serve on the initial Historic Review Board, and, together, the two created the feasibility study for Troup Row, one of

Temple Ahavath Chesed, Jacksonville, Florida.

the city's earliest preservation efforts, under the aegis of the Savannah Housing Authority. Both men continue to be extensively involved in a broad range of civic and cultural activities.

Looking west from the firm's offices, across Columbia Square, one is filled with the sense of what Gunn refers to as the "visual fabric" of a city—the warp and the woof of the old and the contemporary, woven into a pleasing and harmonious whole. It is the kind of weave that has characterized the work and personalities of Bob Gunn, Eric Meyerhoff, and their staff. And it is the kind of blending that flavors the animated discussions of future projects, and of dreams that will undergo the tempering and testing of their skilled hands and supple minds, at the drawing board.

SAVANNAH BANK AND TRUST COMPANY

The original home of Savannah Bank and Trust Company, at the corner of Bay and Drayton streets, as it looked in 1870. That building, and the trolley, are long since gone.

Savannah Bank and Trust Company, founded in the depressed Reconstruction year of 1869, is today the oldest bank in Savannah, the oldest trust company in Georgia, and the seventh-largest bank in the state. In 1970 the bank adopted as its official logo a silhouette image of the steamship *Savannah*, the first steamship to make a transoceanic voyage, sailing from this city for Liverpool on May 22, 1819. Years later this May date was chosen for the annual observance of National Maritime Day. By adopting this attractive and historically significant logo, the bank not only recognizes the important role of the port in the development of the city, but also commemorates the principal objective of its founder to provide financial services for shippers in and out of the Port of Savannah.

The initial capital stock issue of one million dollars, at $100 per share, was fully subscribed in two days in New York City, largely by New Yorkers and a few British nationals. The bank's principal organizer, largest shareholder, and first president was Morris Ketchum, a Connecticut Yankee who had his own New York cotton brokerage firm.

On New Year's Day, 1872, Ketchum turned over the bank's helm to Savannahian Charles Green. Ownership gradually moved

south. Robert W. Groves, who became board chairman in 1932, had purchased controlling interest, literally bringing Savannah Bank into the community; by 1977 more than a half-million shares were owned by some 550 stockholders, of whom almost 90 percent were Savannahians.

The bank survived the series of depressions that, by 1933, had reduced the town's commercial banks to three; on the eve of World War I there had been fifteen. After the Bank Holiday of 1933 the institution's total resources came to $3.5 million; by 1949 that figure was $18 million. By its centennial in 1969, $100 million had been reached, and less than eight years later total resources had topped $200 million.

In 1978 Savannah Bank's stockholders approved the formation of a holding company, the SBT Corporation, with assets comfortably over the $500-million mark. The bank remained the flagship of an organization that, through 1981, acquired banks in the Coastal Georgia communities of Sylvania, Waycross, Vidalia, and Valdosta.

The corporate position was further strengthened in 1984 with the merger of SBT Corporation and First Railroad and Banking Company of Georgia, headquartered in Augusta. Walton K. Nussbaum, Jr., chairman and chief executive officer of Savannah Bank and, subsequently, of SBT Corporation, became president and chief operating officer of the merged organization.

While SBT and its affiliates became, in turn, affiliates of First

Railroad, it was clearly stipulated that each bank would retain and foster its identity in the communities it served.

For Savannah Bank, that identity is woven into deep concern for and dynamic participation in community life and growth. The roster of those who have guided the bank's course is essentially one of deeply respected civic leaders, philanthropists, prime movers in cultural affairs, and catalysts of significant community improvement.

In 1912, with much fanfare, Savannah Bank moved into the handsome fifteen-story building, far left. Its ten-story annex was completed in 1976 and five years later the renovation of the elegant (1823) Hamilton House was finished.

That list would include such memorable figures as Robert W. Groves, board chairman, 1932; Reuben Grove Clark, president, 1948-1964, chairman, 1964-1968; Malcolm Bell, Jr., president, 1964, chairman, 1973-1980; Walton K. Nussbaum, Jr., current president and chief executive officer of First Railroad and Banking Company; and Thomas P. Rideout, current president and chief executive officer of Savannah Bank and a director of the parent organization.

CARSON PRODUCTS COMPANY

A. Minis, Jr., chairman of the board and a director of Carson Products Company, is a man whose roots in Savannah history are lengthy and exceedingly strong. As he puts it, "My family has been here since Georgia became a colony."

His education took him away from the Deep South for a time. A 1922 graduate of Widener College (located in Chester, Pennsylvania, the school was formerly the Pennsylvania Military Academy), Minis took his A.B. in chemistry at Harvard University in 1926, and received an M.B.A. from the Harvard Business School two years later.

Carson Products Company is a major manufacturer and distributor of cosmetic products, including toiletries, of which some 90 percent are developed specifically for the burgeoning ethnic market. The firm's lines span a wide array, including hair-care and skin-toning products, depilatories, after-shave creams, and lotions. Located at 64 Ross Road in the Savannah Industrial Park, the firm occupies an extensive complex consisting of three buildings and a warehouse that presently occupy some 150,000 square feet.

The Carson organization currently sells both nationally and internationally. At present, there are 140 employees; in the early 1950s some fifteen original employees helped to generate first-year sales of approximately $250,000. The firm—always a force to be reckoned with—has come a long way indeed.

Carson Products Company had its beginnings in 1951, when Minis and Lester Karow acquired Morehouse Manufacturing Company, Inc., a fifty-year-old men's toiletries concern. In 1954 a reorganization grew out of differences of

perception as to the direction the company should take if it was to prosper and grow. Minis was given control of the firm, while Karow was to receive a royalty for the duration of his and his wife's lives.

It was also in 1954 that the company moved from a second-story location, in the Central of Georgia Railway warehouse, to a newly constructed building of approxi-

mately 15,000 square feet in Savannah Industrial Park. Utilization of a one-floor operation realized labor savings that, in themselves, were sufficient to pay carrying charges on the increased investment.

During the late 1950s operations were conducted through three separate corporations, all under Minis' control. Atlantic Trading Company owned the land and building in which manufacturing took place, Morehouse Manufacturing Company was the production arm, and sales were conducted through Carson Sales Corporation.

Growth and acquisitions went hand in hand. In 1963 Galenol, Inc., an Atlanta-based distributor of Dr. Fred Palmer cosmetic products, was purchased, and the operations brought to Savannah. In 1965 Godefroy Manufacturing Company, a well-established St.

Louis producer of hair dyes, was acquired and added to the Savannah operations.

As growth progressed healthily, the operational structure was refined and tightened. In 1966 Morehouse Manufacturing Company was renamed Carson Chemical Company. The following year saw the merger of Atlantic Trading Company (the corporate "landlord"

Typical of the commercial vitality of present-day Savannah is Carson Products Company's 150,000-square-foot production, warehousing, and administrative complex.

entity) with Carson, so that all operations were brought under single corporate ownership. The present name, Carson Products Company, was adopted in 1975.

Carson, which has its own research and quality-control laboratory, maintains an extremely active research program that both improves existing products and develops new ones. Gold Magic Shaving Powder was introduced in 1970, Dark and Lovely Hair Color in 1972, and Dark and Lovely Hair Relaxer in 1978. At the present time six new products are ready for national and international introduction, while several others are undergoing rigorous testing.

SAVANNAH GAS COMPANY

This final section of *Eden on the Marsh* is designated "Partners in Progress," denoting the harmonious linkage of a community's businesses to its own multifaceted growth. Nowhere is this more evident than in the story of Savannah Gas Company and its paramount role in the restoration and revitalization of the oldest section of this city's renowned National Historic Landmark District. The section, known as Trustees' Garden, dates to the birth of the Royal Colony of Georgia in 1733. It was the first experimental botanical garden and agricultural station in the nation.

The history of Trustees' Garden is tightly woven into the saga of Savannah Gas Company and two of the vibrant personalities intimately associated with it. Essentially, the tale of the garden is one of high hopes and early splendor, ebbing into dismal decay, followed ultimately by revivification and new beauty as a national example of urban renewal, undertaken by a private company some twenty years before that concept began to take hold.

Organized in 1849 as the Savannah Gas Company, the firm is today one of the oldest continuously operated utilities in the nation. In 1850 it received its first contract from the City of Savannah to light 200 gas street lamps, at thirty-three dollars per lamp, from "dark to daylight." That same year the firm purchased—from the federal government, for $6,549—the property containing old, abandoned Fort Wayne, and for the next 103 years it was the site of the gas-manufacturing plant.

Fort Savannah, a dirt fort built in 1762 on the orders of Georgia's founder, General James Edward Oglethorpe, overlooked the Savannah River from the highest ground in the area, and was meant to

serve as a bastion against Spanish forays from the south. After the War of Independence, it was renamed for the Revolutionary hero, General "Mad Anthony" Wayne. A brick fort built in 1812 now occupies the site.

Every Eden presupposes a garden; so it was here. Oglethorpe and his powerful backers, among them King George II, had envisioned the ten-acre garden site as, principally, a place to cultivate mulberry trees, their leaves to feed the silkworms that would provide essential silk for England. With the failure of this venture, the area became a residential section, prior to and after the fort was built.

The dawn of the nineteenth century found the "Old Fort" section a thriving center for seafarers and the increasingly brisk pace of the city's maritime life. But original sections are often lamed by fashion, as a growing populace moves from the core—in this case south, away from the river. And so, for nearly 100 years after the growing utility purchased the fort site, the area came increasingly to fit a designation suggestive of toughness and decay: the "gashouse" district.

But it was a vital time for the company; the success of gas streetlights brought increasing requests for home lighting, and by the 1870s the practice was widespread. The next significant change came in 1881, with the introduction of gas cooking, followed eight years later by gas water heating.

It was not until the World War I era that the substance was used to heat homes—and the cornucopia of gas power was later to offer refrigeration, air conditioning, and clothes dryers as well. From the inception of the utility until the local advent of natural gas in 1953, Savannahians were served by "manufactured gas," produced by

To most observers, this was, in 1946, a pitiful slum area that was beyond redemption; to Mary Hillyer, it contained the seeds of a dream of revitalization and attractive housing.

the ejection of live steam over molten coke.

In its 136 years the company has had but five changes of ownership. The most recent was in January 1966, when it became an operating

division of Atlanta Gas Light Company, the largest natural gas distribution firm in the Southeast with over 950,000 customers in 209 cities and surrounding Georgia areas. L.J. Hill, Jr., corporate vice-president, heads the Southeast Georgia Division in Savannah. Since 1903 its strong community identity, as Savannah Gas Company, has remained unaltered by these changes.

The unique tale of the pioneering urban-renewal project focused on the old Trustees' Garden area that had its beginnings in February 1945, when H. Hansell Hillyer and his wife, Mary MacLaren Hillyer, arrived in town. Hillyer, then president of the St. Augustine (Florida) Gas Company, had pur-

Atop the ramparts of what had been Fort Wayne, guarding old Savannah's river approaches, Savannah Gas Company erected its plant after purchasing the site in 1850.

This is Mary Hillyer's realized dream, thanks to her persistence and the encouragement and support of her husband and Savannah Gas Company.

chased the assets of the local utility; the resulting entity, through expansion, became the South Atlantic Gas Company in January 1946, which it remained until the 1966 merger.

Following the acquisition, Hillyer and his associates found it necessary to purchase a short street and its facing properties that bisected the gasworks. The company was thus in the unenviable position of owning some of the most unsightly, dilapidated houses in the entire Old Fort district. Razing all of the structures seemed the obvious so-

lution. But, visiting the festering slum with her husband and standing waist-deep in weeds in a vacant lot, Mary Hillyer saw through the ruin to a suddenly crystallized vision: the restoration of the original Royal Colony's botanical garden as the focal point of a handsome residential area, attractive to anyone with a feeling for its historic import.

With distinct misgivings, Hillyer agreed to let his wife try her hand at renovating one of the worst buildings, which had inspired the book, *The Damned Don't Cry,* a searing tale of slum life. If the restoration failed to attract the "nice" people Mary envisioned as tenants, Hansell would use the refurbished space for company offices.

Working with her own rough sketches as guides for local contractors, Mary Hillyer completed the renovation and found an eager tenant, a renowned female physician and cancer specialist from New York. She was but the first of the "nice", and often notable, individuals to call Trustees' Garden Village home.

In all twenty-three buildings underwent the transforming effect of Mary Hillyer's vision; after completion of the first eleven, the Hillyers purchased the redeemed site from the company, as well as adjacent property that yielded another twelve revitalized structures. Some years later Savannah Gas repurchased the entire section, which includes fifty apartments, twelve

commercial offices and retail outlets, and the nationally famous Pirates House restaurant.

Much of the rest is history. The nation heard about Mary Hillyer's accomplishments when American Broadcasting's Paul Harvey did a radio show from Savannah in 1956 lauding her work. National publications, such as *The Saturday Evening Post, Holiday, House and Home,* and *The New York Times,* have carried features on the area, and the hardworking visionary who made it possible.

The garden proper, a botanical wonderland echoing the glory of its royal beginnings, has delighted and refreshed countless thousands yearly. It was perhaps the single element closest to Mary Hillyer's heart, remaining so to this day. It proved an equal source of satisfaction to Hansell Hillyer, and the company he headed, until his passing in 1977.

The words of W. Lee Mingledorff, Jr., a former mayor of Savannah, provide a fitting epilogue. He said, "Perhaps the most significant feature is that ... it was sponsored by a private company. The restoration of private property, on this scale ... is always a major contribution to a community."

ANSLEY AND SUTTON CONSTRUCTION COMPANY

Frank Ansley and James Sutton have been working partners for the better part of a quarter-century. "Working," that is, in the sense that Carl Sandburg or Robert Frost—honored poets who knew firsthand the taxing use of muscle driven hard by mind—would have used that word.

There is an underlying sameness about the men, as though each had been hewn from the same length of southern oak, with its innate strength. Their lives have been spent out of doors, working hard, and that good seasoning goes all the way through. Most important, they seem to savor what life brings

Concrete-encased, this ceramic cooling tower was the first in the Southeast. It was built in 1980 for Savannah's Memorial Medical Center.

firm has left its solid mark on hundreds of projects in the Savannah area and along the shimmering necklace of barrier islands that rim the Georgia and South Carolina coasts.

The company had its beginnings in 1967, when the two men decided to pool their respective experience and bought out Carson & Scott Construction, a small bridge and foundation builder. Ansley and Sutton's roster of clients has

their way.

What it has brought, in terms of their work, is indeed very important in Coastal Georgia, where the life of the water is never far from serious and continuing consideration. Ansley and Sutton Construction Company specializes in, but does not limit itself to, bridges and bridge foundations, docks and pilings, and bulkheads, the solid underpinnings that enable landsmen to move easily and safely to and from the lure of the water. As subcontractors or, in many instances, general contractors, the

Dataw Island, located off the South Carolina coast, was linked to the contemporary world by this Ansley and Sutton bridge, built in 1983.

ranged from governmental agencies to world-class resort developers, from international engineering firms to *Fortune* 500 companies— and some out-of-the-ordinary individuals as well. Among them is a cultivated lady who shares her private island paradise with deer, wild pigs, donkeys, alligators, eagles, mink, venomous snakes— and some of the country's finest

poets, painters, and writers, who come by invitation to work and meditate.

For the U.S. Department of the Interior, the firm has worked in one of the nation's wilderness jewels, the Okeefenokee (Swamp) National Wildlife Refuge, as well as the Savannah Wildlife Refuge, a primal setting for rare waterfowl and other marsh denizens, within sight of Savannah's Talmadge Bridge. Nearby Hilton Head Island, South Carolina's storied millionaire's refuge, is peppered with Ansley and Sutton construction such as its hospital foundations and several of its lavish resort-residential "plantation" enclaves, involving tide gates, bulkheading, and pilings by the thousands.

Together with a regular cadre of a dozen employees, supplemented by as many as a dozen more when required, Frank Ansley and James Sutton may find themselves up in the air, as well as at water level; the concrete cooling tower they built for Memorial Medical Center, one of the first in the Southeast, was one such instance. Be it library or office building, pile driving or paving, heart of town or wilderness setting, these master builders and their skilled workmen craft integrity and solid experience into each new project.

SAVANNAH AIRPORT COMMISSION

Savannah International Airport brings travelers to within eleven miles of the nation's most extensive National Historic Landmark District.

Savannah, firmly established as the leading South Atlantic seaport, has borne the designation of "port" city for over 250 years. It boasts another port, only eleven miles from the heart of its famed National Historic Landmark District, that is of ascending importance to rapidly increasing numbers of private and business travelers, as well as a growing range of commercial interests. That is Savannah International Airport, administered by the Savannah Airport Commission, under the executive direction of Eldon E. Davidson, a rangy native of Cape Cod, Massachusetts, whose professional career spans close to a half-century of military and commercial aviation.

The relatively recent "international" designation indicates that the airport has U.S. Customs Service facilities available. The city has been linked to the history of commercial flight for at least sixty-five years, and that history has been guided by the commission for over thirty of those years. Daffin Park, a prime municipal recreation area, was the site selected in 1918 for the first city airport. Miniscule by today's standards, it then consisted of twenty acres, the runway length some 2,500 feet.

In 1928 the city bought a 730-acre tract southwest of the Daffin

site. Opened in September of the following year, the new airport became a regular stop on Eastern Air Express' New York to Miami service. An official city resolution in 1932 proclaimed it "Hunter Field," in honor of Savannahian Frank Hunter, a legendary World War I flying ace and distinguished Army Air Corps command general in World War II. In 1940 the city acquired 600 acres northwest of town, and on the eve of Pearl Harbor work began on what is now Savannah International Airport.

Known initially as Travis Field, then as Savannah Municipal Airport, the new facility opened on October 1, 1950, with a Delta Airlines flight; now, as then, Delta serves Savannah, as one of five major airlines offering regular service.

The Savannah Airport Commission was created in 1955 by act of Georgia's General Assembly. Five commissioners, appointed by the city's mayor and aldermen, serve staggered terms. Administrative responsibility rests with the executive director, who meets monthly with the commissioners and serves at their pleasure. The pleasure is evidently mutual, for Davidson has held the position for twenty-one years. A career Marine flyer, he holds an advanced degree in meteorology, and launched a second ca-

reer in airport administration in 1962, coming to Savannah two years later.

There have been quantum leaps in growth over the years. Boardings have mounted from 37,655 in 1961, to over 400,000 in 1984. The original 600 acres have mushroomed to 3,500, with additional acquisitions planned; there are currently 80,000 square feet of terminal space. Early in 1983 a new air cargo facility, costing in excess of one million dollars, offered 36,000 square feet of warehousing and manufacturing space at ground level, together with 11,500 square feet of second-floor office space. Runways of 7,000 and 9,000 feet, respectively, readily handle any existing aircraft including the world's largest, the Air Force C-5A.

The augury of future growth was significantly bolstered in 1984, with federal authorization of Foreign Trade Zone 104, to be run by the Savannah Airport Commission. Consisting at present of twelve acres of GPA land, twenty-five acres of airport property adjoining the runway area, and 6,000 square feet of cargo terminal space along the airport parking apron, the zone is also served by rail and highway. Assembly, modification of goods, or storage is of prime advantage for shippers or consignees. Duty and excise taxes need not be paid until the goods are shipped to the domestic market.

Establishment of the FTZ is another mark of the progressiveness that characterizes the Savannah Airport Commission—and the airport it has guided to healthy maturity.

THOMAS R. TAGGART & ASSOCIATES

Like many another young man of his Vietnam-era generation, Thomas R. Taggart was in a hurry to catch up once he had completed his military service. His easy assurance and relaxed manner, today, belies the impressive range of his professional accomplishments since graduating from the University of Georgia Law School in December 1971.

Noted trial lawyer, coast-to-coast peregrinations as a much-sought-after legal lecturer, former state representative and ranking member of the Georgia General Assembly's House Judiciary Committee, regular contributor to national legal journals, and, betimes, deep into the preparation of a book for a major New York publishing house, Taggart handles these many roles with the aplomb of a gray-bearded solon—but it will be a long, long time before there'll be any gray on this Savannahian's head.

His equanimity was even sufficient to surmount a disastrous fire, in January 1984, that gutted the splendid Georgian-revival mansion in which his firm's offices were situated, compelling the firm's removal to temporary quarters for the next fifteen months. The Cope House, built around 1905, was a Savannah jewel; ironically, the fire that ravaged it took place the very night before representatives of the U.S. Department of the Interior and of the Historic Savannah Foundation were to inspect the mansion, prior to its formal listing as a Registered National Historic Landmark.

Taggart and his colleagues have been back in the substantially renovated structure, located at 1719 Abercorn Street and newly identified as the Taggart Building, since April 1985, as interior work progresses around them.

Thomas R. Taggart & Associates is situated in this Georgian-revival mansion once known as the Cope House. Recently renamed the Taggart Building, it is at 1719 Abercorn Street. Original drawing by Sharon Saseen Dillon

Taggart began the practice of criminal trial law in Savannah in 1972, with John T. Sparkman as his original partner. There followed a slow evolution to the practice of civil law, and it was a period of association with other lawyers that brought commercial law into the firm's venue.

Taggart has achieved no small measure of attention for his successful handling of personal injury, medical and legal malpractice suits, and product liability actions. He is, to date, the first and only Savannah attorney to have won a one-million-dollar jury verdict in a wrongful death personal injury action.

His service in the Georgia legislature—as representative for the 125th House District—took place from 1975 to 1979 and, in addition to his role with the House Judiciary Committee, he served as assistant administration floor leader for then-Governor George Busbee. Taggart subsequently served, through gubernatorial appointment, as a member of the State Crime Commission.

Taggart's professorial role, as a legal lecturer, began in 1979. A faculty member of the National College of Trial Advocacy, he has conducted "advocacy colleges" for trial lawyers at both Harvard and Yale, in addition to the National Judicial College in Reno, Nevada. He is also on the faculty of Regional (or basic) Colleges of Trial Advocacy, held on a nationwide basis under the auspices of the Association of Trial Lawyers of America.

One of some fifteen life members of the Georgia Trial Lawyers' Association, Taggart is also a fellow of the prestigious Roscoe Pound Foundation, named for the famed U.S. educator and legal scholar, as well as a trustee of the Melvin M. Belli Society, a national association of trial lawyers dedicated to improving the quality of trial advocacy in the United States.

Thomas R. Taggart

ROPER OUTDOOR POWER EQUIPMENT

Sears, Roebuck stands squarely behind its Craftsman line and so does Roper, longtime producer of outdoor power equipment for the world's largest and best-known retailer.

"Make it right and make it worth the price." That was the working precept of David Bradley, a pioneer plow maker whose finely crafted farm implements changed the agricultural face of the midwestern states and the central plains territories of 150 years ago. His small Chicago-based firm was one of the predecessors of the *Fortune* 500 company known worldwide as Roper Corporation, and his philosophy continues as the bedrock of the Roper reputation.

Roper Corporation has been part of Savannah for the past decade in the form of the headquarters of The Roper Outdoor Power Equipment Group, the largest of the firm's three operating groups. The company is the world's largest manufacturer of outdoor power equipment, including lawn and garden tractors, rotary lawn mowers, tillers, and accessory products.

One hundred seventy-five employees are quartered in a large, state-of-the-art facility at 12052 Middleground Road. The Savannah offices are home to the engineering, research and development,

"The plow that broke the plains" wasn't drawn by this stalwart—but Roper experience stretches back 150 years to those early plows.

sales and marketing, accounting, quality control, materials management, manufacturing services, and administrative functions.

Group president Harry L. Grumish, commenting on the 1975 move to Savannah, emphasized that, "Roper chose to do business in Georgia because of the state's excellent business climate and because of the high level of productivity exhibited by the work force. Savannah was our first choice as a headquarters location. It's a beautiful city that offers our people an outstanding quality of life."

The Savannah headquarters serves divisional manufacturing operations in McRae and Swainsboro, Georgia; Orangeburg, South Carolina; Williamsburg, Kentucky; and Mississauga, Ontario, Canada. The Georgia plants produce rotary lawn mowers. Riding mowers, garden tractors, and attachments are made in Orangeburg, while the

Kentucky plant manufactures tillers. The Canadian operation, growing out of the 1968 purchase of Moto-Mower of Canada, serves the market for outdoor power equipment in that country.

Roper outdoor products, including the Roper Brand and the Roper Rally line, are almost universally known. However, what is not generally known by the myriad users of Sears, Roebuck's line of Craftsman outdoor power equipment is that it is Roper's Outdoor Power Equipment Group that manufactures a large portion of this time-tested line of products.

Roper Corporation's roots are deep and diverse, going back on one side of the business to David Bradley's invention of his first plow in 1832, and on the other side, to the 1874 birth of the Florence Machine Company, a small manufacturer of oil stoves. Through the years a series of mergers, acquisitions, and name changes have resulted in the present-day company, with twenty-two manufacturing and sales locations and 5,000 employees.

Today Roper Corporation, in addition to outdoor products, manufactures and markets kitchen appliances, lawn utility buildings, venetian blinds, and various coated metal products for the consumer market.

DERST BAKING COMPANY

A sagacious woman once observed that the smell of paradise is that of "a producing bakery, set in a field of blooming roses." Roses or no, for the past 118 years Savannahians have followed their approving noses to Derst Baking Company, which may well be the oldest baking firm in America still operated by direct descendants of the original founder.

The Savannah *Daily News and Herald* of July 29, 1867, duly reported that plague continued to ravage Ireland, that Napoleon II was suffering from lumbago and colic, and that General Custer had taken what was to be his next-to-last stand. That edition also carried the following notice: "John Derst, Variety Baker, Broughton Street opposite Marshall House. Bread, Cakes, and Pies fresh every day. Cakes for Parties and Weddings made at Short Notice."

Thus did a young Confederate veteran serve notice of a venture that has spanned four generations and twelve decades so far.

John Derst was born May 3, 1838, in the small Rhenish village of Pfeddersheim. At the age of seventeen, following his mother's death, he undertook the arduous, month-long voyage to America. His father and three brothers had been part of an earlier wave of German emigrants to the bustling seaport of Savannah; the elder Derst and one brother had died before John's arrival in November 1855. He was met by his two surviving brothers, in whose shoemaking establish-

Captain John Derst (1838-1928), founder.

ment he worked for the next two years.

In 1857 Derst undertook a three-year apprenticeship, and the shape of his future was set. The thoroughness of that training, and his dedication, is evident in the careful record of recipes and procedures he inscribed, in both German and English, in a series of notebooks the Derst family still prizes.

With the outbreak of the War Between the States, Derst, though not yet a citizen, volunteered for service as a private with the De-Kalb Rifles. He knew his share of privation and suffering, having helped in the construction and subsequent defense of Fort Mac-Allister, a coastal fortification south of Savannah.

His last two and one-half years of service actually augmented his earlier apprenticeship, for he became chief baker at the Confederate hospital in Atlanta, to which he had been invalided from the fort. Finally, ten years and a long war after he had begun his apprenticeship, Derst opened his first, modest bakeshop on Broughton Street, opposite Marshall House.

Despite the demands of the fledgling enterprise, Derst found time for extensive community involvement. In 1869 the city had a 55-man volunteer fire department, of which Derst was a member; four years later the fire companies formed military units, and he joined the "German Volunteers" as a private. He achieved the rank of captain, commanding the unit for eleven years. He also served as a city alderman, playing a major role in promoting adequate fire protection for the rapidly growing city, and was a moving force in the beautification of Savannah's many parks.

Of the four sons born to John and Emma Catherine Hartfelder

Derst between 1896 and 1910, it was the first, Edward John, who was to continue and build upon the family baking tradition. Upon coming of age in 1917 young Edward purchased the bakery from his father, for the sum of $3,000, which covered all equipment, ingredients—and good will.

For the next forty years, under the guidance of Edward Sr., healthy growth was the corollary of enthusiastic acceptance of the business and its increasing array of freshly baked goods. Expansion into both house-to-house and wholesale deliveries dictated the move to a new plant on East Oglethorpe Avenue in 1924. The following year Edward Sr. both incorporated the business as Derst Baking Company, and joined the first of two cooperatives under whose labels the firm was subsequently to market two major product lines that remain staples to this day. By the time Captain Derst's richly varied life came to a close in 1928 at the

Edward Derst, Sr. (1896-1965), provided second-generation leadership and set standards for Derst Baking Company that are still closely followed by his son and grandson.

age of ninety, his business had prospered.

In 1949 the organization moved to its present plant, an extensive, one-story facility located on a 26-acre site on Mills B. Lane Boulevard. There are five production lines, devoted to some 150 various baked specialties, and directly outside the plant are four mammoth flour silos, each with a capacity of 400,000 pounds.

The Derst family found a uniquely civic-minded way to utilize a part of the large acreage surrounding the plant. Located in a pleasant grove of shade trees, Sunbeam Park is a comfortable recreational facility, named for the product line that remains the company's mainstay. This facility includes tables and chairs and fully equipped kitchen with indoor and outdoor barbecue facilities and ample parking to allow its use by several hundred people. Sunbeam Park is available, free of charge, to civic and church organizations; its popularity with Savannahians is such that it is booked solid one year in advance.

Edward Sr. had two daughters and a son, Edward Jr. The latter, after World War II Coast Guard service, successfully completed the highly intensive course work at Chicago's American Institute of Baking before involving himself in the family operation. In 1957 Edward Jr. was named president; Edward Sr. assumed the chairmanship, maintaining an active role until his death in 1965. It was in that same year, consistent with Derst tradition, that Edward Jr. bought the business.

Nearly three decades have elapsed since Edward Jr. assumed the leadership, and they have proved highly fruitful. The bakery's expanded product line is marketed in a radius of 150 miles, carrying the Sunbeam, Holsum, and Captain John Derst assortments well into South Carolina, and south to the Georgia-Florida border. It now takes over 460 employees to keep up with what Captain Derst started, and his modest bakeshop has evolved into a business generating nearly thirty million dollars in sales annually.

A fourth generation of Dersts continues the tradition of commitment. Edward III, a graduate of The Citadel, The Military College of South Carolina, and, like his father, a Coast Guard veteran, is executive vice-president. His brother Morgan heads production, while sister Cathy serves as treasurer. Longevity of service has been characteristic of a dedicated corps of employees, many of whom have been valued staff members to three generations of Dersts.

There has been no diminishing of family involvement in community affairs: It was Edward Jr. who built the Sunbeam Park recreational facility, and who deeded to Historic Savannah Foundation a splendid 1820s house, marked for destruction, which he bought, moved, and partially renovated. His wife, Bettye, is active in historical societies, which have played a pivotal role in restoration of Savannah's world-famous National Historic Landmark District. Edward Jr. and Edward III are regularly called upon to serve in a variety of civic projects.

"Not by bread alone . . ." might well serve as a Derst family motto. "Bread coupled with good works" would undoubtedly come much closer to the truth of the matter.

WILMINGTON CABINET COMPANY, INC.

Showrooms, offices, and a 60,000-square-foot manufacturing plant are part of Wilmington Cabinet's complex, from which it serves the Georgia-South Carolina area within a 100-mile radius of Savannah.

"Be there when you are supposed to; provide good service and back up your work; stay right with or, if possible, ahead of trends in the field." Or, consider this: "Despite conventional wisdom, 'nepotism' of an enlightened kind works well for us."

Salty pragmatism of this sort provides the working credo for Wilmington Cabinet Company. Voiced by Mrs. Barbara McGinty, vice-president and co-founder of the flourishing 34-year-old firm, the remarks typify the spirit that knits a cadre of some 80 employees whose service and experience total over 500 years.

In 1951, working from his garage, John McGinty transformed his woodworking hobby into the enterprise he still heads, which grossed over five million dollars in 1984. They saw the opportunity manifest in dissatisfaction, voiced by builders and subcontractors, with rusting problems affecting metal kitchen cabinetry. For the first five or six years profits went back into the business. The young couple lived on Barbara's salary as an employee of the mortgage loan department of a local financial institution. She also handled the paperwork for the new venture in the evenings. Her job provided a solid grounding in the financial aspects

of home building, as well as extensive contacts with builders and contractors.

Wilmington Cabinet's first customer, a prominent local builder, needed built-in kitchen cabinetry for two new homes; three decades later that company, now run by a second generation, remains a satisfied customer. Fine woods were and are John McGinty's first love. Teak, mahogany, cherry, and cypress are regularly used, as well as any other prime wood as requested. Barbara points out that "many firms say 'custom-design.' Our products are 'custom-made,' to the customer's precise specifications."

Wilmington Cabinet is a custom-crafter "to the trade." While it does not solicit retail business, it will do such custom work on request. For the home, the firm creates built-in cabinetry for kitchen, bath, and laundry, counter tops in wood and a variety of other luxury materials and finishes; wet bars; display cases; bookcases; and specialty pieces. Commercial cabinetry and an extensive range of office furniture are also produced, and Wilmington handles complete lines of major appliances from five of the nation's top manufacturers.

The firm's manufacturing plant, offices, and extensive showrooms are located at 311 Johnny Mercer

Boulevard in Wilmington Island, an attractive suburban community nine miles from downtown Savannah. The 60,000-square-foot plant—with computer-plotted woodworking equipment for much of its precision cutting, and 80 employee-specialists—is a far cry from the original backyard operation and husband-wife team. Expanded showrooms and extensive warehouse facilities are replacing the existing outlet on Hilton Head Island, the elegant resort-residential enclave in South Carolina, and there is an additional warehouse on nearby Tybee Island.

Wilmington Cabinet serves the Georgia-South Carolina area within a 100-mile radius of Savannah. Barbara McGinty estimates that 90 percent of all custom cabinetwork in that area, for new construction, additions, and remodeling, is done by Wilmington. Growth from within has made for cohesiveness. Many student employees, upon graduation, join the firm full time, and tuition aid is available for employees seeking to build, or diversify, skills.

John and Barbara have been joined in the business by their children, Lynda and Geoffrey, and the McGintys are heavily community-oriented: John as a Rotarian and Barbara as a board member of the Savannah Chamber of Commerce and as vice-chairperson of Chatham County Hospital Authority, which administers Memorial Medical Center. Many a local agency boasts handsome custom cabinetry or furniture, compliments of a progressive enterprise deeply rooted in the community.

GEORGIA PORTS AUTHORITY

"There is every reason to believe that growth is a permanent condition in the Port of Savannah." The person responsible for that heartening augury can marshal impressive documentation, for he is the seasoned professional who, with the guidance of a group of distinguished citizens appointed by the governor, oversees much of the activity that makes for a healthy port. As executive director of the Georgia Ports Authority, George J. Nichols was alluding to fiscal 1984 figures that buttress Savannah's designation as the number one South Atlantic port.

For that year a record 2.25 million tons of containerized cargo was handled, for a whopping 33 percent rise over 1983; at the same time, break bulk (noncontainer cargo) tonnage was just over 1.8 million tons, another record-setting figure. Not incidentally, 1984 saw Savannah becoming the first U.S. port of call for the world's number one container ship—the gargantuan, 950-foot, 58,000-ton, *American New York,* the current pride of United States Lines. For cargo vessels of this line, Savannah has become the only East Coast port of call other than New York. Several other major international carriers have also designated the port as South Atlantic load center.

One of the preeminent reasons for its success is the happy accident of geography that makes Savannah the "innermost" port on the entire seaboard, placing it closer to inland sources and destinations of cargo. Two rail systems and over 100 motor carriers serve the port, providing the most direct,

thus least expensive, routes to and from the entire southern United States.

For 252 years Savannah has been Georgia's principal portal to the world beyond the seas. The Royal Colony's riches—wine, silk, hemp, flax, and potash—were funneled to England through Savannah. By the early 1800s export trade focused on the crop that made the city the "King Cotton Port of the World." And so it remained, with cotton accounting for nearly 90 percent of all exports, until the early 1920s, when the boll weevil devastated generations of southern cotton crops, changing forever the complexion of the port's activities.

Today's port handles incoming and outgoing cargo ranging from alkalies to Xerox copiers, produced or distributed by a myriad of corporations. The miles-long and -wide sprawl of facilities administered by the Georgia Ports Authority covers some 1,040 acres; in 1948, three years after GPA was formed by the state legislature, there was a 407-acre tract with two million square feet of terminal space, and no berthing facilities.

Savannah's ascendancy to global port of premier importance has come about under the prudent but

imaginative direction of the Georgia Ports Authority, which also administers the more southerly Brunswick-Colonel's Island complex and certain barge-worthy rivers. GPA's major divisions include operations, engineering and construction, finance, administration, public affairs, planning, and trade development. The latter division— with dynamic representation in Norway, Korea, Japan, Greece, and Hong Kong, as well as Atlanta, New York, and Chicago—has garnered domestic and international attention and a mercurially rising volume of trade locally, where Chief Tomochichi and his Creek braves greeted the first white seafarers to come up this grand river long, long ago.

In 1950, looking south across the Savannah River, this was the prospect at Georgia Ports Authority's principal port site.

Today Savannah, the number one South Atlantic port, boasts this colossal cargo center where worldwide imports and exports traverse a seventeen-mile river voyage to or from the Atlantic Ocean.

UNION CAMP CORPORATION

Alexander Calder, Sr., president of Union Bag and Paper Corporation, precursor of Union Camp Corporation.

its president, Alexander Calder, the closing of the contract for the erection of the first unit at Savannah, to cost four million dollars of a pulp and paper plant of the most modern type. . . ."

Construction, begun that fall and completed in the late summer of 1936, brought an incalculable boost in morale to the city—mired like most of the nation in the depths of the Great Depression—and brought, as well, a tangible cornucopia of employment for 500 to 600 people, with an annual initial payroll of one million dollars.

Something very, very big began to happen in and to Savannah in the spring of 1935. Word of it came through the front-page lead story in the Savannah *Morning News,* on May 29. That story began: "The Union Bag and Paper Corporation of New York City, the world's largest manufacturer of bags and . . . other commercial commodities produced from wood pulp, announced yesterday through

Union Bag and Paper Corporation's Savannah plant in the 1930s.

That original investment made possible one paper machine, producing some 150 tons of kraft paper daily; a grocery bag plant; and a woodlands operation to supply the mill with raw material.

Fifty years later the corporate name is Union Camp. That forest-products colossus, with headquar-

ters in Wayne, New Jersey, ranks in the top half of the nation's 500 largest industrial companies. It owns, or controls, over 1.75 million acres of woodlands in the Southeast, has more than 100 major locations in twenty-five states, and conducts international operations in fifteen countries, on five continents. Worldwide, it employs more than 18,000 people.

At the turning of that first half-century in Savannah, the original annual payroll is now over 100 times greater, encompassing some 3,500 employees. If one calculates wages, goods and services purchased, freight costs, raw materials, and exports, the estimated economic impact of Union Camp's Savannah complex on the community is well upwards of $400 million.

Union Camp is the result of the 1956 merger of Union Bag and Paper Corporation and Camp Manufacturing Company. UB&P was itself the outgrowth of several other firms, the eldest being Union Bag Machine Company. It was a patent-holding organization formed in 1861 by Francis Wolle, a Moravian minister and teacher who, in 1852, invented the first paper bag machine. Camp Manufacturing Company was formed in 1887 with the purchase of a lumber-manufacturing operation that, in the 1850s, began production in Franklin, Virginia. In 1966 the merged organizations changed the corporate name from Union Bag-Camp Paper Corporation to its present title.

The Savannah enclave occupies the former site of the Hermitage Plantation, one of the jewels of the antebellum South. Directly on the Savannah River, the massive complex has choice access to water, rail, and highway transport. Six of Union Camp's major corporate divisions are inherent to the local

Paper making at Union Bag and Paper Corporation's Savannah plant in the 1930s.

operation.

The firm's Woodlands Division, headquartered in Savannah, also has operating arms in Alabama, Virginia, and South Carolina. Savannah Woodlands, the largest of these regional operations, manages some 1.1 million acres of company land in Georgia, Florida, and South Carolina. It is directly responsible for purchasing and delivering wood for the Savannah mill and two lumber operations in the state of Georgia.

Also headquartered in Savannah, the Building Products Division includes eight lumber mills, two plywood plants, a particle board plant, and a lumber treatment facility. With an annual production capacity of over 385 million board feet, Union Camp ranks among the top six manufacturers of southern pine lumber.

At the heart of the Savannah operation is the Kraft Paper and Board Division. The enormous pulp and paper mill—the world's largest—converts wood into pulp, and from that manufactures paper and linerboard. Average daily production is approximately 2,850 tons.

In Savannah the largest on-site converting operation is that of the Bag Division; it consists of the retail packaging group, serving customers such as supermarkets, small convenience stores, large discount chains, and fast-food outlets.

The Container Division repre-

sents the single-largest segment of the firm's unbleached converting operations. In Savannah the division is represented by the oldest and one of the largest of the corporation's twenty-five domestic box plants.

Union Camp's Chemical Division is the largest wood-based chemical business totally owned by a forest-products firm. Converting by-products of the pulp and paper mill operations into higher-value, specialized chemical derivatives is the key to the success of the company's chemical manufacturing operations. Such conversions, emanating from Savannah's chemical manufacturing, find their way into products as diverse as inks, paint, and adhesives, as well as bath oils and other skin-care products.

The Savannah complex is also home to two other major corporate operations: the environmental affairs office, and corporate engineering. The former office monitors environmental regulations—as they apply, on a company-wide basis—with particular emphasis on

air, water, toxicity, and hazardous waste. This office also acts as liaison with regulatory agencies on environmental activity.

All of Union Camp's major construction projects are managed by the corporate engineering group. Responsibilities encompass design, purchase, consultant coordination, contractor selection and management, and the coordination of construction with plant operations.

No business biography of this nature—limited physically if not in scope—could hope to do more than sketch the implications of the first half-century partnership of Savannah, its people, and its premier employer and sturdy friend, Union Camp Corporation. Of what began in 1935, thanks to Union Bag and Paper's Alexander Calder, the key word would be that which has always held prominence in the corporate title—the word "Union." For Calder, bringing the operation south to Savannah helped forge the partnership of Savannah and the company. "Let's both pull together," he urged. That long, successful pull has no foreseeable end in sight.

Union Camp Corporation's Savannah plant is located directly on the Savannah River. This massive complex has choice access to water, rail, and highway transport.

THE SAVANNAH COCA-COLA BOTTLING COMPANY

A massive, framed quotation dominates an array of plaques and citations in the reception area of The Savannah Coca-Cola Bottling Company. It reads: "Coca-Cola is . . . a sublimated essence of all that America stands for . . . a decent thing, honestly made." High praise, that, from a legendary newspaperman noted for his unflinching journalistic honesty: William Allen White, editor of the Emporia, Kansas, *Gazette.*

The elixir known as "Coke" has been celebrated in song and story from Poughkeepsie to Punta Gorda. As a local magazine proudly put it, a few years ago: "One of the outstanding . . . contributions Georgia has made to the thirsty world at a rate of more than 155 million times a day in 135 countries around the globe is . . . 'Coke'." The totals have rocketed since then.

The formula, still a jealously guarded secret, was devised in 1886 by an Atlanta druggist, Dr. John S. Pemberton, who concocted the beverage in a three-legged pot, in his yard. By 1892 another Atlanta druggist, Asa G. Candler, had become sole owner and, with friends, formed The Coca-Cola Company. Initially, Coke had been available only as a soda-fountain mix; by the turn of the century

agreements had been struck for the beginnings of a system of locally owned and operated bottling plants around the nation—an empire was born.

Coca-Cola came to Savannah in 1902. J.S. Poindexter, Sr., later bought the franchise, and on March 13, 1905, opened his plant at 13 East Bay Street, and sold thirteen cases of Coke. The Poindexters, husband and wife, had two employees. The bottles were hand-washed and -filled, and distributed by mule-drawn wagons.

It was, and is, a family business. J.S. Poindexter, Jr., became president in 1936, following his father's death; he became chairman in 1971 when his nephew, Paul S. "Peter" Steward, assumed the presidency after eleven years in successive management capacities.

From 1899 until 1954 The Coca-Cola Company had one product, available at soda fountains or in bottles. Since then, a rainbow of soft drinks and diversified food products have joined the "champ." That growth and responsiveness to change has been reflected in Savannah plant operations, according to Steward.

His grandparents had two employees to help serve Savannah; ten counties in southeast Georgia and lower South Carolina are now

supplied by the Savannah plant, its subsidiaries, and 200 employees, of whom 50 percent are in sales. A fleet of 110 vehicles has replaced the mule-drawn wagons, and acquisitions such as that of the Statesboro, Georgia, plant last year set the pattern for the future. The pattern was augmented in September 1985 with the purchase of the Sylvania, Georgia, Coca-Cola Bottling Company.

Savannah Coca-Cola moved into a newly designed plant at 102 Coleman Drive near Pooler in 1980. Its former building, in the city's historic district, was converted into the luxurious Mulberry Inn.

Coca-Cola United of Birmingham, Alabama, purchased the Savannah organization in 1982, together with its subsidiary plants in Hinesville and Claxton. Steward, president of the division, says, "My grandfather sold thirteen cases of Coca-Cola on his first day in 1905. We've come a long way since then, and we'll be going further, for a long time to come."

_____

The modern bottling plant and area headquarters of The Savannah Coca-Cola Bottling Company is located in Pooler, just west of Georgia's "Hostess City."

SAVANNAH LUMBER & SUPPLY CO.

In the last fading years of the nineteenth century, during the Spanish-American War, the structures served as a military hospital, fronting on what was then Shell Road, now Bull Street. It was in the depths of another conflict, World War II, on the first day of November 1943, that they were purchased and became home for the newly formed Savannah Lumber & Supply Co. Located then, as now, at the corner of Bull and Forty-fourth streets, the firm has been in a new and substantially expanded building since 1950, providing it with over 20,000 square feet of enclosed space, together with some 11,000 square feet of yard area, some of which was purchased in 1964 from the Atlantic Coast Line Railroad.

Founder Harrell C. Murray, Sr., had sufficient faith in what he envisioned as the future of the building industry in the Georgia-South Carolina "Coastal Empire" to forego the security of his managerial position with the Savannah Planing Mill Company and establish his own enterprise. Both of his sons were serving their country: Harrell Jr. with the Coast Guard and W. Cambridge, a B-17 pilot, with the Army Air Corps. Undaunted, Harrell Sr., with the aid of his daughter, Ernestine, as bookkeeper; Henry Mobley, as truck driver; and one yardman, commenced business in some 3,000 square feet of space.

Harrell Jr. and W. Cambridge returned to civilian life late in 1945 to help the young company make its mark supplying consumers and building contractors to mount the crest of the postwar building boom. In September 1946 Harrell Sr. and his sons formed a partnership, which was incorporated in 1959 with the senior Murray as president, Harrell Jr. as

First housed in what had been a Spanish-American War military hospital, Savannah Lumber & Supply has been at home in this modern facility since 1950.

vice-president, W. Cambridge as vice-president/secretary, and daughter Ernestine as treasurer.

With the passing of Harrell Sr. in 1971, Harrell Jr. became chairman of the board, retaining a vice-presidency, while W. Cambridge assumed the presidency and Ernestine was named secretary/treasurer. A third generation of Murrays is also represented, in the person of Harrell Jr.'s son, Frank, a twenty-year veteran with the firm. At present there are twenty-four employees.

Approximately 60 percent of Savannah Lumber & Supply's business is transacted with building contractors. Industrial and retail sales accounts form the balance of the firm's volume, encompassing a full range of building materials including yellow pine, fir, redwood, oak, mahogany, and teak, as well as a variety of treated lumber, hardware, insulation, roofing, dry wall, plywood, windows, and doors. The firm's motto is "Everything for Building and Repairs" and "Where the Professionals and Do-It-Yourselfers Buy." They offer

friendly, personalized service.

Harrell Sr. served as Exchange Club president and president of the Building Material Merchants Association of Georgia and was also an honorary life member of the Savannah Jaycees. His sons and daughter have built upon the tradition of community involvement and service.

Harrell C. Murray, Sr., founder, was never far from the business he guided from its inception in 1943 until his death in 1971.

MEMORIAL MEDICAL CENTER

It was a community dream, a tenaciously pursued vision that finally came to fruition thirty years ago. It was a dream of life restored and revitalized, as a living memorial to the 321 men of the community who made the ultimate sacrifice of their own lives, in defense of their country during World War II, and to those veterans who survived to return. And it was the determination of those returning veterans that was of pivotal importance in the realization of that dream.

The shape of that dream was Memorial Hospital, which opened its doors as a 250-bed facility on September 29, 1955, "dedicated to the glory of God and health of mankind, in memory of those who died in the service of their country."

The Savannah of those immediate postwar years was a city of some 48,000, where trolleys still traveled the city's streets and passengers boarded Central of Georgia trains at the splendid old West Broad station, now home to the Savannah Convention and Visitors' Bureau and the Great Savannah

Open-heart surgery, pioneered in southeast Georgia at Memorial Medical Center in 1967, is one of many types of sophisticated procedures performed in the hospital's 28,000-square-foot, state-of-the-art surgery complex.

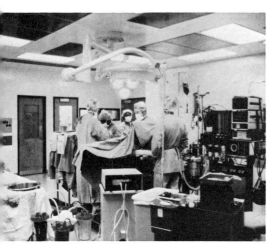

Exposition. College students still attended classes in the palatial Armstrong family home, overlooking Forsyth Park.

It was a time, too, of a groundswell of public and professional awareness of the serious inadequacies of health care delivery. Acute medical services were dispersed among several small institutions: Candler, Central of Georgia, St. Joseph's, and Telfair hospitals, and the Park Avenue and Oglethorpe sanitoriums. The infusion of some federal funds, during World War II, enabled expansion of Candler and St. Joseph's hospitals, but the city continued without 24-hour emergency services, X-ray and laboratory facilities, while operating rooms continued to be inadequate and staffing levels insufficient. No Savannah hospital employed a full-time pathologist, and no institution was accredited for internships by the American Medical Association.

Two events in those postwar years ultimately crystallized in the creation of the new hospital. The first came when the Georgia Medical Society appointed a committee to cooperate with individuals and groups desirous of increasing hospital services in the community. Medical professionals and scores of other concerned citizens realized that, without additional hospital facilities, an epidemic or other disaster would place catastrophic demands on the community's already strained health care system.

The second event was the formation of the World War II Memorial Committee, appointed by then-Mayor Peter Nugent to select a memorial as fitting tribute to the city's fallen heroes. A myriad of worthy proposals were made, but local veterans' groups ardently promoted the construction of a *living* memorial. There followed a

fusing of two deeply felt community desires: the one for a patriotic, tangible remembrance, the other for improved community health care.

In the earliest days of 1949 the desires coalesced under the dedicated guidance of the late Reuben G. Clark. No one would quarrel, if space allowed, with the inclusion of literally hundreds of names of those whose devotion, persistence, and hard work made possible what is now Memorial Medical Center; few, if any, would quarrel with mention of Reuben Clark, a man whose professional achievements were, if possible, overshadowed by his deep and continuing love of his community and his responsiveness to its most pressing needs. Although it was generally known that federal and state funding for a new facility would not be available for

Memorial Medical Center, Inc., launched the region's first hospital-based air emergency medical service in July 1985 when LifeStar began serving a 12,000-square-mile area of southeast Georgia and southern South Carolina.

another two or three years, a joint city/county committee (the precursor of the Chatham County Hospital Authority, created in 1952), chaired by Clark, began serious and intensive preparations.

Groundbreaking ceremonies at the 47-acre site were held, appropriately enough, the day after the

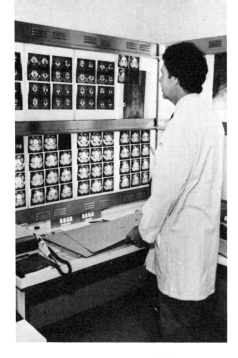

Magnetic resonance imaging, lithotripsy, computed tomography, linear accelerators for cancer therapy and treatment, and Yag and Carbon Dioxide lasers are among the many tools in Memorial Medical Center's lifesaving arsenal of diagnostic and treatment systems.

Pearl Harbor Day observance of 1953. Dedicated on October 21, 1955, the original $4.5-million facility, located at Waters Avenue and Sixty-third Street, was hailed as "one of the country's most modern hospitals," a statement as true today as it was then. Licensed to operate 250 beds and served by some 140 physicians, it featured "private and semiprivate rooms, all with baths, multiposition electric beds, an intercom system to nurses' stations, state-of-the-art X-ray and physiotherapy units, and air conditioning throughout." Perhaps commonplace, today, but futuristic, then.

The history of what, in May 1967, evolved into Memorial Medical Center is, essentially, the history of the quantum leaps in medical science, technological advances, physician-patient and health care-client rapport, and the myriad progressions that have characterized highly progressive medical centers and the broadest spectrum of medicine itself, in the three decades since Memorial first opened its doors. The hospital's reputation as a pacesetter in health care for Coastal Georgia has been continu-

ally enhanced by such additions as its fifty-bed psychiatric unit, named in honor of Hospital Authority chairman Clark; its seventy-bed rehabilitation wing; a fifty-bed nursing home; and a 28-bed minimal care/diagnostic center, all three of the latter representing a $2.2-million enhancement that was completed in 1967. That same year southeast Georgia's first total heart-lung bypass was performed at Memorial.

By 1980 Memorial Medical Center was a full-fledged, 465-bed tertiary health care provider. As a regional medical center, it also serves as the Southeast Georgia Trauma Center, Regional Poison Control Center, Regional Radiation Oncology Center, and Regional Neonatal and High Risk Obstetric Center for southeast Georgia and southern South Carolina. In January 1981 Memorial launched a major construction and renovation effort designed to modernize the center, bringing it to a level of sophistication equal to its regional leadership role. The $33-million project encompassed construction, renovation, equipment, and furnishings; a major feature was a new, five-story patient tower that helped increase the percentage of private patient rooms to two-thirds of the total.

In addition, the 144,000 square feet of new construction, fully renovating the original 1955 structure, has been augmented by such improvements as a new radiation oncology center for cancer treatment, a new day surgery unit, a new 28,000-square-foot surgery complex with ten operating rooms, and new intensive and progressive care units for open-heart, neurosurgery, trauma and general surgery, and medicine patients. Now operational is the center's LifeStar service—the region's only emergency air

medical service. The LifeStar helicopter, medical support personnel, pilots, and maintenance crew are based at Memorial ready to cover the 12,000-square-mile service area within a 150-mile radius of Savannah.

Memorial's thirty-year tradition of bringing the latest wonders of medical technology to the region continues today, with the addition of magnetic resonance imaging, lithotripsy (a nonsurgical treatment for kidney stones), and other new systems to its diagnostic and treatment arsenal.

Another tradition, still vital after three decades, is medical education at Memorial Medical Center. Originally initiated at Memorial to help answer the community's need for additional physicians during the decade after World War II, the medical education program at Memorial, through the affiliation with the Medical College of Georgia, has been responsible for training hundreds of residents over the years. Many of these new physicians have established practices in the community increasing the scope of medical specialties needed to serve the diverse health care needs of all citizens. Medical education at Memorial has been a magnet, attracting new physicians, new technology, and new procedures to the region.

No chronicling of Memorial Medical Center's myriad services would be adequate without mention of its 200-plus-member auxiliary, the volunteers whose hearts, hands, and skills augment health care expertise. All monies from auxiliary-run gift shops and concessions feed directly back into needed equipment—such as laser surgery and other state-of-the-art technical equipment—that keeps Memorial at the very crest of the wave of health care progressiveness.

TRUST COMPANY BANK OF SAVANNAH

"I don't know of any other bank in Savannah that has the goodwill of the people that Liberty Bank has." So said Judge Peter Meldrim, successor as president of the American Bar Association to President and former Chief Justice of the United States William Howard Taft, speaking from his bench while presiding over Superior Court in Savannah in 1925.

Liberty National Bank was the precursor of what, in 1974, became Trust Company Bank of Savannah. And the eminent jurist's comment has been a significant guideline by which those charged with responsibility for the institution's operations have conducted its affairs. It was as the Germania Savings Bank, founded by Captain Henry Blun, Sr., a distinguished Confederate officer, that the institution opened for business on February 10, 1890, with an original capitalization of $50,000. Before year's end its name was shortened to The Germania Bank, its capital raised to $200,000, and it entered the field of commercial banking.

For its first forty-one years the bank had a Blun at its helm. Following the death of the captain in 1912, his son, Major Henry Blun, Jr., became president, serving in that capacity until 1931, when he was named chairman. Initial quarters for the institution were at the northwest corner of Bryan and Abercorn streets. In the wartime climate of 1917 the bank's name was changed from The Germania Bank to the Liberty Bank and Trust Company of Savannah, which became a national institution in 1930.

What is now Trust Company Bank had the distinction of hiring the first female banker in Savannah; Miss Weta Englerth handled the savings department cage from the fall of 1903 for the next forty-seven years. And, further, the bank has had the distinction of coming "home" to its present-day site in the multimillion-dollar brick-and-glass structure that, since 1974, has commanded an imposing prospect of Savannah's premier square, Johnson. It was at this site that The Germania Bank was located, in the city's first multistoried office building, from 1904 to 1926.

In 1933 Liberty National affiliated with Trust Company of Georgia, a 94-year-old, multibank holding company, with assets in excess of six billion dollars. The group currently consists of eighteen full-service commercial banks, with 182 banking locations throughout the state.

Today Trust Company Bank of Savannah operates eleven branches throughout Chatham County, including a facility at Hunter Army Air Field. The bank has enjoyed a close relationship with the armed services, having served both the Air Force and the Army for four decades. The bank was also the first to provide service, in April 1970, at Savannah International Airport.

In September 1984 reciprocal interstate banking laws, earlier enacted in Georgia and Florida, made possible the approved merger of Trust Company of Georgia and Sun Banks, Inc., in Orlando, Florida. SunTrust Banks, as the new entity is known, became the first regional banking company of its kind in the southeastern United States. At the close of 1984 combined assets stood at $15.5 billion. Retaining corporate and local identities, the merged companies have over 450 offices in Georgia and Florida, with a staff of more than 15,000.

Describing the bank's philosophy of management, the chief executive officer of its holding company emphasized that the foci were financial strength, profitability, and managed growth. He added that the bank had set for itself—and achieved—the specific goal of becoming one of the top-performing banking companies in the nation. He further pointed out that the institution is constantly mindful of its responsibilities within the communities where it operates, and continues to devote a generous portion of resources toward the enhancement of the quality of life in those areas.

JOHNS-MANVILLE

Johns-Manville, a multinational company headquartered in Denver, is locally situated in this facility in Savannah.

It all started in a basement on New York City's Maiden Lane in 1858. And it started with a man named Henry Ward Johns, who subsequently took time from his labors to advise his growing public to this effect: "We promise and claim less than many others but shall endeavor, as heretofore, to furnish the best materials of the kind and to make every resource available for their improvement."

What he started was the development of the first asbestos-based asphalt roofing and a number of other insulation products. Twenty-eight years later in Milwaukee, Charles B. Manville and his sons founded the Manville Covering Company, producing pipe coverings and insulation for heating and cooling systems. Within five years the Manville organization was the western distributor for the increasingly popular product line of Johns, who was well out of the basement by then.

In 1901 the two enterprises merged, becoming the H.W. Johns-Manville Company. Just over a quarter-century later Johns-Manville became a publicly owned corporation, listed on the New York Stock Exchange. J-M has the rare distinction of being one of the original stocks making up the world-renowned economic barometer known as the Dow Jones 30 Industrials.

And if the stock has world recognition, a not-insignificant seg-

ment of that world is roofed over, insulated by, wrapped up with, or the partaker of substances filtered through J-M products. Some of those products have long been "out of this world," thanks to the aerospace industry, and their inclusion as vital components of the vehicles of every NASA space flight since 1961.

As a corporate citizen, Johns-Manville has been an integral part of Savannah since the fall of 1956, when its new plant began supplying quality roofing products to

markets throughout the Southeast. Initially, two shifts produced, respectively, shingles and roll goods. Continuing refinements and improvements led to saturated roll goods, coated roll products, laminated shingles, and fiberglass roll goods. Fiberglass shingles continue to be the largest-volume product of the Savannah plant. Perhaps, more appropriately, one might say the largest "area" product, for more than three billion square feet of shingle coverage has been manu-

factured in Savannah since 1956.

The Savannah plant employs over 200 men and women; its annual payroll is close to five million dollars. Yearly expenditures for raw materials, supplies, freight, electricity, and natural gas total in excess of thirty-five million dollars.

J-M, headquartered since 1971 in the foothills outside Denver, is a multinational company with well over 20,500 employees in some 100 plants, mines, and other facilities worldwide. Its Savannah plant exemplifies progressive employee policies that include a benefit package encompassing a retirement plan and educational assistance, in addition to conventional perquisites.

Manville Corporation, and particularly the Savannah plant, led the U.S. roofing industry in con-

Another truckload of Johns-Manville roofing products is loaded for shipment to markets throughout the Southeast.

verting to fiberglass shingles and roll goods, which provide a longer roof life and better fire safety. This product line is distributed by the marketing responsibility of the Roofing Systems Division. Manville is an innovator in the production of fiberglass mat, the base material for Manville's roofing products.

J.C. LEWIS MOTOR COMPANY

J.C. Lewis, Sr., founded the Ford agency that bears his name on November 11, 1912.

J. Curtis Lewis, Jr., president, has guided the firm since 1950.

It isn't every day that a man convinces a metropolitan police department that motor vehicles would serve it better than horses, arranges to take the animals as a partial "trade-in," then does a brisk business selling "used horses" as a sideline to his thriving automobile sales agency. Nor is it every day that a man (son of and business successor to the first), in honor of a valued company associate and friend, donates to a religious group the land on which to build a place of worship. But then no one in Savannah ever characterized either man as "every day," or "just another face in the crowd."

The founder of what has long been one of the major automotive dealerships in southeast Georgia was as memorable a public servant as the astute businessman he was. And what was true of J.C. Lewis, Sr., whose name was synonymous with Ford vehicles from 1912 until his passing in 1942, has proven equally true of J. Curtis Lewis, Jr., who, as president, has guided the firm to its preeminence since 1950, in addition to serving as Savannah's mayor from 1966 to 1970 and

lending his considerable support to a broad range of community and civic enterprises before and since.

For the past ten years a third-generation member of the Lewis family, Walter, now executive vice-president, has been intimately involved with management of the agency—which has added the Mazda and Saab lines to Ford, the company's continuing mainstay. And J.C. Lewis Enterprises—encompassing a diverse range of businesses including television stations in Savannah and Columbus, Georgia, and Columbia, South Carolina; the local Ramada Inn; the Avis car-rental franchise; and an investment company handling real

estate operations—grows, under the watchful, seasoned guidance of the man in whose honor Congregation B'nai B'rith Jacob received the land on which to build Agudath Achim Synagogue.

That man is Sam Steinberg, senior executive officer of Lewis Enterprises and vice-president of J.C. Lewis Motor Company. He was a boy of fifteen, attending business college, when J.C. Sr. hired him as an office assistant in 1917. Sam is currently in his sixty-eighth year with the Lewis organization.

Following the death of the senior Lewis, Steinberg headed the company for eight years, until young Curtis finished high school, college, and military service.

The senior Lewis opened his first agency on November 11, 1912, at 309 Bull Street, directly across from what is now the DeSoto Hilton Hotel. The display area was large enough to showcase one auto—the Ford Model T. When Steinberg joined the firm five years later the sticker price for a Model T was $387.25. Initially Lewis had difficulty obtaining financial backing since bankers—like almost everyone else—thought the contraptions no more than a passing fad.

Public acceptance, spurred by dynamic marketing, has carried the firm through a series of increasingly larger locations to its present twenty-acre site at 9505 Abercorn Street, where more than 100 employees and a huge inventory of new cars and trucks indicate that the "horseless carriage" is here to stay, along with J.C. Lewis Motor Company and, of course, Sam Steinberg.

Walter N. Lewis, executive vice-president and the third-generation family member to be involved with management of the agency.

BEN FARMER REALTY, INC.

This contemporary facility at the geographic center of Chatham County is headquarters for the fifty specialists who make up the Ben Farmer Realty organization.

The idea of a haunted house is not the sort of image to foster happy days or pleasant dreams for a realtor. Yet, for Ben and Connie Farmer, whose first office was in just such a house, the only spirit that has been present in their lives for the past ten years has been that of success, to judge from the flourishing condition of Ben Farmer Realty.

Their present building, at 6349 Abercorn Street, consists of some 15,000 square feet (of which some 9,000 is used for Farmer enterprises, the balance for much-sought-after rental space). It is a far cry from the three-bedroom house on White Bluff Road where the Farmers started out, with some unpleasant psychic manifestations as live-in neighbors. Such things as typewriters that turned themselves on and off, lights that would flick on of their own volition, the sound of footsteps on the staircase, and attic doors eerily opening and closing convinced the Farmers that relocation was something to look forward to.

The firm, which in September 1975 consisted of the Farmers, five sales agents, and a receptionist, nonetheless did some three million dollars worth of business that year. Ten years later the staff had grown to four management personnel, forty agents, and five clerical employees, and the annual volume is now comfortably in excess of thirty million dollars.

Initially, the firm focused exclusively on residential resale. With extensive expansion in 1977 the scope has broadened to include property management, commercial real estate sales, insurance, new construction sales, and the largest prelicensing school in Savannah.

Ben Farmer, Savannah's Realtor of the Year in 1975, has served as a national instructor for programs of the Realtors' National Marketing Institute, and as a member of the board of directors of the Savannah Board of Realtors. A native of Goldsboro, North Carolina, he is a 1967 graduate of that state's Belmont Abbey College. While a student there, he met and

married Connie, the daughter of an Air Force officer. For five years after graduation he was with the Sears, Roebuck organization, serving in a management capacity in four southern states.

In January 1973 Farmer joined his brother in Savannah as part-owner and sales manager of Town and Country Realty, selling his interest two years later to found Ben Farmer Realty, Inc., of which he is president. Connie Farmer, co-owner, general manager, and secretary/treasurer of the firm, is a professional model and instructor for one of the leading modeling agencies and schools, and is often called upon to judge regional teenage modeling contests.

Innovative marketing techniques and an intimate knowledge of the constantly fluctuating real estate market in Savannah, its environs, and nearby South Carolina are characteristic of the organization. In 1976 Ben was a founder of both area multilisting and computerized multilisting services. He is demonstrably proud of the vigor of the organization's prelicensing school which, according to the Farmers, has graduated more fledgling real estate agents than any other in this region; Ben estimates that some 2,000 individuals have successfully completed the institution's course work.

Ben Farmer Realty, Inc., is a member of both the Savannah and Georgia Realtors' Associations, the Savannah Chamber of Commerce, and Savannah Homebuilders' Association, and the corporation holds a residential broker's license in Georgia and a nonresident South Carolina license.

GREAT DANE TRAILERS, INC.

When you see a sleek and gleaming trailer on the road, chances are the trailer and its mud flaps will bear the image of a large, alert, short-haired dog. Great Dane is the name, and building a variety of specialized trailers is the serious game at which this Savannah-based firm ranks second in both the nation and the world.

Great Dane Trailers, Inc., had its origins in 1900 as the Savannah Blowpipe Company, a fabricator of the dust- and chip-collection apparatus utilized throughout the Southeast by sawmills, furniture

A 1930 Great Dane trailer hitched to a vintage Studebaker truck/tractor.

plants, and planing mills. By 1912 the business was fabricating light structural steel products, and with twenty-five employees had moved to a new location on Lathrop Avenue, the area that is still home to the immense complex of the present-day company. In 1931 the original firm was incorporated as The Steel Products Company.

Sensing the economic implications of the improving highway system of the Southeast, the firm undertook the design and manufacture of truck trailers. The best of the breed were being built by a Greenville, South Carolina, man who, in 1930, began calling them "Great Danes," because of his admiration of the stamina and durability of these prized European

work animals. He was hired by The Steel Products Company, and thus began the legend of these quality trailers, now well into their sixth decade worldwide.

Those original Great Danes were sixteen- to twenty-foot flatbeds with three- to six-ton capacities (some of today's models, double the length, handle sixty-ton payloads). By 1934 the line also included tank trailers and enclosed trailers, or vans. Tightening highway regulations, anticipated by the company, led to a stressed-skin van of lightweight design that be-

came the principal Great Dane product.

World War II production of some 12,000 trailers for the government garnered the firm five Army-Navy "E" for excellence awards. The 1940s and 1950s were a pioneering time for The Steel Products Company. In the early 1940s it created the refrigerated trailer field with a produce van incorporating a wet ice bunker, cooled by a motorized blower system; it continued this lead with its first factory-finished refrigerated van, followed by the refrigerated

aluminum trailers that met the demand of the Florida perishables market and became the standard for the eastern United States.

By 1953 trailer production was exceeding six million dollars annually, and sales outlets were established in thirty-one cities in eighteen states throughout the East. In 1958 the company changed its name to Great Dane Trailers, Inc.; the following year redesigned lines of vans and tank trailers, largely made of aluminum, were introduced. Great Dane was an early, and highly successful, entrant in the railroad piggyback and maritime container fields, producing its first order of the former in 1961, and of the latter in 1963.

In 1966 Great Dane announced a $2-million expansion program, doubling trailer production. A year later it became a subsidiary of United States Freight Company, the world's largest forwarder. The parent firm subsequently chose the name Transway International Corporation as a more accurate reflection of its multifaceted services.

Between 1972 and 1983 Great Dane added three manufacturing facilities, each with its own area of specialized production, to the burgeoning operation at its Savannah plant, which alone produces 150 trailers per week. The others are located in Memphis, Tennessee; Brazil, Indiana; and Jacksonville, Florida. Sales outlets currently include thirty-six dealerships and seventeen company-owned branches, located in the United States, Canada, and the United Kingdom.

Anyone who uses the highways can attest to the proliferation of Great Dane trailers on America's roads—as can the well over 3,000 Americans involved in the design, manufacture, sale, and repair of Great Dane products.

JOHNSON, LANE, SPACE, SMITH & CO., INC.

July 1985 marked the fifty-second anniversary of the founding of Johnson, Lane, Space, Smith & Co., Inc., an event of which it is very proud. Not only is Johnson Lane the only New York Stock Exchange member firm headquartered in Savannah, it is the only member firm with its home office in the state of Georgia.

In 1933 the company started with offices in Savannah, Atlanta, and Augusta. The seven original stockholders had been associated with the corporate division of the Citizens & Southern National Bank prior to the enactment of the Glass-Steagall Act, which prohibited banks from engaging in the underwriting of stocks and bonds. The seven founders were Thomas M. Johnson, president; Julian A. Space, vice-president and treasurer; Allen Crawford and Freeman N. Jelks, vice-presidents; Remer Y. Lane, secretary; Craig Barrow, Jr., vice-president and manager, Augusta; and Hagood Clarke, vice-president and manager, Atlanta. With the exception of Crawford, all of the founders are still represented in the firm through their children and/or grandchildren.

With $25,000 in capital and the blessing of C&S, Johnson Lane opened its headquarters in the imposing old Hibernia Bank Building. The Savannah office still occupies that same location today, but that's not to say Johnson Lane hasn't grown over the past half-century. At the end of the most recent fiscal year, assets reached the $435-million mark, and the firm currently employs more than 400 people in nearly twenty offices located throughout Georgia, Florida, and the two Carolinas.

The philosophy upon which Johnson Lane was founded was to serve the needs of the individual investor, and it is still committed to that purpose today. Additionally, the company is very active in financing the expansion of industry, which is one of the principal ways of benefiting local communities. By raising capital for corporations, Johnson Lane indirectly helps provide jobs and services for the individual; by assisting municipalities with financial projects, the firm participates in the betterment of the community. Among its client list are such familiar names as Citizens and Southern Georgia Corporation and its South Carolina counterpart, Citizens and Southern Corporation; Days Inns of America, Inc.; First Railroad and Banking Company of Georgia; H.W. Lay & Co.; Ryans Family Steak Houses, Inc.; Savannah Electric and Power Company; Savannah Foods & Industries, Inc.; Sikes Corporation (formerly Florida Tile); and Union Camp Corporation.

In its early years Johnson Lane dealt primarily in unlisted securities and municipal bonds, but in 1957 it chose to become a member of the New York Stock Exchange and an associate member of the American Stock Exchange. Today the firm executes transactions in all of the nation's leading securities markets and offers a complete range of financial services to both individual and institutional investors and issuers.

A few years ago, the company adopted the deep-rooted, wide-spreading live oak as its corporate logo. Because the great evergreen tree is known for its strength, shelter, and long life, Johnson Lane's stockholders felt it symbolized what they stood for. Certainly, the firm's commitment to the Southeast is firmly rooted since it has been a vital part of and contributor to the region for over fifty years.

But what of the future? Says the company's president, David T. Johnson, "We will always be here to help."

The headquarters of Johnson, Lane, Space, Smith & Co., Inc., is located in the imposing Hibernia Bank Building.

L.P. MAGGIONI & COMPANY
ESTABLISHED 1870

Escape from a seminary in Genoa, Italy, adventures as a cabin boy on a blockade-running vessel during the War Between the States, shipwreck and rescue along Florida's Gulf Coast, a friendless young immigrant who meets and wins the girl he loves, and many struggles—then success that ultimately leads to his family's international reputation as a purveyor of delectable specialty foods.

These circumstances are part of the history of a Savannah family that has been a renowned supplier of oysters and a variety of seafood and other delicacies for over 115 years. The runaway seminarian was Louis Paul Maggioni; his "personal" Ellis Island was Cedar Keys, Florida. The girl was Natalie Bettelini, whom he met and courted during his travels in his first job as a pencil and notions salesman.

Shortly after their marriage, the young couple moved to Savannah. In 1870 the enterprise that has

Louis Paul Maggioni (1848-1897), literally cast ashore in the New World, labored to develop a dream still vital after four generations. Courtesy, Melanie Finocchiaro

thrived as L.P. Maggioni & Company had its beginnings as a small retail market specializing in fresh oysters and fish. Expansion into a wholesale venture was well under way by the time of L.P.'s death in 1897. Under the leadership of L.P.'s son, Gilbert Philip, the wholesale operation prospered. Perhaps most significantly, it was G. Philip who sensed the potential of canning saltwater delicacies, and, in time, this encompassed not only oysters and clams, shrimp and crabmeat, but vegetables as well.

At the time of the firm's seventieth anniversary in 1940, it then had some 2,500 employees, a fleet of 137 fishing vessels of various kinds, and a string of eleven canneries and plants along the coast from South Carolina to Florida.

According to L. Paul Maggioni, company chairman and grandson of the founder, the firm operated as many as fourteen plants, close to its major oystering beds, during the pre-World War II years. It was also a prime customer of vegetable and citrus growers in the Southeast. During the 1920s and 1930s the company maintained shad fishing camps along Georgia's Ogeechee River, manned during the January-April season by Italian fishermen brought from New York.

Even the residue of large-scale oystering operations is profitably utilized. Oyster shells have paved many a secondary road, crushed shells provide poultry feed, and, ground finely, the shells, rich in calcium carbonate, make excellent fertilizer.

In recent years the firm has tightened the focus of its enterprises, specializing almost exclu-

Natalie Bettelini (1854-1915) met and was courted by Louis Paul Maggioni during his travels in his first job as a pencil and notions salesman. Courtesy, Angela Beasley

sively in the production, canning, and distribution of oysters, marketed under the "Daufuski," "Mermaid," and "Crystal Bay" labels. Each enjoys its enthusiastic partisans, in various parts of the Southeast, and as far afield as Utah, Nevada, Wyoming, and Maine. Currently the firm maintains one major cannery, at Lady's Island, South Carolina.

Company headquarters, since 1968, are part of a well-kept office-warehouse at 25 Telfair Place, on Savannah's west side. There the third and fourth generations of the Maggioni family oversee the healthy enterprise. L. Paul, as board chairman, shares his long years of "hands-on" experience with sons Ralph Philip and Philip Joseph, president and vice-president, respectively, and son-in-law J.R. "Roddy" Beasley, also a vice-president.

OGLETHORPE REAL ESTATE AND CONSTRUCTION

"I would get bored imitating projects already done . . . if it would simply be a 'carbon-copy,' I wouldn't want to do it." In the building business, where the success of a given type of construction often translates into "it worked—let's repeat it," a statement such as the above is both fresh and arresting.

Tom Campbell, president and owner of Oglethorpe Real Estate and Construction, brings such freshness of approach both to his profession and the balance of his life. His most recent endeavor—the Abercorn Oaks Office Park, at 5859 Abercorn Expressway—is a distinctive expression of Campbell's innovative approaches. The initial building of the complex, consisting of 10,000 square feet of quality office space, has the structural atmosphere of the part of the world in which it is situated; it purposefully evokes the nineteenth-century flavor of the architecture of the Georgia-South Carolina coastal "Low Country."

Approximately one-third of the space is headquarters for the Oglethorpe organization. From it, upwards of twenty sales associates handle the primary business of the realty "arm" of the firm—residential resales and property management. Campbell himself is involved in syndication of commercial ventures, development of office space, and direct management of both businesses. The balance of space in the park's pilot building is given over to professional offices.

While Oglethorpe's real estate operations command his close attention, Campbell readily ac-

knowledges that the construction enterprises absorb much of his focus because, "I *like* to build." Attesting to that are, among other projects, the twenty energy-saving homes that garnered Oglethorpe the first-ever Good Cents Home Award of Savannah Electric and Power Company.

Currently in the forefront of Campbell's plans is limited cluster building of what have been referred to in national professional publications as " . . . tiny houses . . . appealing on a human scale." These are affordable one-and-a-half story, two- and three-bedroom houses of cedar clapboard. This project would entail building several houses to give the feeling of a small community, with completely finished bedroom, bath, kitchen, great room, and foyer downstairs, and with upstairs plumbing; buyers would complete interior finishing of the upstairs bedroom and bath.

Campbell has been active professionally in local real estate and construction since 1973, following several years of teaching in Savannah-Chatham County schools. His experience, prior to starting Oglethorpe in 1976, included a period as sales manager, assistant broker, and, eventually, vice-president of a major local realty-construction firm. A native Missourian, he arrived in Savannah by way of Australia!

Fresh out of Central Missouri State University in 1967 with a

bachelor's degree in education, he and a fraternity brother decided to see a bit of the world; Australia was the bit they chose. Armed with one-way tickets to Sydney and youthful confidence that "something would turn up," they boarded a Pacific cruise for the two-week voyage. Something did indeed turn up: on the first day at sea, Tom saw Nita Pierce, the tall, lovely blonde who ultimately became his wife. They met; they dated in Sydney during the months she remained visiting relatives; and they wrote regularly after she returned to Savannah. Tom, who'd secured a teaching position, finished out his year's contract, flew to Savannah, and began teaching locally.

Yes, they are living happily ever after; much of that comes of the "Kids Helping Kids" Christmas toy project, carried out through Savannah-Chatham County schools, that Nita and Tom started in 1982. The program, through which children bring toys to their own schools for redistribution to families whose holidays might otherwise be very lean, has seen some 20,000 toys gathered through 1984. The reception has been so enthusiastic that in 1984 Tom had to enlist the Southside Optimist Club, of which he is a past president, to handle the project. He and Nita, who teaches at Groves High School, are still happily involved behind the scenes as Mr. and Mrs. Claus.

The pilot building of Abercorn Oaks Office Park, home of the Oglethorpe organization, embodies the feeling of Coastal Georgia architecture of the late nineteenth century.

SMITH & KELLY COMPANY

Elton Allen Smith, co-founder.

The Smith & Kelly Building, at the corner of Drayton and East Liberty streets, has been the firm's home since 1984.

Lawrence Kelly, co-founder.

with enough left over to circle the earth and provide a carpet base from Savannah to Disneyland!"

The encyclopedic wealth of detail concerning the multifaceted shipping industry is the stock in trade of this veteran, and the firm that is fairly launched into its second century as a fixture of the Savannah maritime scene. Smith & Kelly Company had its origins in 1870 in the vision and partnership

The enormous variety and mammoth volume of products and materials passing through the Port of Savannah each year have long since earned it the designation of number one South Atlantic port. And no small part of that volume is handled by the 115-year-old firm of Smith & Kelly Company, steamship agents, freight forwarders, and stevedoring contractors.

Kurt Nanninga, a courtly gentlemen who would look as much at home at the helm of a huge freighter as he does behind the board chairman's desk at Smith & Kelly, is a walking repository of maritime fact and legend, as it has accrued around the salty environs of Savannah's waterfront. "I'll bet you didn't know," he says, "that if all the jute arriving in this port in a single year was put in one giant roll, there'd be enough to lay a twelve-foot strip over every paved street and highway in Georgia—

of two men who clearly recognized this port's potential. Elton Allen Smith, of Philadelphia, and Lawrence Kelly, of Brooklyn, had, by 1890, been granted a company charter—Smith became president, Kelly, vice-president—which, in addition to granting the firm the right to engage in all facets of shipping, gave it the privilege of conducting the business of "watering the highways, streets, and lanes of Savannah," for certain fees, to be collected from the city and property owners.

Steadily accelerating growth and success has developed into Smith & Kelly's three locations, each very close to the unceasing activity of the river. From 1870 to 1955 it was located at 28 East Bay Street; from 1955 to 1983 it occupied extensive quarters in the Georgia Ports Authority's Ocean Terminal Building; and, since the beginning of 1984, the firm has occupied its own, handsome, four-story building at the corner of Drayton and East Liberty streets, known as the Smith & Kelly Building.

In addition to Georgia branch offices in Atlanta and Brunswick, the eighty-employee firm has active branches in Charleston, South Carolina; Jacksonville, Florida; and Chicago, Illinois.

The Smith & Kelly name remains representative of over a century of solid service to the Port of Savannah and all who do business there.

CLYDE BRUNER ENTERPRISES

"I know of no more encouraging fact than the unquestionable ability of a man to elevate his life by a conscious endeavor." The words are those of the nineteenth-century naturalist and writer, Henry David Thoreau. "Any person not working to his or her full potential is wasting the God-given gift of life." Those words were voiced recently by the same man who, as a young high school graduate, hitchhiked to Savannah a quarter-century ago, a family Bible under one arm, a modest suitcase under the other. Both articles were graduation presents from his farming family, in the South Georgia community of Metter. It seems safe to say that, had they met, Mr. Thoreau would have looked approvingly upon young Clyde Bruner, making his way down a dusty road toward the wide world and its opportunities.

That family Bible has a prominent place of honor in the handsome suite of offices occupied by Clyde Bruner Enterprises, located at 116 Oglethorpe Professional Court, on Savannah's bustling south side. Pretentiousness, a calamity that often attends success, has no place in Bruner's scheme of things, in which both gratitude and humility figure prominently.

Bruner's first job, upon arriving in Savannah, was with Union Camp Corporation; it was followed by some nine years as a salesman with Derst Baking Company. The young family man was dealing determinedly with responsibilities that would have crushed a lesser person; two of his children were severely afflicted with Downs Syndrome, and he was working three jobs, meeting "medical bills that were eating me alive," as he fought to avoid having the children put in an institution for special care.

Thus, on October 15, 1971, the Krispy Chic chain of fast-food res-

Clyde Bruner, founder of Clyde Bruner Enterprises which includes the Krispy Chic chain of restaurants and the Blue Dolphin restaurant, with son Christopher on his lap, son Keith (standing, left) and wife Ginny (right).

taurants—which, by the end of 1985, will number fourteen—had its beginnings in a "without frills" store on Montgomery Crossroads at Waters Avenue. With a $5,000 loan, the bare rudiments of used equipment, and two part-time employees, Bruner was on his way, with chicken fried in such a manner as to keep them coming, by the tens of thousands, in the fourteen years since. In that first store on the first day, according to Bruner, "I sold $196 worth of chicken. I was on 'Cloud Nine.' I never expected those kinds of sales to begin with."

That first store, finally closed in April 1980, was replaced earlier that same year by his seventh restaurant, two blocks from the original location. "I wanted a new store," Bruner says, "for the comfort and convenience of all those customers who made my early success possible." The firm's Garden City store, at Highway 21 and Minus Avenue, is known as Krispy Chic Express, and represented a new concept—that of a drive-through-only emporium.

In October 1983 Bruner moved on an impressively successful tangent with the opening of Clyde Bruner's Blue Dolphin, a family-style restaurant, specializing in seafood and fine beef, located on Mall Boulevard, hard abreast Savannah's most extensive shopping

complex. Its resounding popularity, however, has in no way diminished the Bruner dream of a continually expanding and far-ranging chain of Krispy Chic outlets.

Despite the pace of what, to most dazzled observers, seems to be an unbroken succession of 24-hour business days, Bruner makes substantial time to enjoy his four sons. Success has not bred the country out of the boy, and Clyde Bruner and his wife, Ginny, take much pleasure from the 1,600-acre beef cattle farm they acquired five years ago, near Clyde's hometown of Metter. The herd, consisting of some 1,200 to 1,400 head, supplies the choice beef served at the Blue Dolphin.

The farm, which had been a long-standing dream of the Bruners, is virtually self-contained, in that the entire family is involved in its operation, including breeding of the cattle. Only the slaughtering is done elsewhere. And the two boys Clyde Bruner fought to keep, care for, and love remain a cherished and integral part of the family's life.

KONTER REALTY COMPANY

In his first inaugural address, John Rousakis, Savannah's four-term mayor, characterized his city as "a sleeping princess," dreaming of her proud past. He asked his new constituency to help awaken her, so that the past could flow into the dynamics of both the present and an equally proud future.

Partners both professionally and personally, Harriet (left) and Larry Konter have guided the growth of Konter Realty Company since its inception in 1961.

The revitalization of that regal lady has dramatically complemented the living repository of tradition contained in the nation's largest urban National Historic Landmark District.

Population growth, including business and industry, attests to the continuing health of a community; one of its concomitants is the expansion of real estate endeavors. If Konter Realty Company is any index, the future of Savannah and surrounding Chatham County is bright indeed.

Konter Realty is Savannah's largest real estate firm, currently producing over 500 sales annually of residential properties, plus commercial and investment sales with a total property value in excess of thirty-five million dollars. Its property management division alone accounts for gross assets of over ninety million dollars and maintains monthly rent rolls of some $500,000.

The firm, founded by Larry and Harriet Konter in 1961, began in a small, two-room office in Savannah's Realty Building. It remained there, through several expansions of office space and staff, until December 1966, when it moved to new headquarters at Paulsen and Sixty-ninth streets. The building, designed expressly for Konter's operations, had its office area more than tripled through additions in 1971, 1977, and 1979.

Continuing growth dictated the opening, in 1979 and 1981, respectively, of additional offices at 11149 Abercorn Expressway and at 206 Johnny Mercer Drive on nearby Wilmington Island. In the latter year Konter also established a resort office (Vacation Rentals, Inc.) on Tybee Island.

Now the corporate headquarters building with 9,300 square feet, housing all facets of the Konter companies, is located at 5801 Abercorn. The firm—now in its twenty-fifth year—continues its dynamic growth.

The Konter group of companies consists of these entities: Konter Realty Company, Konter Management Company, Konter Construction and Konter Homes, Konter Real Estate Institute, Vacation Rentals, Inc., and Halak, Ltd., a development company. The business has maintained a strong family orientation. Larry Konter is president; his wife, Harriet, is administrative vice-president; son Stanley is vice-president of Konter Realty and president of Vacation Rentals; and son Jerry is treasurer of Konter Realty and president of Konter Construction and Konter Homes.

Larry Konter is past president of both the Savannah Board of Realtors and the Georgia Association of Realtors, and has served as a regional vice-president for the National Association of Realtors. Harriet, 1985 president-elect of the Georgia Association of Realtors, is currently president of the Savannah Board of Realtors.

Jerry (left) and Stanley Konter have earned their executive positions in the family business through extensive experience in the multifaceted organization, and both have college degrees in real estate.

NEAL-BLUN COMPANY

The year was 1897, and much of the world basked in the golden somnolence of the waning Victorian era. William F. McKinley prepared to assume the duties of the nation's twenty-fifth presidency, an administration that was to end tragically in 1901. Savannah, still a city of less than 50,000, moved toward the century's end under Mayor Peter Meldrim. On November 20 of that year the enterprise known today as Neal-Blun Company had its formal beginnings as the Neal-Millard Company.

Its president, B.B. Neal, and his associate, F.P. Millard, began business—with an initial capitalization of $7,500—at the southwest corner of Bay and Whitaker streets, hard abreast the busy waterfront. The firm's articles of incorporation showed "an intent to . . . conduct business in building materials and related products. . . . " That intent has been vigorously and successfully developed over the intervening eighty-eight years.

In 1907 Captain Henry Blun, president of what was then The Germania Bank, bought an interest in the firm, which thereafter was known by its present name. That same year the company moved to its own building at 14 West Bay Street. For the next forty-four years, during which the firm remained at that same location, Savannah's healthy growth had a corollary in the expansion experienced by Neal-Blun Company.

Then, as now, the firm specialized in mill work, hardware, and other finish items for the construction industry, and in its early years it offered a comprehensive line of paints and varnishes of its own manufacture. Mule-drawn wagons, rail, and steamship were the modes of transport for customer deliveries, when both the century and the business were young. The company

Downtown Savannah in the early 1920s. The building at left was home to the Neal-Blun Company from 1907 to 1951. The Hyatt Regency Hotel has replaced it as a neighbor of City Hall (right). Courtesy, Historic Savannah Foundation

turned to the vehicles of a gentleman who once spent a great deal of his leisure time not far from Savannah. "We were the first building material distributor in this area to have a salesman driving a Model T Ford," recalled John McIntosh, Neal-Blun's third president.

In 1930 A.C. Neff acquired the Blun interest in the firm, becoming its second president in 1939, following the death of B.B. Neal. By the time Neff assumed its presidency, the organization's wholesaling to recognized building supply dealers was being carried on within a 125-mile radius of Savannah; in the immediate Savannah area its focus was on contractors, builders, and large industrial accounts, selling both wholesale and in job lots.

To satisfactorily accommodate accelerating demands of the post-World War II building boom, Neal-Blun found it necessary in 1951 to move to its present site at 3500 Montgomery Street, just south of Victory Drive. There the firm has extensive showrooms and offices, as part of 100,000 square feet of covered delivery and pickup storage areas, in addition to outdoor space, located on its own rail spur of the Seaboard Coastal Line.

John M. McIntosh, a World War II pilot and an established figure in local real estate and construction circles, acquired an interest in Neal-Blun in 1958 and eight years later became its third president. He was succeeded in 1975 by his son, A. Neff McIntosh, a great-grandson of the organization's founder, B.B. Neal. John M. McIntosh, Jr.—the brother of A. Neff McIntosh and thus another member of the enterprise's fourth generation of management—was elected president in 1981.

Neal-Blun Company currently has over ninety employees and ten trucks to service its market area, which reaches into Florida, from Pensacola on the Gulf to St. Augustine in the east. A wholesale branch is maintained in Jacksonville. An important segment of its South Carolina business, extending as far north as Myrtle Beach, is Hilton Head Island. Georgia, as far west as Columbus and Macon, provides a flourishing market.

MERRITT W. DIXON III

Merritt W. Dixon III, Savannah entrepreneur who, through his insurance, real estate, and building and land development enterprises, has become a legend in his own time.

One comes to anticipate the larger-than-life in a city as festooned with legend as are its noble oaks with gray-green whispers of Spanish moss. Such a city is Savannah; just two years past its 250th birthday, it waits with unabashed enthusiasm for the celebration of its 300th. And unabashed enthusiasm, shot through with zest for the daily contest that is life, characterizes the chairman of the board of Dixon Sheehan Titus Insurance, who is something of a legend in his native city, in his own, vastly enjoyed, time.

Merritt W. Dixon III can no more be neatly pigeonholed as a highly able insurance executive than as a canny real estate wizard and eminently successful builder-developer, though he is all of those things. His robust interest, fueled by deep enjoyment, spills over into yachting, high-speed, oceangoing racing boats, and a rapt fascination with helicopters. Only one thumbnail characterization might be apt: He is nothing if not an expansive man, with an aura of largeness both of deed and of gesture.

It becomes readily clear to the listener that the Dixon men were cut from the stuff of which legends are made. His grandfather, James M., was one of Savannah's more colorful mayors, and Merritt III's father, Merritt W., had his own construction company at an age when most young men have yet to decide what it is they want to do. He was well known throughout the Southeast as a road builder, and then retired, a highly successful man, at the age of thirty-five! Merritt III is quick to point out that he considers his father's most significant verbal legacy to him to have been this taut piece of advice: "I found it on my own. You do the same."

And so he has, although his father and artistic mother saw to a solid grounding for him. He received his secondary education at one of the Northeast's finest private institutions, the Hill School, in Pottstown, Pennsylvania. Those years tell a tale of a genial boy from the Deep South bewildered initially by an alien way of life, but determined to make his way among "sophisticated young Yankees."

Typically, his story is laced with laughter, and those school years rank among his four "most significant lifetime experiences." The others were a stint as a car salesman; the Dale Carnegie Course, which taught him "the importance of a positive attitude"; and, early on, a summer job as a laborer, which found him compelled to carry, all day long, a forty-pound Stillson wrench, which "wore me down, and kept me off the streets at night."

After graduating from the Hill School, Dixon enrolled at Atlanta's Georgia Tech University. Three years later, in January 1951, a National Guard mobilization came, in response to the worsening Korean Conflict, and he was called for Air Force service. Returning to Savannah in 1952, he married the former Janet Barnett, and promptly embarked upon another of his "significant experiences," selling automobiles for his father-in-law, and having three children: Merritt IV, Lysa, and Jim.

Another aspect of his entrepreneurial talents surfaced when, in 1953, he became president of Par-

kersburg Water Corporation, serving the elegant Isle of Hope section of Savannah. Under his guidance, the number of customers served rose from twenty to over 400. In 1957 Dixon bought into the Peters Insurance Agency, which—as Dixon Sheehan Lane, then Dixon Sheehan Titus—he continues to head as chairman of the board.

The agency has, since the late 1960s, been housed in what at casual glance appears to be one of Savannah's handsomest Colonial-era town houses, at 123 East Charlton Street. Handsome, indeed; eighteenth century, no. Designed and built by Merritt III after a year of detailed research, it is a new "old gem," its interior paneling and cornices milled from 200-year-old boards from old cotton

Merritt W. Dixon III stands at the edge of the Hyatt Regency Savannah Hotel's helipad overlooking the Savannah River.

warehouses.

By the mid-1960s Dixon was well launched on another major and continuing aspect of his career, the construction business. Between 1964 and 1974 he built a series of Howard Johnson Motor Lodges in or near Savannah, as well as in Manning, South Carolina, and Brunswick, Georgia. With the advent of U.S. Interstate 95, the major north-south, East Coast "funnel," Dixon scored a major coup with the construction of two lodges (Savannah, 1973, and Brunswick, 1974) at strategic intersections with I-95. The former, the Gateway lodge, has parlayed its prime location, at a main feeder into Savannah, into a volume of business that makes it number two in the entire Howard Johnson chain—and fifteenth of all motor lodges in the nation. These properties have been managed by his oldest son, Merritt IV, for the past ten years.

But the project for which Merritt III is best known—which had its voluble detractors and partisans long before its actual opening in April 1981—is the 356-room Hyatt Regency Savannah Hotel. With Mitchell Dunn as co-developer, Dixon guided the twelve-year, $26-million construction through some exceedingly tricky waters.

Facing on Bay Street, the seven-story hotel literally straddles a portion of River Street, the famed waterfront promenade and restored area that is a magnet for tens of thousands of visitors annually. It is a potpourri of smart restaurants, chic shops, galleries, and lively cafés, nestled in renovated antebellum cotton warehouses, where the atmosphere breathes "then."

The Hyatt Regency Savannah, a massive study in angularities and crisp geometrics, is distinctly "now." It affords its well-fed and luxuriously lodged guests the unique experience of two regularly used rooftop helicopter pads, breathtaking views of enormous freighters and cruise ships passing within 150 feet of their windows, and a real live freight train running through the hotel, down on River Street. No other hotel, anywhere, can make that claim!

Merritt III says, matter-of-factly, "It puts over 80,000 visitors on the streets of Savannah each year. Before this development, the city collected $10,000 annually in property taxes on this site; the hotel puts more than $180,000—plus some $350,000 in room taxes—in the city's coffers each year."

Within the past year Dixon launched the 114-room St. Joseph Inn, a handsomely appointed and artfully landscaped complex on the city's south side, with five restaurants, ten theaters, and a large, diversified shopping mall in its immediate neighborhood. While each current project becomes his "pet," he was literally all things to all aspects of this inn, from conceptualization to construction. He designed the furniture, room and suite layouts, walkways, and amenities. The inn boasts a swimming-pool-size, outdoor, heated jacuzzi, as well as its own helipad, affording almost instantaneous service to Savannah International Airport.

Reflecting his fondness for helicopters, Merritt Dixon III built a floating helipad at his previous waterfront home. And then there is the 52-foot, 98,000-pound yacht that he had built and outfitted to his express specifications in Singapore in 1970. To which add a number of fast offshore racing boats. Asked what's next, Dixon smiles and gives the names of his racing boats: "Who, Me?" "It's Me," and, now, "Not Me."

METALCRAFTS, INC.

A new roof and renovated steeple for Savannah's historic Independent Presbyterian Church had to be consistent with the "feeling" of the structure.

Much of the premium-quality work performed by Metalcrafts, Inc., is, unfortunately, only to be admired by those in low-flying airplanes, but it is unanimously appreciated by those within the wide array of structures securely roofed by this well-established Savannah firm. But that roofing, significant as it is, represents only one of two operational areas for which this family-owned business is noted. Heavy- and light-metal fabrication and erection (the company's hallmark from its outset), sales, and installation round out its range.

As Metalcrafts, Inc., the enterprise came into being in 1968, when it came under the ownership of Evans, Clarence, and Lemuel Lancaster. A fourth brother, Thomas, joined the organization the following year. Its origins, however, are shared with another Savannah business, Great Dane Trailers. The parent firm, Savannah Blowpipe Company, founded in 1900, fabricated the sheet-metal dust collection systems once in standard use in sawmills and furniture factories throughout the Southeast.

In 1968 Jim Nettles, a fellow church member of E.J. "Evans"

Whether it's a twelve-inch flotation ball for a chemical tank or a hefty segment of a much-larger installation (pictured), the firm's motto remains: "If you can explain or draw it, we'll design and build it."

Lancaster, offered the Lancasters a chance to buy what had been Savannah Blowpipe; Nettles said he would back the brothers, and offered them the option of buying him out in five years' time. The three brothers were then employed, in supervisory positions, with a large sheet-metal and roofing company in the area.

The Lancasters went to that firm's management, discussed their proposed undertaking, and offered to space out their departures so as to avoid disruption of their employer's business. His answer was terse: "Leave right now!" And so they did, and on August 13, 1968, Metalcrafts, Inc., began. From the outset it did well, to the extent that the Lancasters were able to buy out their benevolent backer well before the stipulated five-year period elapsed.

E.J., the original president, passed away in May 1982. At that time Clarence "Pete" Lancaster became president; L.A. "Lemuel"

is vice-president and manager of the metalworking division; and Thomas is vice-president and manager of the roofing division. W.D. Rahn, assistant vice-president, is in charge of shop fabrication.

The brothers have built a seasoned staff of some ninety employees, and the company's products and installations are to be found in a 150-mile radius of Savannah, including some of the more elegant resort locales along the Georgia and South Carolina coasts. The success of the enterprise has occasioned a total of three moves for the firm—and an increase of twenty times the original plant space. Since 1984 Metalcrafts has been at 2501 Tremont Road, on Savannah's west side, in a 30,000-square-foot building tailored specifically to its needs.

Not all of the firm's finely crafted work is hidden from the admiring eyes of the public. One of Savannah's most splendid old churches, the Independent Presbyterian Church, on Bull Street, had both its roof redone and its magnificent steeple completely refurbished, in copper, in a massive 1972 renovation, of which Metalcrafts is justifiably proud.

SOLOMONS COMPANY

Born in Georgetown, South Carolina, in 1816, Abraham A. Solomons was only fourteen years old when his father died. The oldest of eight children, he shouldered much of the financial responsibility.

At age nineteen, he received from the Medical Society of South Carolina his license to "carry on the business of Apothecary and Druggist." With this license and his brothers Joseph and Moses, he traveled to Savannah, Georgia, where, in 1845, he established an apothecary shop at Whitaker Street and Bay Lane.

In those days, each pharmacist made his own drugs from comparatively few basic materials. Accordingly, these first Solomons recognized there could be no substitutes for integrity and dependability. These virtues were rewarded by loyal patrons, most notable of whom were Robert E. Lee and Alexander H. Stephens.

Although prosperous during its early years, Solomons Company shared with the rest of the South hardships caused by the War Between the States. Medicines were the contraband of war. Quinine, then a wholly foreign product, was so valuable and scarce that blockade runners risked everything to secure it. The Savannah Benevolent Association and Solomons Company secured, compounded, and dispensed this vital drug to the community.

At war's end an impoverished people and heavy demand for medicines seriously jeopardized the company's finances. After Lee's surrender, A.A. Solomons traveled north to meet with the firm's creditors. America's great manufacturers showed faith in the small southern firm and made arrangements that the business might continue.

In 1876 just as the firm regained

In need of larger quarters, in 1847 Solomons Company moved to this building at the southeast corner of Barnard and Congress streets. Third from left is A.A. Solomons. Fourth from right is I.A. Solomons.

financial health, the dreaded yellow fever epidemic again struck Savannah. In forty-six days 5,542 cases were reported. Through death or flight, Savannah's population fell from 30,000 to 17,000. Again, Solomons Company and the Savannah Benevolent Association helped the community weather the crisis.

When A.A. Solomons died in 1899 at age eighty-three, his brother Joseph succeeded him and directed the company until his death in 1921 at age ninety-five. Isaiah Solomons, son of the founder, directed the business from 1921 until 1929. His sons, Abraham A. Solomons II and Isaiah A. Solomons, Jr., directed the company from 1929 through 1962.

In 1962 Philip Solomons, great-grandson of the founder, became president of Solomons Company. He oversaw the successful merger of Savannah's three drug wholesalers: Solomons Company, Reeves-McTeer, and Columbia Drug. Philip's wife, Shirley, and the fifth generation, sons Philip, Ralph, and Richard, hold positions

With a regional reputation for compounding prescriptions, Solomons Company received this request from Robert E. Lee. Among other historic memorabilia, this letter is a family treasure.

of responsibility in the firm today.

No business endures over 140 years unless it treats customers and employees fairly. From horses to tractor-trailers, pencils to computers, employee dedication has been a testimony to the American work ethic.

Thirty-five of today's 100 employees represent over 950 years with Solomons. Thus is the history of Solomons Company inextricably interwoven with the people and history of Savannah.

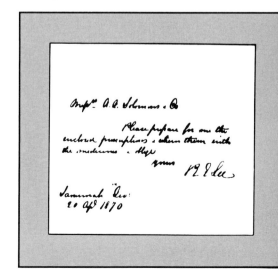

M.J. HOGAN & COMPANY INC.

England's venerable Poet Laureate, the late John Masefield, wrote often and well of ships, the sea, and the men for whom these lures never lose their fascination. But whereas Masefield's "salty dogs" went down to the sea in ships, a brotherly trio of local Irishmen unfailingly goes down to the Savannah River where—day in and day out, year after year—the ships come to them.

Jerry Hogan is president of M.J. Hogan & Company Inc., a line-handling firm that moors and unmoors every seagoing vessel that uses the Port of Savannah. Together with his brothers, Jimmy and Jack, vice-presidents of the venture, and a seasoned cadre of dockside veterans, members of the International Longshoremen's Union, they meet every ship coming into port—and theirs is a calling demanding readiness 24 hours

a day, seven days a week, 52 weeks a year.

Jerry started M.J. Hogan & Company Inc. in 1975, but the firm is a proud part of an unbroken line of family succession stretching back to the end of the nineteenth century. The Hogan brothers' grandparents, on both sides, made their homes in what was actually the oldest section of Savannah, where General James Edward Oglethorpe and his small band of colonists first gathered in 1733. That area, which came to be known as the "Old Fort" section, was predominantly Irish at the turn of the century. It was on Bryan Street, within sight, sound, and savor of the river, that the Dyer and the Hogan families lived.

Only those who have lived in one of the world's great port cities can truly know the extent to which the close proximity of the harbor, or the waters that link city and open ocean, can influence the atmosphere of such a city. In Savannah, even those living or working as much as forty city blocks away from the river are regularly reminded of the maritime quality of life when the hoarse, booming sound of a seagoing vessel's horn echoes over the city, signaling its arrival or departure.

So it was with the Hogan brothers' grandfather, William Dyer, living near the Savannah River in the Old Fort when this century was emerging. Day or night, at the sound of a ship's horn, the young man would literally run to the waterfront to help tie up incoming freighters and other vessels. For him, at first, this

was done for the pure "fun of it," and as a courtesy to the ships and their captains. Noting his eagerness, willingness to be of help, and promptness, one kindly mariner suggested to the lad that he make a business of what he loved doing and charge for his services.

So he did, and the first phase of what has become the family enterprise began as Dyer and Company. The elder Dyer remained active in the business until his death shortly before World War II.

With the advent of that war the pulse of the port and the pace of its shipping industry quickened. All through those arduous years, and for some time afterwards, the burgeoning family business was managed with optimum efficiency by Mary Dyer Hogan, who nonetheless found time to be a full-time mother to the Hogan brothers and their sister, Jan. Mrs. Hogan continued to head the firm until 1953, when it passed into the hands of the late William J. "Billy" Dyer, an uncle. It was known as W.J. Dyer & Son, until Jerry purchased it in 1981, incorporating it as part of M.J. Hogan

Jerry Hogan, president, directs the docking of one of the more than 1,900 ships handled by the firm in 1984. Photo by Nancy Heffernan

Jerry Hogan (in dark glasses) oversees a crew, all seasoned dockside veterans, in the mooring of one of the thousands of seagoing vessels to enter the Port of Savannah. Photo by Nancy Heffernan

& Company Inc.

The Hogan brothers retain crisp memories of what Jerry says "always seemed like middle-of-the-night trips" with their mother to the docks to meet incoming ships. Both Jerry and Jimmy began their apprenticeships very early; as pre-teens, they would often handle ships' lines themselves, to help their mother when company line handlers didn't show up on time for a docking. The deep admiration, love, and respect of the Hogan brothers for their mother is abundantly clear when they speak of her success in what is preeminently the calling of hardy men. A chief regret of Jerry's is that Mary Hogan did not live to witness the world-class role that the Port of Savannah now plays, for she had been deeply troubled by the post-World War II decline in tonnage handled; the resurgence came too late for her to exult over.

During 1984 the firm handled close to 1,900 ships; that would average out to more than five per day. However, arrivals and departures do not lend themselves to averaging, thus the continuing 24-hour alert that is a fact of life in the Hogan's business. Deep water and weather set their own rules; as Jerry points out, "Tides control what we do on the river, and the ship's draft determines the tide level in the channel necessary to bring it in or out. And many ships like to dock at night, so they can load or unload early in the morning." While bad weather poses no problem for those mooring the ships, fog does. "It's the one thing that can keep a ship from entering or leaving port," says Jerry.

The Hogans require four hours' notice of an arrival or departure, so they can alert and transport the four to six longshoremen necessary to moor or unmoor the vessel, under the Hogans' supervision. After tugs have maneuvered a ship to the dock, it requires about a half-hour to secure it, with two men each handling bow and stern lines; two men generally can unmoor a vessel. Hardest to handle are the mammoth tankers which, due to their size, have to be secured to "dolphins" (clusters of pilings away from dockside). For such ships, line handlers use a flat-bottomed boat with a fifteen-horsepower motor, jockeying into position to pull the ship's lines to the dolphins.

Jerry Hogan's wife and literal helpmate, Ellen, and his three children are very important to him, as is his role as president of the Propellor Club of the U.S. Port of Savannah, and his duties as a member of the national executive

M.J. Hogan & Company Inc. moors and unmoors every seagoing vessel that uses the Port of Savannah. Photo by Nancy Heffernan

committee of the Propellor Club of the U.S., both highly significant maritime associations.

There is another absorbing interest in his life. Jerry Hogan is Irish, through and through. And so is Savannah on the 17th of March each year, when upwards of 300,000 visitors flock to the city from all over the continent to help celebrate the second-largest Saint Patrick's Day parade in the world. Its planning requires the tactical sense of a field marshal and the unfailing cheerfulness of a true Irishman. Jerry's love of the day and its festivities has been lifelong, and that love has found significant official roles for him for the past five years.

From 1981 to 1983 Hogan was parade adjutant; in 1984 and 1985 he was vice-chairman; and in 1986 he will be chairman of what requires 364 days' planning for a successful outcome. He views his role in its preparation as an honor and a welcome responsibility. Perhaps because, as he says of his life's work, "Standing there early in the morning ... seeing the ship coming up to you is really relaxing. This is not a job, it's just something I enjoy."

CRITZ, INC.

By 1940 H. Dale Critz (fourth from left) was well established at West Bay and Broad streets. With him for the next forty-two years was the late Wallace Butler (third from left), who retired in 1982.

"'Gone Fishin'." The words conjure up a hand-lettered sign propped up in the window of a small business in a southern town wrapped in the somnolence of a midsummer's afternoon. Consider this as a contemporary alternative: there's no sign in the window, for there will always be a well-trained, courteous staff to help, six days a week; the business, nearly fifty years old, is progressive and prosperous; the community is indeed Deep South, but it is the vital home of the premier port of the South Atlantic coast.

And the fishing? How about a week or two of big-game fishing each January in the Florida Gulf Stream? And perhaps two weeks in the spring off the northern coast of Yucatán in the Gulf of Mexico. Follow this, late in the fall, with another week or two in pursuit of giant black marlin along northern Australia's Great Barrier Reef. To give these excursions a bit of balance, throw in some grouse shooting, late in August, on the Scottish moors.

How does that suit you? It suits Dale C. Critz, president of Savannah's Buick, Mercedes, BMW, and GMC light-truck franchises, just fine. Critz, Inc., at 7000 Abercorn Street, is a well-tended shop, even when the boss is away. Its five acres of modern showrooms and state-of-the-art repair facilities

house an inventory of better than three million dollars' worth of fine cars, sold throughout a marketing area that includes Chatham, Bryan, Effingham, and Liberty counties in southeast Georgia, as well as nearby Jasper County, South Carolina.

Critz's talent for selling automobiles is undoubtedly a reflection of his father's skill in the business—as is his love of, and expertise in, the rarified world of international big-game fishing. The late H. Dale Critz, a native of Little Rock, Arkansas, bought what had been the Savannah Automobile Company, a Buick-Pontiac dealership, late in 1938. As Quality Motors, Inc., it remained at the original West Bay and Broad streets location until 1948, although in 1945 an additional Buick showroom was added, at Jones and Barnard streets. From 1940 to 1974 the firm dealt exclusively in Buicks.

Within a year of opening the agency, H. Dale found himself in a position to buy his first deep-sea fishing boat—and the family tradition of serious angling was set. H. Dale was one of a select group invited to fish off Cuba in the 1950s in the legendary marlin tournament sponsored by the equally legendary Ernest Hemingway. In 1963 H. Dale helped organize the world-class Masters' Invitational Tourna-

ment, held in Palm Beach each January; one of its most coveted prizes is the Dale Critz Memorial Trophy, donated by Dale C. in honor of his late father.

Dale C., a Duke University graduate and former Naval officer, joined the firm in 1957. In 1974 and 1976, respectively, he secured the BMW and Mercedes franchises, and in 1984 General Motors also named Critz, Inc., to handle its GMC light-duty trucks. While Dale and his wife, Lila, share a love of deep-sea fishing, community involvement is also serious business with them. Dale has served on the board and as president of Historic Savannah Foundation, and was a trustee of Candler Hospital from 1965 to 1982. Lila, a member of the board of Telfair Academy of Arts and Sciences, was president of the Junior League of Savannah in 1970-1971.

A third generation of Critz men, in the person of Dale Jr., has been and will be actively involved in the business. Between graduating from the University of Virginia and recently completing studies for his MBA from the University of Texas, Dale Jr. spent over two years with the agency, selling BMW's and Mercedes cars. He is soon to embark upon further training with a GM dealer elsewhere in the country, after which he will return to the Critz organization, either in Savannah or at the firm's dealership in West Palm Beach, Florida. And, who knows? Perhaps the lure of the "big ones" will find him girdling the globe, with ready rod and reel, in times to come.

HUNTER, MACLEAN, EXLEY & DUNN, P.C.

The firm of Hunter, Maclean, Exley & Dunn, P.C., has engaged in the general practice of law since 1879 when Walter G. Charlton, a graduate of the Law Department of the University of Virginia, formed a partnership with N.C. Collier, who was later United States judge in New Mexico.

The firm of Charlton & Mackall, afterwards Charlton, Mackall & Anderson, stood high at the Savannah Bar, numbering among its clients some of the most important interests in Savannah and surrounding Chatham County.

J. Randolph Anderson joined the firm in 1891 and practiced with it until his death in 1950. In addition to serving as lieutenant governor of Georgia, he helped put together the railroad lines which became the Seaboard Airline Railroad, now the Seaboard System Railroad. The firm has acted as system-wide general counsel for the SCL in employment discrimination and other matters and still serves as Seaboard's local counsel.

In 1903 the firm became Anderson, Cann & Cann. One of its

J. Randolph Anderson helped guide the firm to a preeminent position during the course of nearly sixty years' practice, most of them as a senior partner.

specialties was maritime law, a practice it established through acting as a regional representative of various London protection and indemnity clubs. It continues to handle "P&I" matters and represents an expanded number of maritime interests.

In 1945 Anderson, Cann & Dunn formed a seven-man firm when it merged with Connerat, Hunter & Cubbedge. That same year the organization moved to its present address in The Savannah Bank & Trust Company Building. The connection between The Savannah Bank (now a part of First Railroad and Banking Company) and the law firm was and still is a strong one.

Known as Hunter, Maclean, Exley & Dunn, P.C., since 1980, the law practice now includes more than thirty-five attorneys and at least as many paralegals, secretaries, and support staff. The firm's members have a tradition of public service. E. Ormonde Hunter and Spencer Connerat served in the Georgia General Assembly. Walter G. Charlton and George Cann were superior court judges. Sam Cann was district attorney, and both William Mallie Exley and Mark Silvers were chairmen of Savannah's Metropolitan Planning Commission.

The present senior partner, Malcolm R. Maclean, a graduate of Harvard Law School, is a former mayor of Savannah. W. Brooks Stillwell presently serves as a city alderman and Robert Glenn is president of Historic Savannah Foundation.

Service to community became, during the past seven decades, mil-

Colonel E. Ormonde Hunter's distinguished career has embraced the legal profession, active duty in both world wars, and service as a state legislator in Georgia.

itary service to country for many associated with the firm. Connerat and Hunter served in World War I, and during World War II Hunter rose to colonel while in the China-Burma-India Theater. Both Maclean and J.P. Houlihan commanded fighting ships during that conflict, while Exley was an Eighth Air Force navigator. Finally, Viet Nam service drew Arnold Young, F. Saunders Aldridge, Lee C. Mundell, and Roland Williams to active duty.

A substantial amount of work continues to be done on behalf of nonprofit entities such as St. Joseph's Hospital, Chatham County Hospital Authority, Protestant Episcopal Church in the Diocese of Georgia, Inc., Historic Savannah Foundation, and others.

Hunter, Maclean, Exley & Dunn, P.C., is the largest law firm in the state of Georgia outside of Atlanta.

S.A. ALLEN, INC.

Sam A. Allen, the company's founder, was an Arkansas native who grew up working with forest products and who was renowned for his pluck and resourcefulness. He started his pulpwood marketing business in 1925 in Pine Bluff, Arkansas, supplying pulp and paper mills in that state and in Louisiana. On May 18, 1936, after moving to Savannah, he delivered the first load of pulpwood to what was then Union Bag & Paper Corporation, becoming the "dean" of that company's wood shippers. That initial shipment was followed, during the next few decades, by millions of cords of wood. This set the basis for the long-standing, cordial relationship between the two businesses. Union Camp Corporation, currently celebrating its fiftieth anniversary, remains a valued client of S.A. Allen, Inc., which in 1986 observes its own fiftieth year in business.

Following World War II service, Sam D. Allen (now company president) and his brother, Harold, joined their father in the business. At the time of the senior Allen's death in January 1947, the firm's identity was still that of a supplier of timber to pulp and sawmills, although Sam A. maintained a small garage, with one mechanic, to service timber hauler's trucks. With the advent of "wheel" or circular saws, the mechanic serviced these as well.

In 1954 the Allen firm sold the last of its holdings of some 4,800 acres of timberlands to Union Camp. Later Allen contracted to cut on those same lands for Union Camp. Among the Allen company's major timber customers, in addition to Union Camp, are the Georgia affiliates of such major corporations as Rayonier, Georgia Pacific, and Interstate.

In 1957 Harold Allen left the business, and two years later Sam D. bought out the family interests and became sole owner. It has been a quarter-century since the firm took on, as a distributor, a line of hydraulic loaders that could be adapted to wheeled tractors. And it was during the 1960s that the Allen organization moved increasingly into the distribution of hydraulic pumps, motors, and related components.

In 1972 S.A. Allen, Inc., added to its Allen Hydraulics division, having bought out the Parker-Hannifin distributorship that had been started by one of Sam D.'s sons and a systems engineer employed by Allen. Sam D. Allen, Jr., manages the firm's hydraulics branch in Wilmington, North Carolina, while his brother, Steve, is in charge of data-processing operations and manages company headquarters, on Pine Barren Road in Pooler, just west of Savannah proper. The eldest of the third-generation Allens, Andy, left the business seven years ago to design and build engines for Class C racing cars.

Despite the range of his responsibilities as company president, Sam D. makes time for a heavy load of professional, civic, and community obligations. Furthering his father's deep concern for intelligent forest management, Sam has been a member, since its beginning, of the Georgia Forestry Association. At the state level, he served as a state representative for two terms in the Georgia General Assembly. A former vice-president of the Georgia Baptist Convention, Sam recently completed the second of two five-year terms as a trustee of Southeastern Baptist Theological Seminary, located in Wake Forest, North Carolina, and served as chairman of the trustees for two years.

The firm delivered its first load of pulpwood to Union Camp Corporation in May 1936. In the nearly fifty years since, it has been followed by several million cords of wood. Pictured below are Sam A. Allen (in suit, standing near rear of lead truck), Sam D. Allen (behind cab of lead truck), and Harold W. Allen (standing by door of third truck). Courtesy, Union Camp Corporation

E.L. MOBLEY, INC.

The late Robert Frost was a sterling poet, and the ultimate farmer-philosopher. One of his best-known poems, "The Road Not Taken," addresses life's choices: the path one chooses not to follow, and the road, " . . . that has made all the difference."

Had Elton L. Mobley not chosen to "take" typing, rather than high school French, there is a strong likelihood that the man who became "dean of Savannah's customshouse brokers" would never have established one of the South Atlantic Seaboard's best known and most experienced firms of customs brokers and freight forwarders. The founder of E.L. Mobley, Inc., began life as the son of a tenant farmer in Chinquapin, North Carolina; the youngest of nine children, he was the only one to attend college.

Typing struck the enterprising farm boy as a practical skill to acquire and, he says, "led me into the customs business" since it was a job requisite. After World War II the young, newly married ex-GI studied nights at what is now Armstrong State College, earning his degree in business administration.

Mobley supplemented his veteran's educational benefits by working for a finance company and, subsequently, a real estate firm, before cutting his teeth as an import clerk with a local customs brokerage. During the course of some five years with the firm, he rose to the position of import manager and, after coupling a year's study with his experience, successfully completed the rigorous customs broker's examination in the spring of 1962.

Mobley thus became the youngest customs broker in Savannah, and that same year he started his own firm. The story of the com-

The Mobley family (clockwise from top left): Richard E., Paul E., Elton L., and Virginia J. Mobley.

pany's first office, at Bee Road and Victory Drive, is a story of a kindness done and a kindness later richly repaid. The office had been that of a realtor who, upon moving, gave the use of the office, together with his secretary and bookkeeper, to the young veteran. When, five years later, the Mobley organization had successfully grown to the point where a Charleston, South Carolina, branch office seemed advantageous, it was the son of that friendly realtor who became its manager and who, in 1971, bought that "arm" of the business.

Mobley's original staff consisted of himself and his wife, Virginia. In the fall of 1969 Virginia Mobley attained her license, becoming the second fully accredited female customs broker in the state of Georgia; her licensing made possible incorporation in 1970 since the firm then had the requisite pair of licensed brokers.

The need for improved, expanded space occasioned a series of moves and the corollary need for additional staff over the next ten years. On the first day of 1980 E.L. Mobley, Inc., with a staff of thirteen well-qualified specialists, took up its present quarters at 21 East Bay Street, close to the river that is an international conduit of the goods the firm sees through every aspect of import/export procedures, to or from inland destina-

tions.

A second generation of the Mobley family is very much in evidence in the business. Richard E. Mobley, president of the company since 1983, went his dad one better, in the realm of "youngest broker" laurels. At the age of twenty-one he took the customs broker's examination, sailed through with flying colors, and prior to his twenty-second birthday, in July 1975, received the certification that gave him the distinction of becoming the youngest licensed customs broker in the nation. Brother Paul Mobley manages the firm's satellite office, located at Atlanta's Hartsfield International Airport.

Elton, Virginia, and Richard have each played significant leadership roles in local and national industry associations, and both Elton and Richard are deeply involved with the Savannah Port Society, the 148-year-old organization that runs the International Seamen's House, a mission to merchant seamen visiting the Port of Savannah. Soft-spoken about deeply held religious beliefs, the Mobley family's "atmosphere" can be felt in the cohesive quality of their business and the people who make it up.

ATLANTIC MUTUAL FIRE INSURANCE COMPANY
SOUTHERN BANK AND TRUST COMPANY

The imposing antebellum mansion at the southwest corner of Bull and McDonough streets has enjoyed—for the span of its 140 years—the happiest of symbiotic relationships with Chippewa Square, which it overlooks. In this instance, the "living together" has been mutually advantageous because the Stoddard-Hull-Barrow House enjoys the exceedingly pleasant prospect of Chippewa Square—and is an integral part of what, visually and atmospherically, makes the square so pleasant.

It was in 1844 that silversmith Moses Eastman began construction of the house at 17 West McDonough Street. In 1848 it was purchased by John Stoddard, a wealthy planter and merchant. Joseph Hull, who bought the house in 1893, instituted major renovations, including the addition of a third story, as well as the extension, to the full height of the second story, of the elegant, rounded colonnade at the front of the house. During the course of the next sixty years this regal structure was the town residence of such persons of prominence as the Barrows and the Gordons.

In February 1953 the local evening newspaper carried a story announcing purchase of the mansion under the headline: "Fine Old Home to be Wessels' Firm's Offices—Three Companies Acquire Gordon House on Bull Street." Thus began the identification of the Wessels family with this historically important and aesthetically valuable structure, in what was the first significant commercial use to be made of such a building, ensuring its continuing, viable role in the life of what was to become the nation's largest National Historic Landmark District. The businesses in question were the Atlantic Mutual Fire Insurance Company,

what was then the Southern Savings and Loan Company, and the Atlantic Insurance and Investment Company.

The Stoddard-Hull-Barrow House was in its thirtieth year when there arrived in Savannah a man who forthrightly listed his occupation as "capitalist," which, for him, took the form of constructing houses and rental-property buildings. That man was Frederick Wessels, patriarch of a clan whose history has been interwoven with that of Savannah and Chatham County ever since. He and his wife, Anna, were the parents of Frederick Wessels, Sr. (1877-1950), whose stamp upon the business and community life of the city was both deep and long lasting. Those multiple influences have been continued and vigorously implemented by the succeeding generations bearing the Wessels' name.

A lifelong Savannahian, Fred Sr. was educated in local public schools and in 1893 started his business career as an office boy with Savannah Insurance Agency. In 1905 he organized the German Mutual Fire Insurance Company, which, twelve years later, took the Atlantic Mutual name. Started, in Wessels' words, with "$5,000, faith in the Lord, prayer, and hard work," the company has long been a national concern, its assets in the millions, with agencies throughout the United States.

In 1916 Wessels was the prime mover in the establishment of Southern Savings and Loan Association, which, in the late 1970s, became a full-service commercial institution, under the name Southern Bank and Trust Company. Since its inception the institution has placed primary emphasis on loans to disadvantaged groups. In 1922 Fred Sr. formed Atlantic Insurance and Investment Company,

general agent for some of the nation's largest fire insurance and casualty companies.

From 1907 to 1913 Fred Sr. served as Savannah's city marshal, operating the fledgling insurance business after regular hours at city hall. It was, however, in the worlds of banking and insurance that his business acumen made itself most evident. At the time of his death in 1950, he was president of both Atlantic Mutual and Southern Savings and Loan, chairman of Atlantic Investment and Insurance, and president of both Merchants & Farmers Mutual Insurance Company and the Southern Union Insurance Company.

A lifelong communicant of the Lutheran Church, Fred Sr. was well known throughout the United Lutheran Church of America, and his particular interest in its Newberry (South Carolina) College was acknowledged when, in the late 1940s, the school conferred upon him the honorary degree of Doctor of Laws. His civic and community endeavors—and the honors that accrued as a consequence—were numerous and varied.

Long active in the Savannah Chamber of Commerce, he was the 1934 recipient of its Lucas Trophy for the year's most outstanding contribution to the city. In 1939 he received the Golden Deeds Award, tendered by Savannah's Exchange Club, for his early efforts on behalf of what was unquestionably his most notable contribution to the betterment of the community: his long service as chairman of the Housing Authority of Savannah.

His wife and helpmate, in the truest sense of the word, was Adeline Kuck Wessels, whose devotion to her community was of an intensity and perseverance to match her husband's. Her work in the interests of children stands out

the parlor with antiques and Oriental rugs, which continue to add to the charm of the house.

Fred Jr. assumed leadership of the companies upon his father's death, and presided over the formal commencement of business at the new location. Building effectively and imaginatively upon his father's successes with the various Wessels' enterprises, Fred Jr.'s stewardship (interrupted only by service to his country during World War II) was vital to the position of eminence they enjoy today.

A devoted Lutheran like his father, Fred Jr. was also deeply interested in Newberry College and other church-affiliated institutions. Long active in community politics, he served for twelve years as a Chatham County Commissioner.

Following Fred Jr.'s death, leadership of the Wessels' companies passed to his sons, Frederick III and Charles H. At present, there are four distinct operations: Atlantic Mutual, Southern Bank, Atlantic Insurance and Investment, and Southern Union Company, which handles real estate development.

Fred III, active in a variety of roles with the various concerns since graduation from Newberry College in the late 1950s, is chairman of the bank and president and chief executive officer of the other three companies. Charles H., a graduate of Wittenberg University, Springfield, Ohio, and of the University of Georgia Law School, is a former Navy lieutenant-commander. During the course of three senatorial terms in the Georgia General Assembly, he was chairman of the Judiciary Committee and of the State Ports Subcommittee. He is currently chairman of Atlantic Mutual Fire Insurance Company and serves as vice-president and general counsel of the other family businesses.

Chippewa Square's elegance derives from such elements as the 1840s Stoddard-Hull-Barrow House, home to the Wessels' family businesses since 1953. Its utilization for contemporary business purposes was precedent setting.

distinctly: long involved, locally and at the state level, with Parent-Teacher Associations, she served for a number of years as state PTA president. In addition to instituting one of the earliest school hot lunch programs, she did pioneering work in the field of child abuse—work that was furthered substantially by her grandson, Charles H. Wessels, through his efforts during the course of his three terms as senator in the Georgia General Assembly.

Rosalie Wessels, Fred Jr.'s wife, was the catalyst in the purchase of the Stoddard-Hull-Barrow House. She also restored and decorated

THE POLOTE CORPORATION

High school boys, riding their bicycles, are given to dreaming the passing dreams of adolescence. Making after-school deliveries for a drugstore during his years at Savannah's St. Pius X High School, Benny Polote did his share of dreaming, while pedaling along.

It was a persistent dream, seeing him through a year as a merchant seaman, after high school, and a stint as a lab technician for American Cyanamid Company; the sole black in the lab in those days, he was, within eighteen months, the chief steward of the department. The dream was deferred—but it never lost sharp focus.

In the late 1960s Polote began to put a working foundation under his dream, when he went to work for a local subcontractor, C.E. James & Son. It was there that he got his first taste of the construction business, and saw the approach that, with determination and hard work, would enable him to realize that dream of being his own boss.

Today, as both chairman and president of the multimillion-dollar construction firm The Polote Corporation, he is indeed his own boss, as well as a hands-on source of inspiration to the seasoned force of engineers and skilled construction people who have helped make the name "Polote" a respected one in the building industry throughout the

Benjamin Polote, chairman and president of The Polote Corporation.

Southeast, and well beyond.

TPC has gotten high marks for a range of successful projects that have earned it a solid ranking among "the most diversified, fast-growing, black-owned ... construction firms in the United States," according to one industry spokesman.

The company began business in 1971 as Polote Home Builders; it was restructured in 1973 as Polote Builders, Inc., and in 1975 landed its first major contract, for the Savannah Model Cities renovation project on Thirty-seventh Street. Locally, projects have also included the Westside Comprehensive Health Center, work at Savannah International Airport, the on-campus home of Savannah State College's president, Dr. Wendell G. Rayburn, and, currently, successive phases of the massive renovation and supplemental construction of the Telfair Arms condominium complex at the southeast corner of Forsyth Park.

TPC's first commercial construction job was at the Dublin, Georgia, Veterans' Administration Center; another USVA project was the Service Building at the Na-

tional Cemetery in Chattanooga, Tennessee. A broad, highly diversified range of government construction contracts—undertaken for an impressive number of major federal agencies—have included air traffic control towers in Chattanooga and Orlando, Florida; correctional institutions and law enforcement training centers; the Mammoth Cave (Kentucky) National Monument; building modifications at Robins Air Force Base, Warner Robins, Georgia; and a number of Army Corps of Engineers projects in Georgia and the Carolinas, which included major portions of the Richard B. Russell and Tennessee Tombigbee dams.

"In all," Benjamin Polote says, "Savannah-area projects account for no more than 15 percent of our business. From Texas to Washington, D.C., we've been busy—and operations in Saudi Arabia and Egypt are under study." The Polote Corporation's headquarters is at 1810 Mills B. Lane Avenue, in a clean-lined, elegant building that is part of the dream of a man bent on "being his own boss."

Polote's corporate headquarters, at 1810 Mills B. Lane Avenue, has a Mediterranean "feeling," reflecting Savannah's subtropical climate.

CHATHAM STEEL CORP. & RELATED COMPANIES

The Telfair Academy of Arts and Sciences, Historic Savannah Foundation, Congregation Agudath Achim, United Way of the Coastal Empire, The Savannah Symphony, Savannah Ports Authority, United Jewish Appeal, Savannah Area Chamber of Commerce, and Savannah Theatre Company. Other than tremendous importance to the cultural, religious, civic, and economic life and well-being of the community they nurture, what do these seemingly disparate organizations and institutions have in common?

Among other things each has been served and its goals or mission furthered by the volunteer participation over the course of the years—usually at a significant decision-making level—by one or more members of the Tenenbaum family. Community service projects do best when put under the guidance of a person with a proven capacity for "getting things done." So it is with the Tenenbaums.

The business, which now consists of several related organizations, had its origins in 1915, when Samuel Tenenbaum started a scrap-metal company in Savannah. The patriarchal Tenenbaum had come to the United States in 1911 from Europe; his wife, daughter, and three sons had remained there until 1921, by which time Tenenbaum had saved enough to arrange for their passage to America.

Following their graduation from high school, sons Albert and Ralph joined their father in the Chatham Iron & Metal Company, which became the major scrap processor in the Coastal Georgia area. The third son, Meyer, went on to pre-law studies, graduating from Emory University Law School in Atlanta, Georgia. He practiced law for approximately ten years before entering the family business.

A major expansion took place in 1938 with the formation of Chatham Pipe & Supply Company, specialists in the wholesale plumbing, heating, and industrial supply business. Later, during World War II, Chatham Iron & Metal's activities as a supplier of scrap for vital war production needs received federal recognition through a Scrap Producer Merit Award, conferred by the War Production Board.

The surging postwar economy found the Tenenbaum's recognizing and acting upon the need in the area of a full-line, carbon steel warehouse. Thus Chatham Steel Corporation—the third, largest of the three entities making up Chatham Industrial Group—was formed. Chatham Steel's progress has been one of unbroken ascent, leading to distribution centers in Columbia, South Carolina (1969); Orlando, Florida (1982); and Birmingham, Alabama (in late 1983).

All of the third-generation males of the Tenenbaum family are active

Ralph, Meyer, and the late Albert Tenenbaum (from left), and their respective sons have continued to guide the multifaceted business to its prominence in the Southeast.

Samuel Tenenbaum, founder of the scrap-metal company in 1915 that preceded Chatham Steel Corp. & Related Companies and established the business principles and the tradition of community involvement observed by the family to this day.

in the management of Chatham Industrial Group's enterprises. Samuel's sons, Meyer and Ralph, are presidents, respectively, of Chatham Steel and Chatham Pipe & Supply. The third son, Albert, is deceased; his son, Arnold, is corporate vice-president and treasurer. Meyer's son Samuel is corporate vice-president and general manager of the Columbia operation. Ralph's sons, Sheldon and Bert, are, respectively, vice-president/purchasing, and operations manager of the Orlando division. A brother-in-law, Ronald Kronowitz, is manager of the scrap division, Chatham Iron & Metal. And the tradition of community commitment, instilled by Samuel in his sons, fares handsomely in the custody of the third generation.

HIXON BATTERY COMPANY, INC.

Franklin O. "Frank" Hixon, founder.

For more than forty-three years Hixon Battery Company had been a respected Savannah manufacturer of storage batteries that power everything from the largest diesel trucks and yachts to wheelchairs and small riding lawn mowers. Today the firm is a well-known wholesaler and retail distributor of storage batteries.

Since 1969 its plant and headquarters have been at 1304 East President Street. Making and marketing batteries might seem to betoken a masculine enterprise, yet from its inception it was a husband-and-wife endeavor and, since 1974 and the passing of Franklin O. "Frank" Hixon, the firm has thrived and grown handily under the astute direction of Elfreda M. Hixon and Sandra Hixon Wells, the mother-and-daughter team that has lent family continuity and strength to the business.

For some ten years prior to World War II, Frank Hixon was an able and respected sales representative working out of Savannah for two of the nation's foremost storage-battery makers. With the advent of the war he contributed to the national effort as a shipfitter.

Well aware that many of the essential materials for battery manufacture necessary for the war effort were unavailable, he reasoned that the repair of existing batteries would provide a much-needed service. Using the telephone directory to canvass likely prospects, Elfreda turned up scores of eager customers. Frank would repair batteries during shipyard off-hours, and Elfreda would pick up and then deliver the rejuvenated batteries.

The part-time service soon became a full-time business, necessitating a move from the Hixon's garage to warehouse space at Barnard and River streets. With the end of the war and the availability of requisite materials, the couple decided to manufacture new batteries under the Hixon name. In 1952 Hixon Battery struck heavy pay dirt when it won the contract to supply all batteries necessary for the mammoth construction project of the Savannah River Nuclear Plant, located near Aiken, South Carolina.

While continuing success has dictated some changes over the years, including a series of moves to larger facilities, certain vital elements remain the same. Quality and reliability—which Frank Hixon insisted upon in every battery bearing his name—still dictate manufacturing and servicing and, as important, continuity of family ownership embraces the dedicated knot of long-term employees of the firm. As Sandra Hixon Wells notes, "There is no employee turnover rate at Hixon." Skeptics have only to talk with A.P. Smith who, at age eighty-four, hasn't the remotest thought of discontinuing what he has done since 1946, when Hixon asked him to join his new enterprise. "Like father, like son" prevails in the Smith clan: A.P.'s son, Jimmy, the shop foreman, has been with Hixon Battery for close to thirty-five years.

Elfreda Hixon, company president and owner, leaves day-to-day direction of Hixon Battery Company to daughter Sandra, who serves as secretary/treasurer and general manager. In 1983 the Hostess City (Savannah) Chapter of the American Business Women's Association named Sandra Woman of the Year. A director of the Savannah Chamber of Commerce and a trustee of Savannah Vo-Tech School, she was, in 1984, appointed by Governor Harris to serve on the board of the Job-Training Partnership Act Program.

Following Frank Hixon's death in 1974, the business passed into the capable hands of his wife, Elfreda, and daughter, Sandra Hixon Wells.

LYNES REALTY COMPANY

Soon to dwarf all but one of its neighbors in the downtown Savannah of 1924, the Realty Building is shown here just six months prior to completion on November 28, 1924.

For nearly twenty years countless thousands of Savannah-area motorists, utilizing the network of roads known as the "Westside Bypass," have had their progress eased greatly by the limited access, north-south parkway linking De-Renne Avenue to West Bay Street. That highway—officially known as W.F. Lynes Memorial Parkway—is a functional tribute to the memory of the prominent realtor and community leader who founded Lynes Realty Company in 1929.

Judge William F. Lynes, Jr., whose ex-officio title stemmed from service as chairman of the Chatham County Commission (1961-1964), devotedly spearheaded a range of community projects that would have reflected substantial credit on an individual who found time for nothing else. In Lynes' case, the spectrum of civic projects that flourished under his able leadership was an "after-hours" backdrop to his professional success.

President of both Lynes Realty Company and Lynes Mortgage Company, he has also served as president of both the Savannah Real Estate Board and its state-wide counterpart. A regional vice-president of the National Association of Real Estate Boards, he sat

on that group's prestigious Washington committee as well. Judge Lynes' community activities included a variety of leadership roles with the American National Red Cross, and in 1958 and 1959 he was vice-chairman and chairman, respectively, of the United Community Appeal. A member of the boards of the Union Society of Savannah and the Chatham County Tax Assessors, he also served on the board of education.

In February 1973—some eight years after his father's death—William F. Lynes III joined the firm as a sales associate. The ensuing years have been fruitful for Bill and the revitalized organization he has headed, as president of its various companies, since November 1978. His effective progression through a series of increasingly demanding capacities within the businesses was augmented by post-college professional training through more than a score of intensive courses, covering every aspect of real estate and complementary operations.

Following Judge Lynes' death, the firm had changed management and direction several times; development, property management, and mortgaging were viable, but sales operations became stagnant. Under Bill III's direction, a dramatic turnaround has been realized. Lynes now has fifteen full-time sales associates. The company is active in residential, commercial, farmland, property management, and commercial leasing. With the addition of the hotel/motel sales division in 1980, Lynes now participates in sales of hospitality prop-

erties throughout the Southeast.

Under the aegis of Realty Building Associates, of which Bill III is a general partner, acquisition and massive renovation of the Henrik Wallin-designed Realty Building, at 24 Drayton Street, was accomplished in the early 1980s. Erected in 1924, the certified historic structure is a ten-story, 51,000-square-foot building that is both the firm's headquarters and one of its most elegant leasing properties.

The company's development team is presently engaged in two projects on nearby Wilmington Island: Shad River is a 23-acre, 150-unit complex, and Shad's Grant a 37-acre, 96-lot single-family subdivision.

The ten-story splendor of the Realty Building made it a source of great pride in the surrounding business and financial district.

SAVANNAH PATRONS

The following individuals, companies, and organizations have made a valuable commitment to the quality of this publication. Windsor Publications and the Coastal Heritage Society gratefully acknowledge their participation in *Eden on the Marsh: An Illustrated History of Savannah.*

Advanced Transport Systems, Inc.
S.A. Allen, Inc.*
Ansley and Sutton Construction Company*
Atlantic Mutual Fire Insurance Company
  Southern Bank and Trust Company*
Atlantic Wood Industries, Inc.*
Brasseler USA, Inc.
Clyde Bruner Enterprises*
Callaway Gardens Country Store
Dr. and Mrs. Gerald E. Caplan
Carson Products Company*
Chatham-Effingham-Liberty Regional Library
Chatham Steel Corp. & Related Companies*
Coastal Divers & Pollution Control Inc.
Critz, Inc.*
Derst Baking Company*
Merritt W. Dixon III*
Electrical Machinery Company
Ben Farmer Realty, Inc.*
Ferguson Enterprises, Inc.

Foley House Inn*
Georgia Ports Authority*
Dr. and Mrs. Samuel M. Goodrich
Great Dane Trailers, Inc.*
Gunn & Meyerhoff A.I.A. Architects, P.C.*
J. Michael Hemphill, M.D.
Hixon Battery Company, Inc.*
M.J. Hogan & Company Inc.*
Hunter, Maclean, Exley & Dunn, P.C.*
Hussey, Gay & Bell, Inc., Consulting Engineers*
Johns-Manville*
Johnson, Lane, Space, Smith & Co., Inc.*
KEMIRA, Inc.
Konter Realty Company*
Lee and Clark, P.C.
J.C. Lewis Motor Company*
Catherine Theresa Lingenfelser
Lynes Realty Company*
L.P. Maggioni & Company*
Charles C. Martin
Memorial Medical Center*
Metalcrafts, Inc.*
E.L. Mobley, Inc.*
Neal-Blun Company*
Nowell and Associates, Architects
Oglethorpe Real Estate and Construction*
J.C. Penney
The Polote Corporation*
D.J. Powers Company, Inc.*
Chris Roddenberry, Inc.
Harry E. Rollins, M.D.

Roper Outdoor Power Equipment*
Savannah Airport Commission*
Savannah Bank and Trust Company*
Savannah Chapter of the National Society of the Daughters of the American Revolution
The Savannah Coca-Cola Bottling Company*
Savannah Fast Freight, Inc.
Savannah Gas Company*
Savannah Lumber & Supply Co.*
Smith & Kelly Company*
Solomons Company*
Southeast Coastal Properties
Thomas M. Stanley, M.D.
Stevens Shipping & Terminal Co.
Thomas R. Taggart & Associates*
Trust Company Bank of Savannah*
Union Camp Corporation*
United Daughters of the Confederacy Savannah Chapter #2
WAEV/WSOK Radio
Wilmington Cabinet Company, Inc.*

*Partners in Progress of *Eden on the Marsh: An Illustrated History of Savannah.* The histories of these companies and organizations appear in Chapter 9, beginning on page 148.

The interior of the Independent Presbyterian Church, drawn by a nineteenth-century draftsman, is shown in a view from the pulpit to the oversized, double-door entrance. Courtesy, Georgia Historical Society

SELECTED BIBLIOGRAPHY
BOOKS

Abbot, W.W. *The Royal Governors of Georgia, 1754-1775.* Chapel Hill: The University of North Carolina Press, 1959.

Anderson, Mary Savage; Barrow, Elfrida DeRenne; Screven, Elizabeth Mackay; and Waring, Martha Gallaudet. *Georgia: A Pageant of Years.* Spartanburg, South Carolina: The Reprint Company, 1974.

Axley, Lowry. *Holding Aloft the Torch: A History of the Independent Presbyterian Church of Savannah, Georgia.* Savannah: The Pigeonhole Press, 1958.

Ball, Lamar Q. *Georgia in World War II.* 2 vols. State of Georgia, 1946.

Barrow, Elfrida DeRenne, and Bell, Laura Palmer. *Anchored Yesterdays.* Darien, Georgia: Ashantilly Press, 1956.

Bell, Malcolm, Jr. *Savannah Ahoy!* Savannah: The Pigeonhole Press, 1959.

Bell, Malcolm, Jr., and Iseley, N. Jane. *Savannah.* Savannah: Historic Savannah Foundation, Incorporated, Morris Newspaper Corporation, and N. Jane Iseley, 1977.

Bolton, Herbert E., and Ross, Mary. *The Debatable Land.* Berkeley, California: University of California Press, 1925.

Burke, Emily. *Pleasure and Pain: Reminiscences of Georgia in the 1840s.* Introduction by Felicity Calhoun. Savannah: The Beehive Press, 1978.

Burlington, Roger. *Machines That Built America.* New York: The New American Library, Inc., 1953.

Coleman, Kenneth. *American Revolution in Georgia, 1763-1789.* Athens: University of Georgia Press, 1958.

Coleman, Kenneth. *Colonial Georgia—A History.* New York: Charles Scribner's Sons, 1976.

Coleman, Kenneth. *Georgia History in Outline.* 3d rev. ed. Athens: University of Georgia Press, 1978.

Coulter, E. Merton. *A Short History of Georgia.* Chapel Hill: The University of North Carolina Press, 1933.

Coulter, Merton, ed. *The Journal of Peter Gordon, 1732-1735.* Wormsloe Foundation Publications, no. 6. Athens: University of Georgia Press, 1963.

Coulter, Merton, ed. *The Journal of William Stephens, 1741-1745.* Wormsloe Foundation Publications, nos. 2 and 3. Athens: University of Georgia Press, 1958; 1959.

Davidson, Marshall, B., ed. *The Horizon History of the World in 1776.* New York: American Heritage Publishing Co., Inc., 1975.

Davis, Harold E. *The Fledgling Province.* Chapel Hill: The University of North Carolina Press, 1976.

DeBolt, Margaret Wayt. *Savannah: A Historical Portrait.* Virginia Beach: Donning Company/Publishers, Inc., 1976.

Dittmer, John. *Black Georgia in the Progressive Era, 1900-1920.* Blacks in the New World, edited by August Meier. Urbana, Chicago: University of Illinois Press, 1980.

Drago, Edmund L. *Black Politicians and Reconstruction in Georgia: A Splendid Failure.* Baton Rouge: Louisiana State University Press, 1982.

Fancher, Betsy. *Savannah, A Renaissance of the Heart.* Garden City, New York: Doubleday & Company, Inc., 1976.

Gamble, Thomas, Jr. *Bethesda.* 1902. Reprint. Spartanburg, South Carolina: The Reprint Company, 1972.

Gamble, Thomas, Jr. *The Mayor's Report, 1900, and a History of the City Government of Savannah, Georgia from 1790 to 1901.* Compiled from official records. Savannah, 1901.

Gamble, Thomas, Jr. *Savannah Duels and Duellists, 1733-1877.* 1923. Reprint. Spartanburg, South Carolina: The Reprint Company, 1974.

Granger, Mary, ed. *Savannah River Plantations.* Savannah Writers' Project. 1947. Reprint. Spartanburg, South Carolina: The Reprint Company, 1983.

Harden, William. *A History of Savannah and South Georgia.* 2 vols. 1913. Reprint (vol. 1). Atlanta, Georgia: Cherokee Publishing Company, 1969.

Harden, William. *Recollections of a Long and Satisfactory Life.* Savannah: Review Printing Company, Inc., 1934.

Hartridge, Walter Charlton, and Murphy, Christopher, Jr. *Savannah.* Columbia, South Carolina: Bostick & Thornley, 1947.

Hessel, Milton. *Man's Journey Through Time.* New York: Simon and Schuster, 1974.

Historic Savannah. Savannah: Historic Savannah Foundation, Incorporated, 1968.

Jones, Charles C., Jr., LL.D. *Biographical Sketches of the Delegates from Georgia to the Continental Congress.* Cambridge: Houghton, Mifflin and Company, 1891.

Jones, Charles C., Jr. *The Dead Towns of Georgia.* Collections of the Georgia Historical Society, vol. 4. 1878. Reprint. Spartanburg, South Carolina: The Reprint Company, 1974.

Jones, Charles C., Jr., LL.D. *The History of Georgia.* 2 vols. Georgia Heritage Series, nos. 1 and 2. 1883. Reprint. Spartanburg, South Carolina: The Reprint Company, 1965.

Jones, George Fenwick. *The*

Salzburger Saga. Athens: University of Georgia Press, 1984.

Kelso, William M. *Captain Jones' Wormslow.* Wormsloe Foundation Publications, no. 13. Athens: University of Georgia Press, 1979.

Killion, Ronald G., and Waller, Charles T. *Georgia and the Revolution.* Atlanta: Cherokee Publishing Company, 1975.

Kull, Irving S., and Kull, Nell M. *A Short Chronology of American History: 1492-1950.* New Brunswick, New Jersey: Rutgers University Press, 1952.

Lane, Mills, ed. *General Oglethorpe's Georgia: Colonial Letters, 1733-1743.* 2 vols. Savannah: The Beehive Press, 1975.

Lane, Mills. *Savannah Revisited: A Pictorial History.* Savannah: The Beehive Press, 1969.

Langer, William L., ed. *An Encyclopedia of World History.* Boston: Houghton Mifflin Company, 1952.

Lawrence, Alexander A. *Storm Over Savannah.* Athens: University of Georgia Press, 1951.

Leckie, George G. *Georgia: A Guide to Its Towns and Countryside.* American Guide Series, revised and extended by George G. Leckie. Atlanta: Tupper & Love, 1954.

Levy, B.H. *Savannah's Old Jewish Community Cemeteries.* Macon, Georgia: Mercer University Press, 1983.

McPherson, Robert G., ed. *The Journal of the Earl of Egmont.* Wormsloe Foundation Publications, no. 5. Athens: University of Georgia Press, 1962.

Morrison, Mary L., ed. *Historic Savannah.* Savannah: Historic Savannah Foundation, Incorporated and The Junior League of Savannah, 1979.

Most Delightful Country of the Universe, The. Introduction by Trevor R. Reese. Savannah: The Beehive Press, 1972.

Myers, Robert Manson, ed. *The Children of Pride.* New Haven: Yale University Press, 1972.

Nichols, Frederick D. *The Architecture of Georgia.* Savannah: The Beehive Press, 1976.

Olmstead, Charles H. *Art Work of Savannah.* Chicago: The W.H. Parish Publishing Co., 1893.

Our First Visit in America. Introduction by Trevor R. Reese. Savannah: The Beehive Press, 1974.

Perdue, Robert E., Ph.D. *The Negro in Savannah, 1865-1900.* New York: Exposition Press, Inc., 1973.

Perkerson, Medora Field. *White Columns in Georgia.* New York: Rinehart & Co., Incorporated, 1952.

Rauers, Betty, and Traub, Franklin. *Sojourn in Savannah.* 6th rev. ed. Savannah: n.p., 1984.

Reese, Trevor Richard. *Colonial Georgia.* Athens: University of Georgia Press, 1963.

Savannah Writers' Project. *Savannah.* American Guide Series. Savannah: Review Printing Co., 1937.

Saye, Albert B. *New Viewpoints in Georgia History, 1732-1789.* Athens: University of Georgia Press, 1943.

Sholes, A.E. *Chronological History of Savannah.* 1900. Reprint. Savannah: Kennickell Printing Co., 1975.

Sieg, Chan. *The Squares: An Introduction to Savannah.* Norfolk: Donning Company/Publishers, 1984.

Simms, James M., Rev. *The First Colored Baptist Church in North America.* New York: Negro Universities Press, 1969.

Stevens, William Bacon. *A History of Georgia.* Vol. 2. Savannah: The Beehive Press, 1972.

Temple, Sarah B. Gober, and Coleman, Kenneth. *Georgia Journeys.* Athens: University of Georgia Press, 1961.

Von Reck's Voyage. Edited by Kristian Hvidt with the assistance of Joseph Ewan, George F. Jones, and William C. Sturtevant. Savannah: The Beehive Press, 1980.

Waring, Joseph Frederick. *Cerveau's Savannah.* Savannah: The Georgia Historical Society, 1973.

White, George, M.A. *Historical Collections of Georgia.* New York: Pudney & Russell, Publishers, 1855.

Wilson, Adelaide, and Weymouth, Georgia. *Historic and Picturesque Savannah.* Boston: Boston Photogravure Company, 1889.

OTHER SOURCES

Belcher, John C., and Dean, K. Imogene, eds. *Georgia Today: Facts and Trends.* Athens: University of Georgia, 1960.

Bell, Laura Palmer. "A New Theory on the Plan of Savannah." The Georgia Historical Quarterly 48 (June 1964):147-65.

Campbell, Julia H.; Hawes, Lilla M.; and McClendon, Robertine K. "Downtown Architectural Survey." Chap. 4D. Unpublished. Savannah, 1967.

Georgia Historical Society, Collections of. Savannah.

Godley, Margaret W., and Bragg, Lillian C. *Stories of Old Savannah.* 2d. series. Savannah: n.p., 1949.

Gunn, Robert D.; Wood, Raiford J.; Gordon, Arthur; and Hartridge, Walter C. "The Squares of Savannah." Unpublished. Savannah, August 1961.

Hollingsworth, Dixon. *Indians on the Savannah River.* Sylvania, Georgia: The Partridge Pond Press, 1976.

Lattmore, Ralston B. *Fort Pulaski.* National Park Service Historical Handbook Series, no. 18. Washington, D.C.: U.S. Government Printing Office, 1961.

McIllvaine, Paul. *The Dead Town of Sunbury, Georgia.* Hendersonville, North Carolina: n.p., 1971.

Old Fort Jackson-Coastal Heritage Society Archives. Savannah.

Pageant Book Celebrating the 200th Anniversary of the Founding of the Colony of Georgia. Issued by the City of Savannah. Savannah: Review Printing Company, 1933.

Robertson, James I. *The Civil War.* Washington, D.C.: U.S. Government Printing Office, 1963.

Savannah News-Press. Savannah.

Todd, Helen. *Mary Musgrove: Georgia Indian Princess.* Chicago: Seven Oaks, 1981.

INDEX

212

BOOKS IN THE WINDSOR SERIES

ALABAMA
The Valley and the Hills: An Illustrated History of Birmingham and Jefferson County, by Leah Rawls Atkins
Historic Huntsville: A City of New Beginnings, by Elise Hopkins Stephens
Mobile: The Life and Times of a Great Southern City, by Melton McLaurin and Michael Thomason
Montgomery: An Illustrated History, by Wayne Flynt

ARIZONA
Scottsdale: Jewel in the Desert, by Patricia Myers McElfresh
Tucson: Portrait of a Desert Pueblo, by John Bret Harte

CALIFORNIA
Heart of the Golden Empire: An Illustrated History of Bakersfield, by Richard C. Bailey
California Wings: A History of Aviation in the Golden State, by William A. Schoneberger
Harvest of the Sun: An Illustrated History of Riverside County, by James T. Brown
Los Angeles: A City Apart, by David L. Clark
Sacramento: Heart of the Golden State, by Joseph A. McGowan and Terry R. Willis
San Bernardino County: Land of Contrasts, by Walter C. Schuiling
International Port of Call: An Illustrated Maritime History of the Golden Gate, by Robert J. Schwendinger
Stockton: Sunrise Port on the San Joaquin, by Olive Davis
Ventura County: Land of Good Fortune, by Judy Triem

COLORADO
Life In The Altitudes: An Illustrated History of Colorado Springs, by Nancy E. Loe

Denver: America's Mile High Center of Enterprise, by Jerry Richmond

CONNECTICUT
We Crown Them All: An Illustrated History of Danbury, by William E. Devlin
Hartford: An Illustrated History of Connecticut's Capital, by Glenn Weaver
New Haven: An Illustrated History, edited by Floyd Shumway and Richard Hegel
Stamford: An Illustrated History, by Estelle F. Feinstein, and Joyce S. Pendery

DELAWARE
The First State: An Illustrated History of Delaware, by William Henry Williams

FLORIDA
Fort Lauderdale and Broward County: An Illustrated History, by Stuart McIver

GEORGIA
Eden on the Marsh: An Illustrated History of Savannah, by Edward Chan Sieg

IDAHO
Boise: An Illustrated History, by Merle Wells
Idaho: Gem of the Mountains, by Merle Wells and Arthur A. Hart

ILLINOIS
Chicago: Center for Enterpise, by Kenan Heise and Michael Edgerton
Des Plaines: Born of the Tallgrass Prairie, by Donald S. Johnson
Prairie of Promise: Springfield and Sangamon County, by Edward J. Russo

INDIANA
At the Bend in the River: by Kenneth P. McCutchan

The Fort Wayne Story: A Pictorial History, by John Ankenbruck
Indiana: An Illustrated History, by Patrick J. Furlong
Muncie and Delaware County: An Illustrated Retrospective, by Wiley W. Spurgeon, Jr.
Terre Haute: Wabash River City, by Dorothy J. Clark

IOWA
Cedar Rapids: Tall Corn and High Technology, by Ernie Danek

LOUISIANA
River Capital: An Illustrated History of Baton Rouge, by Mark T. Carleton
New Orleans: An Illustrated History, by John R. Kemp

MARYLAND
Baltimore: An Illustrated History, by Suzanne Ellery Greene
Maryland: Old Line to New Prosperity, by Joseph L. Arnold
Montgomery County: Two Centuries of Change by Jane C. Sween

MASSACHUSETTS
Boston: City on a Hill, by Andrew Buni and Alan Rogers
The Valley and its Peoples: An Illustrated History of the Lower Merrimack River, by Paul Hudon
Heart of the Commonwealth: Worcester, by Margaret A. Erskine

MICHIGAN
Battle Creek: The Place Behind the Products, by Larry B. Massie and Peter J. Schmitt
Through the Years in Genesee: An Illustrated History, by Alice Lethbridge
Jackson: An Illustrated History, by Brian Deming
Kalamazoo: The Place Behind the Products, by Peter J. Schmitt and Larry B. Massie

Out of a Wilderness: An Illustrated History of Greater Lansing, by Justin L. Kestenbaum

Saginaw: A History of the Land and the City, by Stuart D. Gross

MINNESOTA
Duluth: An Illustrated History of the Zenith City, by Glenn N. Sandvik

City of Lakes: An Illustrated History of Minneapolis, by Joseph Stipanovich

Saint Cloud: The Triplet City, by John J. Dominick

St. Paul: Saga of an American City, by Virginia Brainard Kunz

MISSISSIPPI
The Mississippi Gulf Coast: Portrait of a People, by Charles L. Sullivan

MISSOURI
From Southern Village to Midwestern City: Columbia, An Illustrated History, by Alan R. Havig

At the River's Bend: An Illustrated History of Kansas City, Independence and Jackson County, by Sherry Lamb Schirmer and Richard D. McKinzie

Joplin: From Mining Town to Urban Center An Illustrated History, by G.K. Renner

Springfield of the Ozarks, by Harris and Phyllis Dark

MONTANA
Montana: Land of Contrast, by Harry W. Fritz

NEBRASKA
Lincoln: The Prairie Capital, by James L. McKee

Omaha and Douglas County: A Panoramic History, by Dorothy Devereux Dustin

NEVADA
Reno: Hub of the Washoe County, by William D. Rowley

NEW HAMPSHIRE
New Hampshire: An Illustrated History of the Granite State, by Ronald Jager and Grace Jager

NEW JERSEY
Morris County: The Progress of Its Legend, by Dorianne R. Perrucci

A Capital Place: The Story of Trenton, by Mary Alice Quigley and David E. Collier

NEW MEXICO
New Mexico: The Distant Land, by Dan Murphy

NEW YORK
Albany: Capital City on the Hudson, by John J. McEneny

Broome County Heritage, by Lawrence Bothwell

Buffalo: Lake City in Niagara Land, by Richard C. Brown and Bob Watson

Harbor and Haven: An Illustrated History of the Port of New York, by John G. Bunker

The Hudson-Mohawk Gateway: An Illustrated History, by Thomas Phelan

A Pictorial History of Jamestown and Chautauqua County, by B. Dolores Thompson

Between Ocean and Empire: An Illustrated History of Long Island, by Dr. Robert McKay and Carol Traynor

The Upper Mohawk Country: An Illustrated History of Greater Utica, by David M. Ellis

A Panoramic History of Rochester and Monroe County, New York, by Blake McKelvey

Syracuse: From Salt to Satellite, by Henry W. Schramm and William F. Roseboom

NORTH CAROLINA
Greensboro: A Chosen Center, by Gayle Hicks Fripp

Raleigh: City of Oaks, by James E. Vickers

Cape Fear Adventure: An Illustrated History of Wilmington, by Diane Cobb Cashman

Made in North Carolina: An Illustrated History of Tar Heel Business and Industry, by David E. Brown

OHIO
Butler County: An Illustrated History, by George C. Crout

Springfield and Clark County: An Illustrated History, by William A. Kinnison

OKLAHOMA
Heart of the Promised Land: An Illustrated History of Oklahoma County, by Bob L. Blackburn

OREGON
Lane County: An Illustrated History of the Emerald Empire, by Dorothy Velasco

Portland: Gateway to the Northwest, by Carl Abbott

PENNSYLVANIA
Allegheny Passage: An Illustrated History of Blair County, by Robert L. Emerson

Erie: Chronicle of a Great Lakes City, by Edward Wellejus

An Illustrated History of Greater Harrisburg, by Michael Barton

The Heritage of Lancaster, by John Ward Willson Loose

The Lehigh Valley: An Illustrated History, by Karyl Lee Kibler Hall and Peter Dobkin Hall

Williamsport: Frontier Village to Regional Center, by Robert H. Larson, Richard J. Morris, and John F. Piper, Jr.

The Wyoming Valley: An American Portrait, by Edward F. Hanlon

To the Setting of the Sun: The Story of York, by George R. Sheets

216